SEA SOLDIER

My Bull, — I sho'd not have said so much upon war to you, only
I wish you to shew it my friend — and indeed as you know I must
fill my paper, — I really have nothing else to write of, unless I wish
to frighten you with a description of this vile tropical climate,
— I very much lament being within a few hours sail of Trinidad,
& not having it in my power to go there — I co. have bro.t Caroline over.
— I suppose Portsmouth will be our first port, and I hope the
ship will be paid off at Chatham, you will see by the papers the
arrival of the West India Convoy — and I shall hope to find a
letter from you, telling me all the news, every one, that I

From
St. Thomas
and about
America

10/3

may make my arrangements for leave, — I shall certainly pay
you a visit (upon private leave) as soon as the ship arrives, but
it may not be necessary to let any one in London know it
as I will not go there till I have been to Birm.g — for only
consider in 12 months, I have undergone eight changes of climate
from the worst extremes — adieu my dearest sister may all happiness
and serenity attend you — present my best compl.ts to Mr.
Manley, — your ever affec.e Bro.r MW.

Letter by T. M. Wybourn addressed to Emily from America, with postmarks
and remains of sealing wax, torn

SEA SOLDIER

AN OFFICER OF MARINES WITH DUNCAN,
NELSON, COLLINGWOOD AND COCKBURN

*The Letters and Journals of
Major T. Marmaduke Wybourn RM, 1797-1813*

*Collected and transcribed by his sister, Emily Wybourn;
selected, edited and with notes by Anne Petrides and Jonathan Downs*

PARAPRESS LIMITED
TUNBRIDGE WELLS

Also published by Parapress:

England's One Test Wonders, by Roderick Easdale
Ida and the Eye, from the Autobiography of Ida Mann
Into the Blue, by Capt. T.D. Herrick DSC* RN
'Itching after Rhyme', a Life of John Clare, by Arnold Clay
Some Letters From Burma, by Tom Grounds
Wren's Eye View, by Stephanie Batstone

© Anne Petrides 2000
ISBN: 1-898594-69-4

First published in the UK by
PARAPRESS LTD
5 Bentham Hill House
Stockland Green Road
Tunbridge Wells
Kent
TN3 0TJ

A catalogue record for this book is available
from the British Library.

Typeset in Times New Roman by
Vitaset, Paddock Wood, Kent

Printed in Great Britain by
Biddles Ltd, Guildford & Kings Lynn

CONTENTS

The cover design uses details from 'Scene on Deck of the Victory when Nelson Fell' by D. Dighton, and 'Troops Embarking near Greenwich' by William Anderson, both by courtesy of the National Maritime Museum, London,

Captain of Marines, print by Rowlandson

ILLUSTRATIONS

RMM = Royal Marines Museum.
NC = reproduced from the *Naval Chronicle*, by kind permission of the RMM.

ACKNOWLEDGEMENTS

My grateful thanks are due to the following:-

Emily Wybourn, Thomas Marmaduke's devoted sister, who faithfully copied out all his letters after his death into a bound book, thereby ensuring that they are still clearly readable today.

Margaret Payne industriously selected and copied many pages of background material not available to me in Greece; Robert Lambolle put me on the right road to finding the best publisher; Michael d'Arcy, in Canberra, was supportive and enthusiastic on genealogical issues, and Nick Ralph, similarly, on the potentials of the story; Louisa O'Brien, suitably attentive to detail, put the whole text tidily onto a computer; Alison and Jonathan Downs took the text over and embellished it with notes and illustrations, Jonathan immersing himself in the events described. It was Elizabeth Imlay of Parapress who took the plunge and decided to publish, in a far more splendid form than I could have imagined.

Special thanks to Matthew Little, archivist of the Royal Marines Museum, Southsea, and to Major Alastair Donald of the Marines Historical Association for his interest and support, and for putting us in touch with Leslie Garrett, who checked the notes for historical accuracy; also to Brian Newbury of the Parker Gallery, London for his generous help.

The 'Pictorial Plan of the Grand Expedition in the West Scheldt, Aug. 1809' (p.146) is reproduced by kind permission of the National Army Museum, Chelsea.

The following pictures are reproduced by kind permission of the National Maritime Museum, Greenwich: Cover pictures as described on p. v; 'Sir John Duckworth's Passage of the Dardanelles' (p.104), 'Divine Service on Board' (p.120) and Sir George Cockburn as a Colonel, RM (p.197) all © THE NATIONAL MARITIME MUSEUM.

Anne Petrides

ANNE PETRIDES is the great, great, great granddaughter of Wybourn's sister Caroline Shipton, and his letters and journals have been passed down into her possession. She was brought up in Cyprus until the Second World War, which she passed partly at Sherborne School for girls and then in the WRNS (1944-46) in Naval Intelligence. She worked in the Section dealing with the Japanese codes at 'Station X' in Bletchley Park, and has recently contributed to Michael Smith's second volume about the Station, *The Emperor's Codes*. She then worked as a qualified librarian at the National Book League (1950-56), Camberwell School of Art, and the British Embassy in Athens (1967-84). She married a Greek, Harilaos Yannoulis, has lived in the island of Aegina and Athens since 1967 (arriving three weeks before the Junta's revolution took over the country), and became widowed in 1990. She is now President of the Friends of the Strays of Aegina. Her illustrated book *State Barges on the Thames* was published by Hugh Evelyn Ltd, London 1959.

G ✦ R

All Dashing High-spirited
YOUNG HEROES

Who wish to obtain GLORY in the SERVICE
of their Country, have now the finest Opportunity,
by entering that enterprizing respectable Corps

THE ROYAL
MARINES.

Every one must be well aware, that this Honorable Corps, possesses Advantages superior to any other under the Crown. Good Quarters whilst on Shore; on Board, plenty of Beef, Pudding, and Wine after Dinner. Even these Advantages are trifling when compared to the inestimable one

PRIZE MONEY.

Remember the Galloons; when the Private Marine made sufficient Prize Money to render himself and Family comfortable for Life.

Remember these Times may return, it is impossible to say how soon.

Loose no Time! therefore, in repairing to the head Quarters of the 1st Lieu. H. B. MENDS, of the Plymouth Division of Royal Marines, commanded by LIEU. GEN. BRIGHT, or to *Sergeant* GREBBLE, at the *BLUE BOWL, PITHAY, BRISTOL*, where every attention will be paid to them.

Eleven Guineas Bounty
SEVEN YEARS SERVICE.
Sixteen Guineas
UNLIMITED SERVICE.

Boys 5 Feet, *Eight Guineas*, limited Service. *Twelve Pounds*, unlimitted.

NOW OR NEVER, ENGLAND FOREVER.

※ The Bringers of Recruits will be handsomely rewarded.

GOD SAVE the KING.

INTRODUCTION AND NOTE ON THE TEXT

Thomas Marmaduke Wybourn was nineteen when his patron Earl Spencer, first Lord of the Admiralty, obtained him a commission as a 2nd Lieutenant in the Plymouth division of His Majesty King George III's Marine Forces in 1795. Marmaduke was an orphan, with neither influence nor financial resources. Perhaps he had to take whatever job he was offered, or perhaps he chose the Marines because of the apparent prospect of prize money to supplement his pay: he had two elder sisters to support, Emily and Matilda.

Orphans are known to turn to one another to compensate for their loss, and Wybourn, it will be seen, was close to all his siblings, but especially to Emily. A third sister, Caroline, married and moved to Birmingham, and was about to produce a formidable brood of children, but he wrote to her almost as assiduously as to Emily, and in order to fill up the large squares which in that era served as both writing paper and envelope, he kept a careful daily record in his Journal, and often copied large sections into his letters.

Because of the duplication involved, Anne Petrides, a descendant of Caroline, has made a selection from both these sources. Where some overlapping remains, it is because we have thought some extra light, or some new aspect of a situation, is revealed by using both.

Wybourn's confessional tone is very different from the dry voice of the Naval Chronicle, which we have consulted to support the accuracy of his account. During the Revolutionary and Napoleonic Wars, as now, official reports played down the damage, suffering and death inflicted. Take Sir John Duckworth's inward passage of the Dardanelles, for example: 'The damage sustained was very trifling' says the Naval Chronicle, and 'a few shells thrown … among the Turks soon dispersed them,' but through Wybourn's eyes, '700 pieces of cannon opened fire on us, the Ships were cut to pieces in their Ropes, Masts and rigging', 'the slaughter on shore was beyond calculation,' and 'the Houses flew in thousands of pieces'.

The young Lieutenant can little have thought, when he set out so blithely to subdue 'the treacherous Dutch' in 1799, with such high hopes of money and rank, that warfare on a global scale was about to continue for sixteen years and that, for all his undoubted courage and loyalty, he was to gain little from it but his experience. Promotion went by seniority: generally speaking one could not buy it or earn it in the field. Prize money was chronically slow in coming through, by which time large amounts had often been misappropriated by corrupt officials. By subtle changes his tone moves from enthusiasm to humourousness, to irony, and finally to savage sarcasm at the waste of life he observes.

But the life of an officer had its compensations, mainly of a social nature. Wybourn enjoyed company, he enjoyed food (he was usually put in charge of the catering), and he loved the society of 'the dear ladies'. Readers who are mainly interested in the naval and military history preserved in these pages may think we have over-indulged his passion for partying. But we found we could not bear to leave out the wealth of detail on manners and morals of the Regency period which he offers, and which contribute to presenting our hero in the round, and as a continuous voice. In the end it becomes the voice of a close acquaintance whose feelings we have shared for almost fourteen years by sea and land: tossing in the gales off Toulon, cursing vermin inside his hot uniform in Egypt, and enjoying the delights of the 'Navarier' in Cadiz, whatever that establishment may have been.

Because his own spelling lends both period authenticity and also, at this distance in time, a great deal of charm, we have usually retained it, together with his underlinings. His punctuation, however, consisting mainly of commas and dashes for pages at a time, we have presumed to amend, and we hope that the narrative has thereby gained point and accessibility.

Elizabeth Imlay, General Editor

The Delegates in Counsel, print by George Cruikshank

As his story opens, Wybourn is a 21-year-old lieutenant in charge of the 49th Company (of about 100 men) of the Chatham Division of H. M. Marine forces. They are not yet called the Royal Marines. When he writes of a 'detachment', this is the portion of the Division sent to cope with the emergency and billeted in Gravesend. The rest are still at their barracks in Chatham, waiting to be called upon if required, for mutiny is breaking out in the British fleet.

May 29, 1797
Gravesend

My dear Sisters,

What will you think of my long silence? I will not attempt an apology, as I know you will not admit an excuse. I had written to my brother John which I considered the same thing and expecting you last Saturday again put a stop to my writing, and for four or five days previous to Saturday I was at Maidstone, and only returned in time to have received you, had you come. I have now been here, since that time, in consequence of dreadful mutiny amongst the sailors – it is expected they will fire upon this town – I till this moment have not had time to do anything, I have not had my clothes off or even seen a bed these three nights, and all last night & the night before, did not even sit down. Mrs. Dufaur (our lovely cousin) knows how harassed I am, as well as all the officers commanding the detachment, and now again, we are to be upon our arms all night.

2 o'clock in the morning. I have just got an opportunity of a few hours repose, but will finish my letter first. The town is full of Soldiers, and all the Forts & Garrisons are manned, and all the Guns charged & also a Furnace where red hot shot are preparing, as the sailors are going to take the men of War out of the River and carry them to the Nore, where they [may] ride in safety from our Forts; we expect in a few hours to have dreadful doings. All the Horse are here, as well as Military. I was happy in having an opportunity of convincing the General of my zeal, for I volunteered, which pleased him.

I have been shown much favour by my Captain who has entrusted me with posts of importance though it costs me dear, for I am up all night and day.

The Nore mutiny began 20 May 1797, four days after the Spithead mutiny ended. The seamen saw their action as an extension of the Spithead uprising, hoping to make similar gains e.g. more regular payment and a fairer distribution of prize money. Delegates took control of the ships, sending most officers ashore; by the end of the month all but two ships had joined in and the mutineers tried to blockade the Thames from its anchorage at The Nore.

Give my love to my Sister Matilda and tell her to hold herself in readiness by the 3rd of June when I shall fetch you both to Chatham, as there will be a field day on the 4th and a grand concert, and I shall then introduce you to a Clergyman and his beautiful young wife.

Your affectionate Brother
T.M. Wybourn

June 27, 1797
Gravesend

My dear Caroline,

I have just received your very affectionate letter and from your kind inquiries of me, cannot longer delay writing a few lines to you.

You are so good as to ask what service I am upon, and as no one is so able to give an exact account I shall feel pleasure in relating it, as I am now, at least for the present, out of all danger. The Sailors have indeed made a serious disturbance and had nearly shaken the whole Empire, but thank God and I have the vanity to say by <u>us</u> they are suppressed and the ring-leaders in Prison. I, and three others, were the first ordered on that expedition with 180 men, and as we volunteered to go, have no little pleasure in finding we were of the most essential service, and have succeeded in some measure to my most sanguine wishes. At two o'clock in the morning an express arrived at our Barracks for a large detachment to proceed immediately to Gravesend, I was fortunately the first on the Parade, and though not appointed at first on the Expedition, the General from my zeal, as he was pleased to call it, permitted me to take the command of our division, and to the astonishment of the Commandant at Gravesend we arrived there in two hours (9 miles) with the Detachment. I have nothing particular to relate of our situation there, as happily we had not occasion to fire a shot with small arms – for three weeks I had not a thing off, and little sleep of course, called out at all hours in the night under arms. Our men have received immortal honour by their vigilance, and our party consisting of 18 men took possession of a whole ship's company, and brought 32 of them to our guard house.

Shore batteries were trained on the ships. By 10 June some mutinous crews began to surrender as loyal ships appeared, their guns brought to bear.

I was Officer of the guard over them, the other poor officer was killed in the action between the mutineers and marines, only [think] how dreadful. The Boatswain piped all hands on Deck and in a moment, upon a private signal, gave out that all Loyalists should Aft, Delegates forward, upon which a battle ensued, and many were killed, however the marines got the better of them, and when they were brought to me, I treated them like villains as they were. The Capt. of the ship called us divine Marines in his official letter and exclusive of that, we were honoured so highly as to have our names sent to the King, as deserving his notice; we were immediately reported and recommended to the War Office. We went armed with the 30 prisoners under my command to Chatham, and was there detained, and a relief sent to G. to succeed us, we being nearly dead with fatigue. I am high on the list, and our pay raised from the 24th, so, my love, your ambitious brother feels happy.

Emily no doubt has given you an account of our Warlike appearance at Gravesend and all round. Give my love to my nephews and nieces, with kind regards to Mr. Shipton.

I am my dear Sister your affectionate

T.M. Wybourn

On the 14th the leading ship "Sandwich" surrendered. She was stormed and the mutineers arrested. Ringleader Richard Parker and many others were hanged. The Admiralty made no concessions.

The list for promotion went by seniority. It could not be bought (in theory), or even won in the field.

July 7, 1799
H.M.S. "Zealand"
The Nore

H.M.S. "Zealand was a Dutch vessel sezied in 1796 and used for harbour service.

My dear Sister,

I have most glorious news to inform you of, my ambition is, at length, gratified. I am employed in the hottest of the Expedition going forward.

Upon my return yesterday to the garrison from Sheerness, where I had been to make interest to get into the secret expedition, I was ordered for immediate embarcation to this place, from whence I shall be forwarded to Yarmouth to join the "Isis", and relieve Capt. Stransham [Marines]. I am doubly happy at my situation, as I am to command my own detachment. I suppose you have already heard that the most important of anything yet undertaken by England, is the present business, no one can guess the nature of it altogether, as there

H.M.S. "Isis" was a Fourth Rate two-decker of 50 guns. These frigates were often used in northern waters where enemy ships were smaller. Her captain was James Oughton.

are to be several divisions of Forces, which are to be joined by 45,000 Russians.

Holland is certainly the object, the French are quitting it very fast, and the Dutch are exceedingly alarmed and have petitioned the assistance of the King of Prussia, who has declined it.

The Naval department is commanded by Admiral Mitchell, who will hoist his Flag on board the "Isis", so that I am certain of being in the centre of the whole of it. I am so elated, my dear sister, but as you are not unacquainted with my sanguine disposition, you will readily believe me. The only drawback is, that you will be anticipating evils that Soldiers and Sailors never feel, and [I] shall volunteer the moment I see Holland to be disembarked.

I have 50 men I can depend upon, and the junior officer is as hot an Irishman as can be, so that honour and glory must be obtained. I shall expect to be made a Burgher master before I come back.

I am thinking how charming it will be, to be strutting about the conquered towns of the treacherous Dutch, and to shew them that Englishmen can be as humane as brave, for I am resolved (as far as I command) no violence or plunder shall be made use of to the poor wretches in our power. You see how this subject engroces me. I will therefore write again soon, and conclude with assuring you of my love.

T.M. Wybourn

August 3, 1799
H.M.S. "Isis"
The Downs

My dear Sister

I am now going to communicate all the news I can collect of our intended Expedition, some say it is Holland, others France, many declare Vigo, or the Indies, in short it is impossible to guess right, and the places most talked of you may rest assured are the least intended. If it is Holland, they are certainly ready to receive us, their coast being lined with Forts and Troops, but the Orange party are wishing for us, and they are most numerous. The French are beaten on the Continent, and have already evacuated Rome, Sardinia, etc., etc. Buonaparte is entirely ruined and the Austrians and Russians are preparing to enter France, which is in a state of revolution again: and indeed propositions are now set on foot in Paris for an establishment of Monarchy and terms offered. The King of Prussia is also coming into the business, and has applied to us for a convoy to his ships in the North.

Holland must fall, and under every consideration I firmly believe France is our destiny, for we are sure of Holland afterwards.

The Camp at Deal is finished and all ready, and the only thing we have been waiting for is an account of the French and Spanish Fleets consisting of 42 sail of the line, and as many small ships, when Lord Keith's fleet is only about 30 sail. The enemy did not choose to fight though they have been sailing about this month, and are, at length sculked into Cadiz so that our expedition is now immediately going. The Downs is full of ships and they have 30 more coming from Portsmouth, and many from all parts, it is said that there will be above 300 large and small vessels and 150 flat-bottomed boats. All the troops are chosen men, and the seamen as well as Commanders of the bravest Englishmen, nothing can withstand such an armament, besides which we are to be supported by 30,000 or 40,000 Russians if necessary.

This morning all signals and final orders were given to all ships at present here and I suppose we shall be off in a week. I little thought what extravagance meant – here we have the Admiral's Flag and Sir Ralph Abercromby, and his whole train so that there was a general vote in our Mess to sport a most luxurious table.

Yours T.M. Wybourn

August 12, 1799
H.M.S. "Isis"

My dear Sisters,

We took our departure unexpectedly at daylight, and instead of going to Margate, we passed it about eleven o'clock, and Sir Charles Hambleton's division of Ships joined us from there. It was a most glorious sight, nearly 200 Ships in full sail, steering one course, with a gentle breeze, everything appearing in our favour. The British

A line-of-battle ship had a wardroom, inhabited by all senior officers but the captain or admiral. This included the lieutenants, master, purser, surgeon, chaplain and marine officers. It was sited between the rows of officers' collapsible canvas-walled cabins on either side of the ship. Well lit by stern windows, it often projected over the rudder head of the vessel and was some 16 feet wide, its chief constituent a long mess table.

The frigate, smaller than a ship of the line, had no wardroom, but a gunroom instead, positioned aft on the lower deck. There were no stern windows and no light save that entering through open gunports or the gratings to the deck above. Officers had cabins along the gunroom, as in a line-of-battle ship.

colours flying on board every ship, the bands of music of the different regiments playing loyal tunes, and the hills and shores lined with spectators; numerous boats with all the dear ladies rowing round us while we were setting the sails, and remained with us till we outsailed them, duty to our Country not permitting any other attentions which they claim from us. We continued in sight of land till seven in the Evening and I still perceived the Hills of Margate crowded with people with the help of a Glass. We made the necessary signals to our brood and kept under easy sail all night. It was a lovely night, the Moon shone clear and there was wind just sufficient to carry us about two miles an hour. We were in front of these that all the convoy might see our lights and signals. At each side, and in the rear were all the other ships, the sea as far as the horizon was interspersed with ships, the Moon shining on the white sails – not a sound was heard but now and then a Gun fired as a signal.

No romance could picture a more awful and solemn, though glorious, sight nor impress half on the feelings that this Armamant did, as it was viewed from the deck this night. I could not help reflecting on the blessings of our <u>beloved country</u>, and how we alone remain sole masters of the sea, and while no other country dare risk their Ships either secret or public, or even send a vessel out, we were ranging the whole Seas, and now on the point of invading their shores without their being able to resist us, all they can trust to is their Batteries and Forts; they may perhaps send a few of us to glory, but they cannot hold out long, their fortifications will soon be destroyed by our ships, and then the troops will land and snatch the whole Country from them. Who would be anything but an Englishman?

William Pitt was Prime Minister, and Henry Dundas was Home Secretary.

Bumpers were glasses filled to the brim.

Mr. Pitt and Dundas were in the Trinity Yacht and sailed with us all the morning, no doubt they will drink the Expedition in bumpers after dinner, and I hope we may be the instruments of their plans succeeding. I shall give you this day's account tomorrow.

<u>Wednesday 13th</u>. I rose at five, walked the Deck till eight which gave me a voracious appetite for breakfast and as we always have an elegant as well as profuse set out (that is when we can get it) I did not fail to play my part; indeed we are hungry all day at sea.

Vice Admiral Andrew Mitchell in charge of the naval pat of the expedition and subsequently knighted.

10 o'clock: I am just come down from Deck for there are 50 Captains etc., etc., come on board to consult with the Admiral; we expect to see some part of Holland tonight, as the Port we are supposed to be going to is not more than 200 miles from Deal. I have hopes from a calculation that has been made that we shall commence the

SIR ANDREW MITCHELL, K.B

Admiral of the Blue Squadron

THE RIGHT HONORABLE  LORD VISCOUNT DUNCAN

Admiral of the Blue Squadron

attack on my birthday – nothing would afford me more satisfaction than to fire the first on that day, when I shall be 24 years of age.

I feel myself particularly happy in being on board this ship having the Naval as well as the Military Commanders-in-Chief and all the Staff on board, so that if there is a possibility of getting them in my interest, I may be the first landed. I was just now asked my opinion how the detachment would act under my command and as they had been in action before and had behaved remarkably well during the Mutiny, I of course could say everything for them, it will therefore be our post to storm the Forts on shore if we land at all. The General begged I would have them ready at a minute's warning.

At 10 o'clock we saw land 7 leagues off, and the place we shall land at, if the wind will permit, is within two miles of the Hague, the road to it being through a grove of trees the whole way so that we shall have a rural march at any rate. The Pilots say they can land 10,000 Men in two hours at this place.

A heavy gale came on and drove us out to sea or half the convoy might have been lost.

<u>Saturday Evening</u>. I am just up having been in bed since Thursday. I left off where we were in sight of the Dutch coast, but as there are many accidents between the cup and the lip, we were no sooner preparing for the great event, when a most tremendous gale came on and drove us 150 miles North, and out [of] 105 ships we counted only 90. We met with Admiral Duncan and to our surprise we are near the Texel, our route is altered therefore and we are going to dash at it, and take all their ships, also the possession of the Peninsula of land opposite leading to the Continent. The Duke of York & the second division will then join us and proceed up the Country.

<u>Sunday</u>. I received my dear Matilda's letter, brought from Deal by a vessel with dispatches for the admiral. I dined this day with Admiral Mitchell and Sir Ralph Abercromby etc., etc., and had a long confab but the weather continues so bad, it is now uncertain when we can commence the attack & to risk landing the troops would sacrifice thousands.

<u>Monday 19th Aug</u>. A most lovely day, all accidents repaired and no lives lost except about 50 Horses. Counted all the Fleet – Admiral Duncan with his Fleet on one side of us and a Russian Fleet on the other, we are now jogging on for the Texel. I made a most hearty dinner, for the first time played Flute, Backgammon etc., and am now quite happy again hoping all is for the best.

Lieut-General Sir Ralph Abercromby (1734–1801,) commanded the First Division of 17,000 troops. He was known more for his professionalism and integrity than his tactical genius, but was considered the army's most capable soldier. He was chiefly responsible for raising the standards of the corrupt, weak-willed and badly disciplined British army of the late 18th century to make it the fighting force that later went on to wrest Spain and France from Napoleon.

Duncan was Commander of the English fleet in the North Sea. There is no indication whether Wybourn had been present at the Battle of Camperdown against the Dutch fleet, 11 October 1797, a resounding victory for Admiral Duncan only a few months after the mutiny at the Nore.

<u>Tuesday 20th</u>. Admiral Mitchell, Sir Ralph Abercromby, General Hope and the Captain all got into a Frigate and went to consult with Admiral Duncan, [who] although a superior "flag" handsomely declined a command in this business (which his high rank entitled him to) and even gave up six of his ships to join us, so that we are 12 sail of the line, about 40 small men of war and nearly 200 Ships in the whole. Admiral Duncan will remain behind a little way with the rest of his fleet to afford assistance if necessary.

<u>Wednesday 21st</u>. Made signal for Captains etc., etc., the Deck crowded with great men, who made known their final orders, and now the troops are to land in the morning by daylight, and while they storm the Fort, we are to dash into Harbour with 9 sail to attack the Dutch who have 14 ships. As this place is the only one they are not prepared at, our success is certain.

<u>Thursday 22nd</u>. Just as we were within four Miles from the shore, to our mortification the wind again threatens us. Three days has it been calm, and smooth as glass; this morning as soon as everything was arranged, not a soldier on the Coast or any one impediment to our landing, the wind freshened, the sea got so high, no boats could attempt a landing. The Admiral sent his first Lieut. with Col. Maitland into the Texel, with proposal to give up the place and their ships without resistance (a very modest request). The flag of truce is not yet returned, the wind is coming to a storm, all the ships are under weigh again and standing out to sea to avoid a lea [sic] shore. The Enemy rejoicing at our failure: it appears to be a sweet place. I could see all over the Town and Harbour, they have 48 ships of different sorts in the Texel. All their batteries are well manned and they are heating red hot shot; we are but just out of reach of their Guns.

<u>Friday 23rd</u>. Dreadful weather, we are again blowing about, this is unlucky as they will have time to line the coast with Troops. Signals are flying from one end to another. 9 o'clock at night: our officers are just returning in the flag of truce, but nothing official is allowed to transpire.

The Dutch Admiral and all the officers behaved with great respect to ours, made them dine etc., nor did they fail to shew them how well prepared they were to receive us: this however did not dishearten us.

<u>Saturday 24th</u>. Still blowing weather – we are again in sight of the Tex after having been blown 50 miles away, and are in hopes of being able to commence the attack at daylight tomorrow Morning.

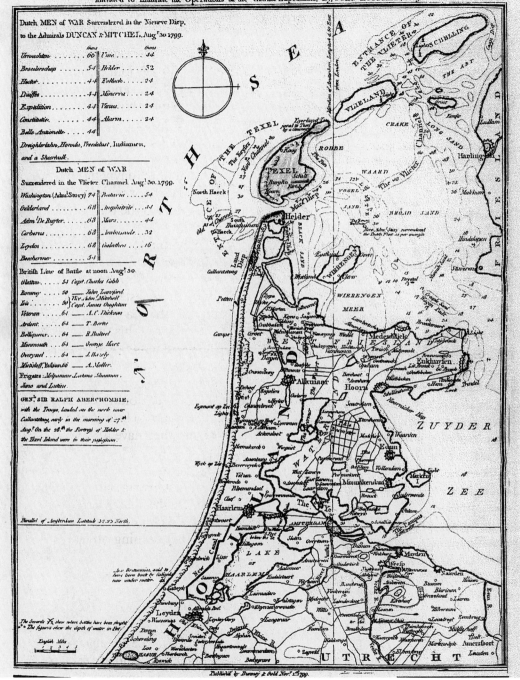

GRAND EXPEDITION.

A MAP of the TEXEL and VLIETER ROADS with the COUNTRY of HOLLAND as far south as the HAGUE:
Intended to Illustrate the Operations of the Grand Expedition; By, JOHN LUFFMAN, Geog.ʳ

Aug 1799

Dutch MEN of WAR Surrendered in the Nieuwe Diep,
to the Admirals DUNCAN & MITCHEL, Aug.ᵗ 30 1799.

	Guns		Guns
Urnachten	66	Unie	44
Broeulerschap	54	Helder	32
Hecktr	44	Pollock	24
Duiffte	44	Minerva	24
Expedition	44	Venus	24
Constitutie	44	Alarm	24
Belle Antionette	44		

Draighlerlahn, Honula, Vreedelut, Indiment,
and a Sheerhulk.

Dutch MEN of WAR
Surrendered in the Vlieter Channel Aug.ᵗ 30. 1799.

	Guns		Guns
Washington (Adm.ˡ Story)	74	Batavia	54
Gelderland	68	Imphitrite	44
Adm.ˡ De Ruyter	68	Mars	44
Cerberus	68	Ambuscade	32
Leyden	68	Galathea	16
Beschermo	54		

British Line of Battle at noon Aug.ᵗ 30

	Guns	
Glatton	54	Capt. Charles Cobb
Romney	50	John Lawford
Isis	50	Rev. John Mitchell / Capt. James Oughton
Veteran	64	A. C. Dickson
Ardent	64	T. Bertie
Bellyiqueux	64	E. Bulteel
Monmouth	64	George Hart
Overyssel	64	J. Bazely
Mutislaff, Bussen 56		A. Moller.

Frigates Melpomene Latona Shannon
Juno and Lutine

GEN.ˡ SIR RALPH ABERCROMBIE,
with the Troops, landed on the neck near
Callantsoog, early in the morning of 27ᵗʰ
Aug.ᵗ On the 28ᵗʰ the Forts of Helder &
the Texel Island were in their possession.

Parallel of Amsterdam Latitude 52.23 North.

The Brittanics said to
have been built be linkwith
now under water.

The Swords ✗ shew where battles have been fought
✗ The figures shew the depth of water in Feet.

English Miles

Published by Bunney & Gold Nov.ʳ 1ˢᵗ 1799.

The British Troops landing in Holland, courtesy of the Parker Gallery

Eight o'clock in the Evening of a beautiful night: we shall drink the usual toasts sweethearts and wives, though many will be downhearted for tomorrow will certainly decide the fate of some of us. We cast lots etc. If it should be me, I have packed up my things and directed them to Craigs Court for you my dear Sisters. Besides which my Uncle will put you in a way to procure all rights, claims and demands on my account, also at Lloyds you will receive my prize money and all other gratuities according to my Will, which I put into my small Trunk. There is a vessel now going with dispatches: the first time we have had leave to send by it.

Uncle Wybourn, senior surviving member of the family, their father's brother, lived at Craigs Court, London, near Charing Cross. It can still be seen, at the top of Whitehal.

Adieu with love to Matilda,
Your affectionate Brother
T.M. Wybourn

he invasion of Holland at the Texel on 27ᵗʰ August 1799 was an ultimately abortive exercise to support a supposed Orange uprising and open a new front for meeting the hitherto triumphant French. It involved 12,000 infantry, 200 cavalry and 600 artillery; the British were to join up with the Russians once on the mainland. Co-operation on this front was poor, resupply of British troops was badly handled and transport was appalling. However, the British did well at Bergen, against a combined army of French and Dutch Batavians, but the ill-disciplined Russians were defeated, causing the British to withdraw; later on 2ⁿᵈ October, the British met the French again at Bergen, this time with success. But four days later they were checked at Castricum and the Commander-in-Chief, the Duke of York, wanted to pull out. The Convention of Alkmaar provided Britain with time enough to retreat, and on 18ᵗʰ October the Duke regretfully left Holland, and the Orange supporters, to the whims of the French and Batavians. See Wybourn's letter of 24ᵗʰ October 1799.

August 28, 1799
Texel

My dear Sisters,

I have just time to give you a few lines, and [the] Express is going with the most glorious news of the success of our brave Troops.

I suppose you received a letter sometime ago, though it is said none will be delivered till a confirmation to Government is arrived of our victories. On Monday we anchored with our whole force along the shore within pistol shot: yesterday we landed 13,000 Men at 4 o'clock in the morning, about 3,000 got on shore first, the Dutch had 6,000 Troops, but strange to say they did not fire a shot till we had nearly 7,000 Men at 4 o'clock on Shore, but hid themselves behind the sand hills; at five a dreadful Battle ensued, the English behaved most nobly under every disadvantage, and in a strange country among sand hills that were occupied by 6,000 Men hid about, all rifle men.

The Dutch immortalized themselves, never were braver men, they disputed every inch of ground by the Bayonet. At 2 o'clock, and not before, we were victorious and drove every man out of the whole peninsula of Holland and at night attacked a fort of 3,000 Men that guarded the harbour and town, stormed it, and took this, as well as several other Forts. The Fleet is sculked further up but many of them are blocked up under their own Batteries by our own people, and we are preparing this instant to go after them, when if we beat them the Island of the Texel will of course fall without assistance of the Troops; but Sir Ralph says he will storm it on the outside next the sea. We are sure of the whole in the course of the day, never was more joy and gladness than on this day.

Frederick Augustus, Duke of York, was Commander-in-Chief of the British Army from 1795. Though a capable administrator, he was not a talented general.

Nearly 40,000 Russians are coming by sea, and I suppose the Duke of York and another large division will immediately come from England and subdue all Holland. We lost 2,000 Men, the Dutch twice that number; all was quiet last night and today not an enemy seen.

What can do more honour to the brave English officers, than the following circumstances. The poor wounded Dutch lying in the field of battle would have been instantly sacrificed by our soldiers for their obstinacy and the great slaughter they had occasioned, but the English placed orange ribbons about them, and thus, instead of their being victims, our soldiers protected them and they were sent on board ships to be taken care of. The first man that jumped out of the [ship] gave three cheers and defied above 200 Riflemen that were peeping about from their hiding places. After about four hours fighting we gained the hills and two brave fellows mounted first, and fired at above 1500 Dutch over just the brow of it; the second man up the narrow pass I saw fall, he rolled over several times down the hill, but got up once more and was carried off by two other men. From that moment nothing could stand against the English. All is now secure and quiet and not an enemy to be seen.

Normally this would indicate they were supporters of William Frederick, Prince of Orange.

I fear the Guns from our ships killed many of our men, as it was impossible to avoid it. One shell burst and wounded several of our

Officers on shore – the shot flew about like hailstones, I wonder only so few were killed.

It is a most glorious sight to see the whole shore and all the Hills crowded with soldiers in all directions, and the whole coast lined with ships.

There is now a fleet in view coming with reinforcements, never was more joy among the Troops on the occasion, or a more seasonable relief, as the soldiers have all been since four o'clock yesterday morning at hard duty without a Tent to cover them, and a stormy night and resting upon their arms for fear of a surprise. We shall now be 17,000 strong which can keep any position until the Russians come etc., etc.

I shall take another opportunity of writing and hope to inform you of more victories. No inhabitants have quitted the towns.

Affectionately yours,

T.M. Wybourn

Sept. 4, 1799
H.M.S. "Isis"
Texel

My dear Emily,

I left off in my last with an account of the landing of the Troops, and though we lost 2,000 Men in the action have gained conquest far beyond all expectation. On the next, the 30th of August we proceeded with a few ships up the Texel harbour, passed all their Forts and 13 Ships that were in the Helder neither manned nor armed: we proceeded then 9 miles up a narrow passage, to attack the Dutch fleet which had retreated as far as they had water enough to sail in. We prepared for the worst as all the enemy's Ships were superior to ours, and just as we had worked our ideas to the highest pitch and at our quarters, and in ten minutes should have blazed away (to use a sea phrase) being by this [time] within shot, the cowards sent their Admiral & a flag of truce, and requested 36 hours to send to the States to know how they should act. We gave them only <u>one</u> hour, and came to an anchor before the whole of them, at the expiration of which time we made preparations to give them a broadside when they struck their colours without firing a gun, and we took possession of 12

Official figures are much higher.

Prize money was a great inducement for naval service. The rewards were divided into eighths. Before 1808, the commanding captain received three-eighths, but one of these eighths went to his flag officer – (if, however, the captain was sailing under direct orders from the Admiralty, he could keep all three of his eighths). Another eighth was divided equally between captains of marines, captains of land forces, sea-lieutenants and masters. Another eighth went to marine lieutenants and quarter-masters of marines, lieutenants, ensigns and quarter-masters of land-forces, boatswain, gunner, purser, carpenter, masters' mates, surgeons and chaplains. Another eighth went to midshipmen, surgeons' mates, marine sergeants and petty officers. The remaining quarter went to the crew and the marines.

beautiful men of War making in the whole 25 Ships of War, besides hundreds of small vessels, all their Dockyards, and the grand harbour their principal dependence; in short this Expedition surpasses everything and the relative consequences of which make it the most important of anything we have done this war.

If we share prize money (and they only share who are in the cause of the enemy's ships striking) I should claim £1,400/1,500 but such an immense armament being in sight, though 16 miles off and of course entitled to share with us I may not get 200, and lastly if they should be returned to the Prince of Orange I shall get nothing at all. I think we should share after such desperate efforts which might have proved fatal to half of us. Such was their supposed safety they said they did not suppose it possible for us to get in, next their army was so strong they were certain we could not effect a landing, and lastly their Forts were so strong they did not fear us, and when we had gained the peninsula and had stormed their Forts etc., etc., they carried their ships up an intricate passage, and such a distance, they said it was impossible we could have the temerity to pursue them, but they pretended to receive us in hopes we should get aground in a channel so bad, but when they found us within a shot of them, they turned about entirely and gave up; many of their Captains actually cried, we could not help pitying them.

News is just arrived on board, the Army has got 24 Miles up the Country, the enemy retreated at all points.

One of our Lieuts. takes this to England as he has the Enemy's Colours consisting of 36 different flags to present to the Admiralty, who will be made a Captain in consequence. This is a most beautiful country but very cold. I need not say anything of our situation and happiness as you will conceive it all when I tell you that glory and honour awaits us. We are perfectly adored by the inhabitants, the ladies are very beautiful, but on the Continent (only 7 miles across) they are as ugly. We are quite worried with their congratulations – all is rejoicing and gaiety here. I am just going to take a plan of the attack made on the first day by the Army. We are going with a small force to reduce a principle [sic] Town about 15 miles up a small sea, that the Army cannot get at. Above 200 Ships are going home today. We remain here with 20 Ships of War probably for a long time.

Give my love to Matilda and Caroline when you write,

Your affectionate Brother

Marmaduke Wybourn

Sept. 12, 1799
Helder Town, Holland

Well my dear Sister here I am at last in a most delightful situation, though almost deaf with the noise of the great guns and mortars.

We landed on Monday last to see service on shore after taking possession of all the Dutch ships. I did all in my power to land this first day, but luckily I escaped that, for hardly is there a man left alive, however we have gained a most glorious Victory, and all Holland cannot drive us away from the possession we have gained. The troops are greatly harassed and distressed for want of relief – poor fellows, about 11,000 besides what have arrived very lately making 20,000 have been keeping 26,000 Dutch and French at bay. We are this moment informed that the Russians are in sight, all the army is highly elated at the news. Holland will be lost to the French before one month. I am so crowded upon with business (for fortune has just put a finishing stroke to my future happiness, but of this in its proper place, you will be astonished as I was myself at the unexpected preferment).

I am uncertain whether I informed you in my last of the surrender of the Dutch Fleet without firing a Gun. The cowardly rascals after keeping us three days at our quarters, and even appeared determined to fight till we got within musket shot of them when Admiral Story wrote our Admiral a letter saying nothing should compel him to surrender, but that he would try the fortune of the day though we were twice his number. And lo! What did he do? Worked our minds up to a phrensy, frightened many of our Midshipmen and gentlemen Volunteers who came out with us, and made many a heart feel as if 5 minutes more would send them to glory. We were not much more than half his force, yet did he strike his colours just as the first broadside was pointed at him – in short you will have the whole of them in England by the time you receive this.

Now my dear Emily rejoice with me, and thank the best of men for his great attention and friendship to me, as almost a stranger. Admiral Mitchell is the man I owe so much to, as he has not only put me into a lucrative situation here, but has recommended me so strongly that what he has made me here, will be the means of my getting confirmed in to the first vacancy at headquarters, most likely, with the interest of my own. I am now Adjutant of the forces, the first appointment on the Staff.

The Helder was taken on 28 August, and 13 Dutch warships and a naval depot were seized. Wybourn landed on 9 September, as Adjutant acting as Administration Officer for the Officer Commanding Land Forces.

Wybourn is especially anxious for money and preferment, because he and his sister are orphans and she is dependant on him.

Wife of his patron, Earl Spencer

On 21 September Admiral Mitchell shifted his flag to the "Babet"; she had been lightened sufficiently for the pilot to take charge (presumably for manoeuvres closer to the mud-flats than could be achieved aboard "Isis"). Mitchell wrote in his letter to the Admiralty: 'I left the "Isis", "Melpomene" and "Juno" with yards and top-masts struck, having taken all the seamen and marines that could be spared from them with Sir C. Hamilton, Captains Dundas and Oughton.' By 15 October Mitchell was back on the "Isis".

We landed 500 men and are now acting under the command of Sir Ralph Abercromby. It is everything I could wish. First I go everywhere my commanding Officer [goes], nothing is done without me. I shall be made known to all the great men here, this I calculate upon at future times. Next, instead of being obedient to <u>all</u> commanders I do nothing but by the <u>commanding officer's</u> orders. I parade the guards, give the word of command etc., etc. In fact I am the responsible man; I have all the writings to attend to, orders etc. and finally am <u>just</u> what I know you can easily picture me. This comes from my always having conducted myself (as my enemies may say) above all others, and not forgetting that restless ambition I know is my foible, but out of evil good will arise. As to the <u>lucre</u>, I am allowed Bon [?] forage, a Horse, forage for that, Contingent money for the Office etc., etc., and Admiral Mitchell has presented me with a regular commission signed sealed etc., which entitles me to double pay. I shall write immediately to <u>Lady Spencer</u> as she will be pleased at my preferment.

I will not attempt to say anything of my friend the Admiral, as all must fall short of the gratitude I feel, but independent of this affair (of which I never dreamt), I really loved the man, he is everything you can conceive a British Admiral ought to be, such grandeur at his Table, fit for a Prince, and yet familiar, even with his Midshipmen at proper times; his study is, to serve all. I never saw him out of temper in 18 days' storm which would have compelled him to quit his enterprise had it lasted but one day longer, for most ships had been without provision two days so that we must have gone home the next.

This is news enough for one day. I cannot conceive how I find time to say so much, for I have not been off my legs since six in the morning till 12 at night. I have never seen such actual service before, and the fatigue of it had nearly laid me up yesterday, four times in thirty-six hours I bled such a stream at my Nose, as to render me insensible with loss of blood; I was obliged to have a Physician, the Major was so good as to insist upon my going to bed and says I should not stir till morning and not then if not well.

Adieu my dearest Girl I long to see you
Affectionately yours
T.M. Wybourn.

October 24, 1799
H.M.S. "Isis"
Texel Harbour

My dear Emily,

    With the most sincere pleasure and comfort, I once more sit down in my own snug little Cabin after all the hardships I have endured since the 9th of Sept. (the first day I could command) to relieve the anxiety I am sensible you must have felt by my silence; I have been remiss, I acknowledge, but not from having forgotten the best of Sisters, but from having been harassed and fatigued beyond measure that positively I have more than once sunk under it and could not have survived much longer in the same manner: indeed now that I am safe, sound in wind & limb and thank God, out of further danger, I will confess the perils I have been in lately have alone occasioned my not writing, as I was unwilling to raise doubts which I knew a description of my sufferings would create in you.

i.e. the first day he had at leisure.

    Will you believe that nothing else but the defeat of our Army prevents my being a prisoner at Amsterdam, or sent to Glory in the event? However my dearest Sister I can now gratify you, and myself likewise, by fighting over again my own battles, and I may be allowed a little latitude, as my sword till now has been a maiden one. How grateful to a young man's feelings is a return from the field of battle when he is cognacious of deserving applause, and the approbation of his commanding officer. Fortune has been more my friend than I could have expected and I have been placed in a situation to acquire the greatest honour and Glory, though at a vast risque, and under every disadvantage. I know not how to express my happiness in words adequate to what I felt when upon my return from Friezland, after two desperate actions with the French and Dutch in which I had only 80 Men under my command against 350. The different Generals, my own Admiral and in short every officer of rank [were] taking me by the hand congratulating me and greatly applauding the conduct of myself and those under me, but gently blaming my rashness in thinking of attacking so great a body when we were only acting on the defensive. You know my ambition. I had been ever since our arrival in Holland aiming at a separate command. We disembarked on the Continent first, here I was only Adjutant and our Battalion was in the rear guard; we soon after garrisoned the Texel Island, here we were only 230 and the Dutch 3,000 but we had a Fort to retreat to which 20,000 men could not take.

As the Army advanced into Holland in the interior we embarked on board Vessels and sailed along the shores of the Zuider Zea, taking every Town as we advanced, aided by the Admiral and all his seamen, though most of our successes were owing to the loyalty of the Inhabitants of the smaller Towns. When we arrived at Enkhausen, the 4th Town in Holland, I was struck with the beauty of the place, and the grandeur of the Streets, most of them being wider than any street in London; a Canal runs through most of them planted on each side with Trees. I have not time to give you a very minute account, [so] shall just pass over the heads of our progress till I come to Friezland, where I have gained immortal Honour, as the Commandant was pleased to call it. I forgot to tell you that there [are] a 100 Bridges in this Town: a Cathedral, Stadthouse, Admiralty and other edifices for the Municipality etc., etc.

Admiral Mitchell soon dissolved the Republican Assemblies, and appointed a Regent and other Officers till the arrival of the Prince. This Town is fortified by the sea on two sides, and by two gates on the other sides. We kept the Town from the whole French army, until the arrival of the English army – at one time they came within shot of us, but were soon convinced they could not take us without an immense loss on their side.

We lived well at this place, but could never be allowed rest, nor had I my clothes off for some weeks. I have actually slept as I have been walking, and dropped on my plate while eating, but this is trifling to our service from that time to the present.

We left this lovely place and charming society for the Town of Lemmer in Friezland about 40 miles across the Zuider Zea and where no English were within the same province; this small Town had surrendered to the English a few days before, and the poor inhabitants after the town was bombarded for a whole day hoisted Orange Colours, but were in fear of having their throats cut by the Patriots and French who had fled upon our appearance in order to assemble a force together.

Never was such joy seen as these poor creatures showed upon our landing. Only myself and three Junior Officers with about 127 Privates: these they thought sufficient to defend them from any misfortune, as they told us the sight of a <u>red</u> coat would frighten them all away such dread had they of the English. But we thought ourselves

Admiral Mitchell had positioned his squadron off Lemmer's fortifications, which jutted into the sea. One of his captains, advised that the town contained a thousand 'determined' regular troops, stationed gun-boats including "Isis's" launch, on two sides of the town and sent the following letter to the commandant of Lemmer: 'Sir. Resistance on your part is in vain; I give you one hour to send away the women and children; at the expiration of that time, if the town is not surrendered to British arms for the Prince of Orange, your soldiers shall be buried in its ruins. I have the honour to be your obedient servant, W. Bolton, Captain of His Majesty's Ship "Wolverine".' The response came back 'To Captain Bolton: Commandant, I have received your summons; the Municipality request twenty-four hours to send to their proper authority to accede to your demands. (signed) P. Van Groutten, Commandant. N.B. Please to send an answer by the bearer.' Bolton replied immediately: 'Sir, I have received your letter, and

in too great danger amongst a country of enemies with only a handful of Military, and about a 100 seamen. There were three sides of the town to guard against any attack by night, and had the enemy one grain of valour, they would have cut us all to pieces long before we began our fortifications.

The inhabitants were mostly loyal and afforded us much assistance, found all the Officers with Horses and raised a Corps of Volunteers, (which we were rather afraid of – by the bye) and 300 workmen; we soon made four Batteries and placed Guns upon them, and set the sailors with their officers to man them. In ten days we were prepared by any attack; the Enemy were now only four miles off entrenched, about 700 of them having embodied on the 12th they attacked us at daylight. The shot flew about like peas. We expected to have been made prisoners before night, as they fought so determined, and were so numerous, but after five hours fighting, the enemy gave it up. We lost very few hitherto. No sooner had they begun to fight with small arms, and were within half pistol shot of us, but (neck or nothing) I begged the Commandant (a Captain of the Navy) to allow me to charge the Enemy with the Bayonet, our men were desperate. We fully expected to die that day and with one accord resolved to reap some glory first.

There was no retreating, we had nowhere to go, and no quarter was expected. Thus determined, our noble fellows rushed on the Enemy without firing a shot till close to them; they flew in all directions, we followed them five miles into the country, killed 18, wounded 60 and upwards, took one Officer and 27 prisoners, with very little loss indeed.

The Papers mention this affair, and I, with much satisfaction, saw my name particularised.

    Adieu
    T.M. Wybourn

have the honour to inform you, that if the Prince's colours are not hoisted in half an hour after the receipt of this, I shall bombard the town.' Bolton then pushed "Wolverine" closer to shore, through the 'oosy flat'. The Dutch then opened fire. Within seconds the entire British squadron blazed away at the town for nearly an hour in which time the enemy threw down its arms and ran. Bolton was not surprised to discover, judging by the strong opposition, that they had been mostly French.

See Letter of Capt. James Boorder on p. 26.

Nov. 2, 1799
H.M.S. "Isis" off the Helder Town
Holland

My dear Sisters,
    We still remain here in the most unpleasant situation blowing continual gales of wind. All the poor fellows that have been serving

on the continent have been many days embarked on board Transports and King's Ships, and now absolutely starving with cold, and at short allowance, unable to get out of the harbour by contrary winds. There are but 3,000 men in Holland now to be embarked, we are much afraid should this weather last, that we shall be blocked up here by the Ice. About 150 Ships are ready for sea would the wind come fair, only one wind will do for us (East) as the Harbour is surrounded with sands, and there is only one single passage for large ships to pass through; how we got in here in the first instance is wonderful as we must pass in full front of all the Batteries and there were 80 pieces of heavy cannon on them when we took the Helder; a proof of Dutch courage however.

We are all most anxiously looking for the pleasure of seeing old England again after our ill successes which is not yet known to us, or what occasions our hasty retreat; some say the Prussians have undertaken to conquer Holland on condition the English will withdraw, there are 30,000 or 40,000 Prussians on the frontiers which no one knows the motive for, others think it is owing to a certain great Man coming here, while the <u>most loyal</u> contend that the object of the expedition is completed, as we came here <u>only</u> to give the Dutch an opportunity of joining our standard and their prince which they have never shewn the least inclination to do (that is, the <u>fighting</u> part of the Country) but on the contrary have disputed every inch of ground by the Bayonet, and certain it is, we did not come to conquer all Holland with such a handful of men, comparatively speaking, for it would be necessary to have 150,000 Men to do that.

Our Army did wonders, no one can form an idea of the <u>miseries</u> they suffered but those that saw it, and had we been here three days sooner (which all know the storm prevented for three weeks after we left England) there would not have been a man to oppose our progress to Amsterdam.

The greatest distress we felt was, after conquering all the Towns we came to and distributing the proclamations which contained an assurance of our force being sufficient to protect them from the Enemy (the Patriots) and the poor creatures hoisting Royal Colours and sacrificing the Patriots to their rage; after all this that the defeat of our Army should oblige us to leave these loyal and generous people to the mercy of those villains, who no doubt will confiscate all their property and put them to death. Such were the situation of my poor friends at Lemmer West Friezland.

I forgot, or had not room in my last to mention the occasion of

'Patriots' were Dutch anti-royalist (anti-Orange) Catholics supporting the French.

our retreat after [so] Glorious an action as we fought and conquered; we had the last action as the papers date of the 24th of October on Friday morning at daylight, and having totally defeated the enemy that day, we allowed our men to refresh and take a little sleep during the afternoon as they had to rest on their Arms as usual in the night.

On Saturday morning a swarm of peasants came in, and so frightened they could hardly speak, informing us that nearly 4,000 of the enemy were marching towards the town, that they intended to stop a little way off till midnight when they would storm the Town and had sworn to give us no quarter; this unfavourable account we kept from the soldiers and sailors and making up our minds as to the event we made every necessary defence, and for my part I had packed up everything and directed them etc.

At 9 o'clock, our ideas were absorbed by those alarming accounts, and we just proceeding to let down the banks of the sea to overflow the Country and thereby prevent the enemy from coming upon us at all quarters when the Capt. Commandant came in to me, and taking me aside requested I would call in all outposts Piquets, Centinels etc., etc., and be under Arms on the Quay in one quarter of an hour without fail, as he had just received an Express from Admiral Mitchell.

All this accomplished leaving most of our things behind, just before we embarked the news of going away had spread through the Town, there was a general consternation; we must obey orders, there was no alternative, Royalists begged on their knees, and the women and children came clinging round us terrified at the account of our leaving them, and saying the patriots would put them to death. Never was I witness to such a scene of distress, we were reduced to the painful necessity of keeping them all off by Centinels, or we should never have got away.

To the honour of our brave officers and Soldiers under my command be it said they came with one accord and volunteered to stay and protect the unfortunate inhabitants with their lives, even after all the seamen had embarked, but the Commandant could not accept our offer. All that could be done was to take them with us, all that we knew to be good people, and write a letter to the French Col. stating that we had <u>compelled</u> the Town and inhabitants to do all they did do. This was done. And after taking all our friends on board Vessels we sailed from the Town, but could only get about a mile off that night; at daylight the next morning we saw the place in possession of the Enemy and the republican General in a Coach and four with dragoons in front: what became of them all God knows. The same at Enkhausen, and all the Towns we passed and had taken. I assure you my dear Emily I would give all I am worth to get away for, to add to other miseries, the Mess is reduced in the article of eating, and to all other comforts I need not say how wretchedly I am off, in short, worse than ever, for having quitted the place so precipitately, I, as well as the rest, left most of my things behind, and what we have we are afraid of trusting to be washed as we are in hourly expecting of sailing, so that after wearing a shirt a week and putting it away, it comes in its turn to be worn again.

    Adieu

    T.M. Wybourn

Dec. 3, 1799
H.M.S. "Isis"
Yarmouth

I have been going to write to you my dear Sister these fourteen days past. I wrote the moment we anchored in dear old England, and some days after I found my letter had not been sent, since which, we have been in the greatest state of suspense expecting orders every moment to sail to Sheerness, so that I have delayed sending it. We this day got sailing orders so that you may now direct for me at Sheerness. We had a delightful passage over towards the latter end, but upon leaving the Texel, had most tremendous gales of Wind for five days that blew us into the centre of the German Ocean and for many days it was impossible to fetch any part of England at all, so that we attempted to make for Scotland and was again driven to sea. The Admiral was upon the eve of bearing away for Norway, however at last we had a fair wind for England, and in three days got close to Northumberland and sailed along the shore in a most heavenly manner viewing all the Towns, Seats, etc., with Castles in our way till we arrived at Yarmouth, when we were complimented with a salute from Admiral Duncan, which we returned, our Band playing "God Save the King". Admiral Story (the Dutch Admiral) came over with us.

    I never enjoyed a ship so much, as the time we were going by Adm.

Duncan, it was a glorious fine day, we had 25 sails set, our gallant Admiral's Flag flying and a fine band of music (formerly Admiral Story's) hardly any wind, and being crowded with the brave Troops who had escaped the common Slaughter in Holland, we were surrounded with Boats, and all the shore covered with people. A Hambourgh Pacquet came in with us and was full of passengers from the Continent with several families of distinction, and many ladies besides.

We played our Band all the way the last few miles, and they seemed highly delighted. Never were poor Divils so happy as we all were, particularly the Troops, at getting ashore having been so long on the passage, without a bed, or common comforts; the last four days we had no fresh water allowed us to wash in, we were in great distress and fatigued to death on the continent and sick at sea; one officer's life is despaired of from extreme fatigue. Indeed we are all more fit to be nursed than to attend our duty. I have no more strength than a child, you would not know me. We shall ever remember the wretchedness we experienced in Holland so wet, so full of Canals and Dykes that the whole country is full of swamps enough to kill any one, and for two months we had not our clothes off ten times. However thank God I am now recovering fast having lived the last few weeks upon all the luxuries of life, added to the pleasure of being on shore. The surgeon doses me with Bark. I am in hopes of going to the Barracks at Chatham on our arrival and get leave for a Month, how delightful is the anticipation of spending Christmas with you, my dear Emily at least, all other dear relatives being separated from us.

'Bark' may be a reference to 'Jesuits' Bark', from the cinchona tree, known also as quinine, the primary drug used to combat malarial fever, though willow bark was also used medicinally.

    Your affectionate Brother
    T.M. Wybourn

Dec. 14, 1799
Sheerness

My dear Sister,

    After some days more of buffitting with the winds and the waves, we arrived here, and are once again on dear old England's land.

    We have disembarked all our poor fellows; while in the hurry of this, I observed some well dressed females looking on, one lady in particular appeared to be much affected, curiosity, or perhaps sympathy, enduced me to wish to see her and I followed them, judge of my surprise when I recognised our lovely young friend Ann W. I found she came to see her Brother Tom on board some ship. To see the disembarkation of the Troops hurt her extremely, for it so happened that she saw them embark for Holland in health, high spirits and well dressed, to see the wretched change that a few months only had made in their appearance was truly affecting – she said I see you have shared the common fate, as you do not look like yourself.

I need not say that I passed a most agreeable time with them, and I received a kind letter from my Uncle Wybourn congratulating me on my safety, with some encomiums on the enclosed letter he saw in the papers, also an invitation for Christmas, when I shall have the happiness of meeting you at least, and in thankfulness that I am permitted to eat another Christmas dinner with the few remaining dear relatives that have always met at my Uncle's table on that day.

Adieu and God bless till we meet

T.M. Wybourn

Oct. 11, 1799
A Letter of Capt. James Boorder to Admiral [Mitchell at Enchuysen]
Lemmer Town West Friesland

Sir,

I have the honour to inform you that at five o'clock this Morning the Enemy made a general attack on this Town in four different parts.

There [sic] advanced party attempted to storm the north Battery. We soon got them between two fires, our tars with pikes surrounded them and they immediately laid down their arms.

Their force was one officer one sergeant one Corporal and twenty-eight men; two of the latter killed. We had no sooner secured our prisoners than they attacked us with the remainder of their force 670 in number, our little Army did wonders. For with sailors and Marines our force was only 157. We fought them for four hours and a half when the enemy gave way in all directions. I immediately ordered the

Marines to pursue them, their breaking down a Bridge prevented their Colours and two field pieces from falling into our hands, but before this was affected [sic] the heavy fires from the Batteries had killed 18 of the enemy and wounded about 20 and on their general attack they had five men killed and nine wounded.

Doubtless Wybourn led his men in the pursuit. See his account on p. 21.

It is impossible for me to speak too highly of the men and Officers under my command. Ist Lieut. Wybourn, also Howard Higgins (2nd) and Gardiner behaved with honour to themselves and credit to their country.

It affords me great satisfaction to inform you that we had not a man hurt.

I am etc.

James Boorder

July 30, 1800
H.M.S. "Isis"
Downs

I cannot avoid writing my dearest Sisters on the subject of your last most melancholy letter, no occurrence of my whole life has occasioned me so much pain. It was a consolation to me to have a dear and affectionate Brother to communicate my most secret thoughts to but now I am deprived of my dearest friend on earth: he was possessed of an honest heart, and being the only companion of my youth, I had fondly hoped when the decline of our life approached, and worldly concerns at an end to have enjoyed this loved Brother's society but alas this was not to be; and I feel now, as if I should never be happy again.

Younger brother John Wybourn had died at Cape Coast Castle.

Do not be offended my dear Sisters when I say that a Brother is everything to a Brother, you are formed for other concerns, and when married the affections must be divided, but brothers are always the same.

O! heavens what a change has a short time made – I feel as if in a dream. It was but the other day I wrote to my dear John reproaching him with his silence, sent him a journal of all transactions since his departure with newspapers etc., etc., much advice also promising ourselves such happy days when he returned. Indeed my dearest

Sisters I am stupefied with grief, added to which we have sailing orders.

We are going with a large Fleet and a kind of Expedition up the Baltic to Copenhagen; some great project is in agitation. Admiral Dickson at Yarmouth is to have the Command. Adieu I have no spirits to add more than that I shall send you an account of our Voyage, and when peace arrives I hope we may be together.

We go tomorrow at daylight. I am a poor one to preach but hope you will try to reconcile yourselves to our present calamity.

T.M. Wybourn

26 August, 1800
H.M.S. "Isis"
Elsingnore [sic]

My dear Sisters,

I have made many attempts to write, and as often found myself unable to proceed, my spirits are however rather better, and some employment my mind has been for some days engaged in has diverted me from those gloomy thoughts which have been long my constant companions since the unhappy event of our dear John's death.

It was my intention to proceed with a kind of journal as you desired, but a most violent gale of wind arose, and at a most unfortunate crisis for we had that day quitted the North Sea and entered what is called the Catagut, a narrow channel between two shores covered with hidden Rocks. Our Fleet was large consisting of 7 sail of the line, and other Vessels such as Gun Boats, Bombs and Transports amounting to 26 in the whole, so that our situation was most deplorable; in this state we remained 4 days as [there was no] possibility of getting into the ocean, or of gaining any port except this we are now in, and that the Admiral had positive orders not to enter, as it is against the Treaty between Denmark and England, however self preservation is the first law, and the Gale continuing the Admiral held a council of War; the result was, to go in at all events, but this was not till two ships had unfortunately perished, one of which we had in tow for a long time, and two line of Battle Ships was only about 4 yards from a reef of Rocks, and were saved by a miracle. However such was the Gale, that we got into this Harbour in a few

Now spelled Kattegat

Bomb vessels, or 'Bombs', had two heavy mortars on turntables firing high trajectory explosive shells. Around 100 feet in length, they were crewed by between 67 and 110 men

18   14   11   8   *Engeltofta*

16   *Light Ho.*   *Gryteskar*   *Grytehaven*

Koll Point   15

Molle Hut   7   *Stabeck*

CATEGAT   11

Kruppern   70   **Engleholm**

Bromby   5   *Wegelholm*

Jonster

Wasby   *Halsehaven*

14   *Hognas*

Vik

Domsten

4   *Kulla*

Havt Chk.   *Gunnanstorp*

Nakke Head   *Lappen*   *Palskop*

Hesborg Hill   *Bozgerhed*

THE SOUND   *Karnan*

Hornbeck   12

Hammar Mill   10

Cronenberg   72   **Helfingborg**

Helfingoer
or Elfineur

Tellgaura   19

Dixen   *Ra*

Hammelbeck   5   11   14   *Tegelbruk*

Sletten   9   *Glomslof*

Nivaae   8   14   12   *Kungsgard*

Sophienberg   11   7   8   *Uronbug*   *Huen I.*   *Saby*

Rong Sted   6   8   *Pihaken*   *Orje*

Smistrup   10   18   *Asmundstorp*

Wabek   6   *Graen*   **Landscrona**

Paper Mill   5   8   30

SpringForbi   12   *Dogstorp*

Taarbeck   18

Scale of Miles   8   *Barseback*

1 2 3 4 5 6

Woods Head   8   7   *Pinhall*   *Fishing Huts*   *Lodkoping*

7   7   *Borby*

Charlotten Lund

4

3   4   10

COPENHAGEN   5   3   4   4

Round Tower
& Observatory   7   **Salt holm**   *N.Flint*   *Jotte*   4

Flaskekroe   *Taurbye*   6   3

Widovre   **Amag**   4

Hongekroe   *Holten derbye*   *S.Flint*   *Trindelen*   **Malmo**

Drage   *Linhamn*

Druc Point   5   3   *Lernacka*

Hvlje   *Fosjo*

6   7   *Bunkeflod*

6   **KIOGE**   *Little Ground*

Eskroe   *Broad*   4   *Hokoping*

6   **BAY**   7   *Ground*   *Koground*

Ekroe   9   10

Chalk   7   *Hollerik*   *G.Hammar*

Halve Slot   **Skanor**

Magleby   7   5   **Falsterbo**   *Trelleborg*

Iorslay Slot   **Steffens**   *Falsterbo*   *Leig*

Holte   **Head**   *Light*   4   *Segelskar*

THE BALTIC SEA

CHART
of
THE SOUND
COPENHAGEN
&c.

S W E D E N

D E N M A R K

Copenhagen from the sea

hours after the Admiral made a signal for that purpose, and without a single sail set went eleven miles an hour, you will easily conceive our danger by this.

I never was more alarmed and even the seamen, for nothing is so dangerous, they say, as a Lee shore, give them sea room and that gale is only thought a Cap full of Wind. We remained in the outer harbour for some time, as we had broken the Treaty; the Danes thought proper to permit us to pass the largest fort in Europe (Elsingnore Castle which stands on a point of land at the extremity of their inner harbour, and when in a state of defence can mount 350 guns).

We are now in the sweetest place in the World, Sweden on one side of us and Denmark on the other and so close that a shot can be thrown from one side to the other. The Country is like a garden and Shrubbery, the Castle is a most elegant structure, it shows three points to the Sea (or rather river) so that no Vessel can pass without leave. All Merchantmen pay tribute, let them be of what nation soever, and men of War must salute it. The Revenue to the King of Denmark from this alone is about 70,000 per annum. The town of Elsingnore is close to us on the Danish side – a little behind the Castle on the side of a wood, or more properly a Grotto, stands the King's Palace, a country residence looking over the sea, and commanding a most heavenly view of the Swedish side, the water, Castle and an extensive country, and in the centre of this channel also a small Island, about 4 miles of ground in it.

On one side of the Palace garden, is the Alcove where King Hamlet was poisoned and which appears in good repair still. It is a very mortifying thing we cannot get on shore, but till we know how the negotiation ends, no leave will be given and so strict is our Admiral that no boats are allowed to come on board or any communication with the shore not even on the Swedish side with whom we have no quarrel, and who have, on the contrary, refused any assistance to the Danes – what could possess them to let us pass this immense Battery we cannot conceive, unless they do not mean to let us pass out again, and therefore hope to bring our Court to their terms. I forgot to tell you that the Castle commands the pass entry and having got by there is no other way to get back again nor can any ship to, or from Prussia, go any other way but this.

Copenhagen is only 12 miles above us, we can just see the Steeples etc., etc. Our force, in case of hostilities commencing, will proceed to the Capital and destroy it immediately. The Marine forces amount to

Wybourn's expedition seems to have had bad luck, although preparations had clearly been made for some sort of discussion with the Danes. The 'Armed Neutrality' pact of Prussia, Sweden, Denmark and Russia was a response to the British practice of stopping and impounding any neutral shipping that might possibly succour France. This northern league posed a real threat to Britain's Baltic trade, on which she depended for grain and timber, hemp and pitch to maintain the fleet. Perhaps this 'expedition' had been intended as an 'armed goodwill' visit, and a reminder that Denmark would probably lose a naval confrontation with Britain. If so, it failed, eventually resulting in Nelson's famous victory where he destroyed nearly the entire Danish fleet within the horrified sight of Copenhagen itself.

800, and there are about 300 Seamen to land to assist us after this. I lament to say the beautiful Castle will be bombarded. We are very busy as you may imagine, for our Ambassador does not think it can be settled; what they meant to do with us, is very strange for it is well known the Danes have 10,000 men on the spot, so that 1,000 will do but little. The weather is getting so cold that in two months the sea will block us up. I do not think our Admiral a <u>Dasher</u> for giving so much time to the Enemy, they will be prepared for us at all points. I hope to have better news for you in my next but the Capt. has just sent to say letters are going immediately, and this is the first opportunity we have had of sending, so Adieu, with Love to all.

    T.M. Wybourn

Journal

Sept. 4, 1800
H.M.S. "Isis"
Elsinore

The Admirals, Captains etc., etc., went in State to dine with the English Consul at Elsinore & passed through the Fleet in grand procession, every Ship manned in the rigging, a guard in the gangway, Drums beating a March and our band playing "Rule Britannia". It was a truly pleasing sight, and that conveyed an idea of the extraordinary superiority of the English; we are here in the Enemy's Gut, without leave and out of reach of their Batterys, which gives us the power to ruin the Kingdom of Denmark – broke the Treaty by so doing – and yet we are courted by the natives, and they tamely submit to the dictate of our Minister at Copenhagen for fear of the consequence of our Fleet, and would offer any terms to get us once more on the other side of the Castle. Received an invitation from Mr. Balfour, our English resident merchant, to dine with him tomorrow, to meet Admiral Dickson and all the heads of the Detachments.

    <u>Friday 5th Sept</u>. Dressed in my gayest apparel to attend Admiral D and the officers of the British Fleet, Capt. O kindly offered me a passage in his Boat. We were received by all the marks of hospitality and English welcome by the Host, a man of princely appearance as

well as manners. When we entered the Dining room we were surprised at the sumptuous entertainment provided and were pleased to find it much in the English style, in short it was beyond our expectation, much profusion. The British Admiral sat in the centre, one side of him Mr. Balfour, on the other the Danish Admiral and the Governors of the Castle, the rest of the company chose their seats, the dinner was served with great regularity, the room well supplied with servants. The table was nine feet broad and twenty-six long. In the middle was a large plateau of silver covered with ornament and figures, down the centre in three rows were all the choicest fruits, sweetmeats etc., etc., at the four corners Fowls, Ham, Fish etc. and one bottle of Port and another of Madeira. After the first course came venison dressed in the Danish way, and after that Turtle, Game etc., etc., also a Duck Pie, a most excellent dish; at this time came two bottles more to each person one of Burgundy another of Champagne, and towards the conclusion of dinner a bottle of Claret, with a few bottles of Hock distributed about the Table. A band of Music under the windows in the Garden regaled our Ears, playing several delightful German airs; Servants from the Parade came continually round with preserves, sweetmeats and fruits of which there was a profusion on the Table, Coffee also; it was a novel sight to look down the table while between thirty and forty people sat in full view of each other from the amazing breadth of the Table, with five bottles before each person exclusive of Glasses etc., etc. All the guests were highly delighted by the hospitality and handsome behaviour of our entertainer and at seven reluctantly took leave.

Nothing could exceed the elegance of this compliment to the British Fleet by an individual who happens to be the only Merchant resident here. His situation is very lucrative and one which a war with the Danes must ruin, but he said with great pleasantry – It had been above 120 years since a British Admiral's flag had been flying in these seas, and as it might be as many more before another was seen he could not deny himself the gratification of wishing to see his countrymen at his Table.

Upon our leaving this hospitable Mansion, crowds of people assembled to see, and followed us to our Boats, it was no insignificant sight to see nearly 40 English Officers in full uniform with the Admiral at their head and all the boats, even, dressed for the occasion. The Guard all turned out to us though they look upon us as enemies and are extremely alarmed; no leave could be given to sleep on shore.

<u>Saturday 6th</u>. Amused myself with fishing with a line of six fathom, it is astonishing how fast the Flounders are caught with a single line, 100 before dinner.

The Officers of the British Fleet gave a dinner at the English Tavern on shore to the Danish Officers, our consul and Mr. Balfour; it was given on shore merely to encourage the Englishman who keeps it, as well as a return for the elegant dinner of yesterday, but which would have been more splendid on board the Admiral's Ship. We this day received sudden orders not to go on shore again, as we sail for England tomorrow.

<u>Sunday 7th</u>. Got the first Anchor up at Daylight, but it was three o'clock before we weighed, the wind in our favour, and all happy at the thought of returning to our blessed Land.

The shores of Denmark and Sweden are so near that it afforded a beautiful prospect, and thousands of people crowded on the shores and housetops. The Admiral saluted with 15 Guns, which was returned by the Castle of Elsinore with the same number. They never give more to any person. We were soon out of sight of this lovely place, the Ship going at 11 knots an hour, and we hope to continue at that rate till we get clear of this narrow channel where we experienced so much danger in coming in, and which our pilot says he hopes we shall be able to do by tomorrow night, with this wind.

<u>Saturday 13th</u>. Anchored in Yarmouth road, after a week's tedious passage here we met a sad disappointment, Capt. M had gone to Elsinore to supercede Capt. O and had taken all our Letters and papers as we unfortunately missed him in our passage home. But we were overjoyed at the event for it informed us that Admiral Mitchell was employed, and that he was in the "Windsor Castle" third in command of the Channel Fleet which consists of 46 sail of the Line. The whole of our officers will join him as soon as possible.

<u>Tuesday 16th</u>. Orders came for us to sail immediately for the Downs which we did, and here on the 18th but were stopped, the Admiralty saying it was a great favour done Adm. Mitchell to suffer the ship to come even here – but that he would have an opportunity of getting his things, his officers and servants round from this place and that the "Isis" must proceed immediately to Yarmouth again; I am at a great loss to determine what to do, whether to go to the Adm. or remain behind. It is pleasant in the "Isis" where I have the command of the Detachment, and in the "Windsor Castle" are four of our Officers with a Capt. at their heads; at any rate I will wait a

short time to see if we are likely to be employed to advantage or honour; if not, I will apply to join the Admiral.

Thursday 22nd. The weather is now so cold I want a fire, this is the fatal climate of our otherwise blessed Land – it being the accession of our beloved Sovereign to the Throne, now 39 years, we drank his health, the band playing.

Wednesday 23rd. It is a miserable day and I am too poorly to leave the Ship or I could be so happy with my friends at Deal where my dear John and I have passed so many happy days in the Wybourn family. There is a large fleet of Indiamen etc., in the Downs, 400 vessels.

I conclude this short journal by observing that it is a grievous thing that we were forced upon thus pouncing upon the Danes, with as little ceremony, as the carnage on board their ships was excessive; but policy obliged us, as they would not secede from the northern alliance.

This passage must refer to the Battle of Copenhagen, fought 2 April 1801.

1801
H.M.S. "Madras"
To the Mediterranean

The "Madras" was a 4th rate frigate of 54 guns..

My good fortune presses her favours upon me so fast that I cannot believe it real. I meet with so much friendship from the General at Quarters, and have been so highly complimented on my military prowess etc., it is a happy omen, for only yesterday I met a Captain who repeated what Lord Spencer said of me, and to crown my glory made me an offer of going on a secret expedition with him which he has been six weeks waiting [to] hear about; I readily accepted the honour he has done me. My letters have all been laid before Lord Spencer. There is an amazing promotion coming out for us, so that you may suppose we are in fine spirits, and we hope to be actively engaged in this defensive War against the Tyrant and hope for peace, when I should try to obtain sweet, delightful "Guestling", a place we all so much admire; and with the produce of the land we might all live, for why has providence thrown me from an element I most admire, to one I dislike? The sea, with all its grandeur, I cannot like.

When you write to Caroline tell her I often think of her and her progeny and when I know to which part of the Globe I am next destined, I will write to her.

Your affectionate

T. Wybourn

In March 1801 Lord Keith landed Abercromby's expeditionary force at Alexandria. The hope was to seize the city, but not the whole of Egypt, to be in a better negotiation position for a future peace with the French, with Britain able to dictate terms in the Levant.

April 1801
H.M.S. "Madras"
at Sea

My dear Caroline,

Agreeably to my promise that I would let you know where the destinies would order me next, know it is to Egypt; so that in time, I shall have seen the four quarters of the World; I regret that I am leaving England at this most delightful season for the scorching lands of Egypt.

"Invincible" (74 guns), wrecked off the Norfolk coast 16 March 1801.

I suppose that you have seen by the papers the great dangers we have been in by being cast upon the Rocks with the melancholy loss of the "Invincible"; all sailing away in health and spirits and in three hours to hear that 400 found a watery grave, and shocking (even to relate), they were obliged to keep the poor sufferers off from entering the boats with oars. Poor Captain Rennie got nearly within reach, but was too much exhausted to proceed.

Paul I of Russia had been considered insane. His formation of the Northern Alliance against Britain had precipitated the strategic attack on Copenhagen at the entrance to the Baltic. He was assassinated on 2 March 1801.

You will ask me if I think that the death of the Emperor Paul will make any difference as to peace; I cannot tell yet. Alexander is highly spoken of and he has sent a letter to George the Third, expressive of his concern of the misunderstanding that subsisted between his Father and his Britannic Majesty. How can we be made amends for the hundreds destroyed in the Catagut?

You will be pleased to find that illuminating for victory is going out of fashion, as I see by the papers that the Lord Mayor has ordered that expense to be appropriated to the relief of the widows and children of those who have suffered.

When you write to Emily tell her how much I am obliged to her for the parcel she sent me, the books also which will amuse me on the voyage. The Bible I hope to find as much pleasure in the perusal of (as I find by her numerous marks in the margin) as she has.

So I find she has sent another of her swains adrift; is she really so hardhearted or is she resolved on a life of celibacy? If I were not a younger Brother I would reprove her. I must now conclude, as the great men are come on board previous to our joining our forces for Egypt.

With love, I am my dear Sister,

Yours affectionately

T.M. Wybourn

June 20, 1801
H.M.S. "Madras"
at Sea

I promised you my dear Emily to keep a journal of such events as should happen from the time I left England but how it has happened that I have omitted this I must account for presently, for not the notice of any one day has, I perceive, been committed to paper hitherto, indeed much subject has not offered that would afford any amusement unless to display my <u>sublime</u> ideas. I should tell you how the Sun (for I am up before it every morning exercising my men), that grand and resplendent luminary of Heaven, appears emerging from the azure horizon gilding the Ocean with a glittering hue and how beautiful to view are the Dolphin giving chase to the myriads of flying fish promiscuously rising, skimming the air like birds to evade them, with sharks, porpoises, and millions of Bonnettas (a sort of mackerel) all appearing upon the surface of the water; never was scene more truly beautiful than we are in the midst of, in the Mediterranean Sea.

We are now steering for Malta, and can just see Sicily on our left. We are gliding along most charmingly, not more sea than on the Thames, and since we left the channel of old England have not had twenty four hours contrary wind.

I have had the curiosity to observe that never less than 33 sails have been set on our ship, except just when we got to Gibraltar, about ten days since, when it blew so strong we could not anchor, and the charming weather for 18 hours was interrupted by a <u>Cap full of Wind</u> which frightened all our troops, then was all gladness turned to sorrow, our sails reduced to three, called storm sails, and with only these, we went nine knots an hour.

What an astonishing thing is a large Ship, only conceive, we have 58 heavy Guns, near 1100 Men and baggage, Camp equipment etc., for the whole Regiment, with Provisions and water for five months on board, and yet we ride securely in defiance of winds and waves over the most dreadful monsters of the deep and visit the remotest quarters of the globe? What man that is at all contemplatively inclined, can behold at night the Ship forcing her way through seas "foaming with madness" in almost opposite directions to the winds, the changes and variety of colours, and the sparkling particles like fire, looking exactly as though we were sailing through a flaming phosphorus, without feeling sensations the most sublime and delightful?

The 26ᵗʰ Regiment of Foot, the 'Cameronians'.

We have the 26ᵗʰ Regiment on board, they came the 28ᵗʰ of May, from that period our little society of only nine members was dissolved, and a new one of twenty eight substituted. I was in glory, as I dearly love bustle and variety, of which you are pretty well convinced. I usurped the chair at the head of the Table and commenced Caterer and sole director of our family; this I did for various reasons, principally because by this means I should have the company and conversation of the first men both of rank and consequence as they sit uppermost on all occasions. In this, I was not mistaken, for amongst others is a Major Gifford my constant left hand neighbour – the moment I saw him, I was prepossessed in his favour, so true it is, as Lord Bacon says, that a pleasing figure is a perpetual letter of recommendation, he is the most pleasing as well as one of the most amiable men I ever met with.

1801
H.M.S. "Madras"
Malta

Charles Hare died 14 July 1801.

We are just making for the harbour of Malta, the Captain of this Ship [Captain Hare] has been dying these three weeks, and as he was born on shore, it seems he is determined to die there, so has ordered the Ship to come to an anchor, as the weather would not admit of his going on shore to sick quarters at Gibraltar. Shocking to relate, the man dies unregretted by his whole ship's company, he was such a tyrant. I am now going to dress for the shore, as I shall have a few hours to look about me while he is removing.

9 o'clock, I am just come on board, and must sit and cool myself before I go to bed, and resume my pen; you can have no conception of the heat, Malta is a perfect oven, no one stirs out all day, but I was resolved to gratify my curiosity.

This place is about a fourth as large as London. The streets are spacious and the houses built of white stone hewn out of their rocks, which rise to a great height above the sea, the glare is enough to blind anyone. I visited the Grand Master's Palace, and the Church of St. John but cannot attempt a description of it, I never could form an idea of its beauty and magnificence, the very Taverns are palaces. I much regret I cannot stay long enough to make a few remarks, but hope to touch there coming back.

Napoleon first made his mark in the French 'Army of the Orient', campaigning in Egypt and Palestine, trying to establish a French empire and threaten British possession of India overland. Opposing him was the Ottoman Empire, assisted by the British forces in the Mediterranean. Nelson, who destroyed the French fleet in Aboukir Bay, and Sydney Smith, who commanded the Ottoman defence of Acre, shattered Napoleon's dreams of empire. He abandoned his troops in Egypt without a sea-link to France. However, owing to the periodic insanity of the Russian Czar, Russian alliances were erratic; after the Dutch failure, there were fears the Czar could mobilize a pro-French northern coalition against Britain. The Mediterranean fleet would have had to pull out and sail to the Baltic, giving the French a chance to reinforce or evacuate. The only answer was to destroy or capture the French army. For this task, General Sir Ralph Abercromby was chosen.

Abercromby was to be supported in his attack on Alexandria by the Turks, but they were totally unprepared for him when the invasion fleet anchored near Rhodes; Abercromby was alone with his force of 16,500 men. No water was available save that carried with him by the navy – the only other water was in French Alexandria which, of course, he was expected to capture. Abercromby was determined that his men should be well rehearsed for the landing on the Egyptian beaches and to this clear thinking the British owed their success. The waiting French numbered 10,000 but Abercromby had boats for only 6,000 of his 15,000 men. Having personally reconnoitred the landing zone, he ordered the assault on the 2nd of March. The boats were caught in a cross-fire which resulted in 700 casualties before they had even reached the shore but, within 20 minutes of landing, the survivors had defeated the French garrison and captured its artillery. A beachhead established, Abercromby landed his supplies and his army began the long march towards the French positions. Early on 21st March the French attacked the British with great impetuosity and a fierce battle ensued, the Highlanders and a French unit hurling stones at each other when they ran out of ammunition, and the British so determined that they were prepared to carry the field with the bayonet if necessary. The French *attacked successfully, particularly with their cavalry, but the battle was won by 9 am, Abercromby mortally wounded. Hutchinson took over and besieged Alexandria with some 5,000 British and a number of Turkish irregulars, then marched on Cairo and nearly provoked a mutiny among his officers. On 27th June the demoralised and homesick French surrendered Cairo, and General Menou left Alexandria to Hutchinson five days later leaving a garrison. Abercromby had died on board H.M.S. "Foudroyant" on 28th March.*

July 15, 1801
H.M.S. "Madras"
Egypt

Camp before Alexandria 4 o'clock in the Morning.

Here I am at last my dear Sisters after a passage the most delightful and the quickest any ship ever had of our size. I was disembarked two days after our arrival & to my astonishment found a large Battalion of my own corps at the Camp doing duty in the front line of our Army, in the very face of the enemy whose advanced posts are not a mile from us; happy am I to say they gained (as usual) the highest honours in the late action, we lost only 170 Men out of 500, and every officer of ours were touched either badly, or slightly.

Wybourn speaks with some pride that every officer was hit; these were men who obviously led from the front, taking the same risks as their troops, if not more.

The Duty is excessively hard, they have remained with the whole army in the same position since 21 of March; but the greater part of the Army went against Cairo and 13,000 French surrendered on the 26th June and are going home. There is only the Garrison of Alexandria, but it is so strongly fortified that the loss of 5,000 Men must ensue to attack it. They have terms offered to surrender but refuse.

Our Army in a few days will amount to fifty thousand men, theirs is only 8,000 and only 3,000 of these are French, so that they must fall, and if they fire a single shot, no quarter is to be shown them. I hope they may be wise enough to submit.

I rode out yesterday to our furthest post, about a mile from our Camp, our horses and the enemy are only a few yards asunder and they drink together. While we were talking to their Dragoons a French officer came up and was extremely polite, asked us the news, and said they were all heartily tired of the place. I was however much alarmed by a whole Troop of Hussars coming furiously up to us with drawn swords. I feared they were offended at seeing four British

View of the French fortified heights, to the eastward of Alexandria

A Turkish Horseman and a Turkish Foot Soldier

officers so near their lines; there was no possibility of retreating as we were too far from our own Picquets so stood our ground; it proved only the relief going round.

The officers of the Troop came up to us, after some civilities we all rode along the Videttes, and upon our turning off to return they all took off their hats. I never mean to go so near them again, in case a violent <u>republican</u>, in his zeal should carry us into their Camp as spies!

We always beat to arms two hours before day, to be ready in case of surprise, and when day breaks, Ravellen [sic] beats and everybody   *Reveille* is dismissed to their Tents till sunset, except the various guards and centrys. It is the most (I was going to say – awfully grand sight I ever saw) at daylight the colours are hoisted, the whole Army drawn up along the position in battle array, and all the Bands, Trumpets, Drums, fifes and Bugles strike off at the same time; it may be heard many miles.

This plain is the most miserable of any in Egypt, not a tree or even a bit of grass, all sand, and scorching as a furnace. Vermin of all sorts but most fleas and ants, scorpions and beetles crawling over one in the night and getting under the clothes, and no man is permitted to undress, or even take off his sword, and in this manner and under Tents only have the Army been ever since they came; not a house, or a hut to be seen anywhere and the natives who are chiefly Arabs and Greeks are much worse objects than the most abject of our Beggars.

The Market is large and well supplied, a Sheep only costs a Dollar, Fowls 36 for a Dollar, Geese four, eggs 750 a Dollar, fruit in great abundance, and almost for nothing: but no vegetables at all except onions & Pumkins [sic]. Alas no Butter. They ride Asses, as horses are scarce, these are most of the particulars of the place and every day is alike. Adieu my dearest Emily, you shall hear from me after we get to Alexandria. Send this to our dear Matilda, and give my love to all friends. I am melting with heat tho' not yet six o'clock. Nor is it possible to write, for vermin.

Your affectionate
T.M. Wybourn

Sept. 16, 1801
H.M.S. "Madras"
Egypt: City of Alexandria

My dearest Sisters,

Nelson's destruction of the French fleet in Aboukir Bay, in the Battle of the Nile in 1798, ruined Napoleon's dreams of a French empire in the east. His most recent actions to which Wybourn must be referring, included the destruction of the Danish fleet at Copenhagen in April and the attack on the French invasion flotilla at Boulogne in August. The short peace came when Napoleon forced Austria and Naples to capitulate; in October the terms of the Peace of Amiens were drafted for final ratification in 1802.

We are now at rest and enjoy the blessing of peace in Egypt, thanks to the gallant Lord Nelson, who determined on a dangerous, yet decisive manoeuvre to accomplish it; you will see it in the papers, and history will transit it to posterity.

The enemy surrendered their last position on the first of this month, and on the 14th a division of them were sent to France: you may easily conceive how happy we are, for besides this honour of conquering the flower of the French Army, we have hopes of quitting the most miserable spot of the whole earth. Decayed buildings, ruins, sand and stones are all we have hitherto seen, with the intolerable heat of a vertical sun, not a cloud have I seen since I have been here, or a drop of rain since I left England to refresh a sickly Army and Navy. You do not hear in England how many are in the hospitals, and nearly half of the officers dead and sick. We have lost our Captain and many officers, above 40 on the sick list, you know not the hardships and miseries we have endured. Holland, bad as that was, was paradise compared to this, however thank God we have gotten through all but the Plague and we are in hopes to be away before the period that that disorder rages at.

I am now in a pretty good house in this vile town, close to the Harbour looking to the sea. This is the first of our getting into the town, the sand hills having been the residence of the Army hitherto. I am attended by a little Imp of darkness who is so rejoiced at obtaining liberty (for she was a slave) that I believe she adores me as her ...?

Presumably the word 'god' has been omitted.

I have just heard that the "Madras" is the last ship to remain here. [Rear Admiral] Sir Richard Bickerton stays to regulate the departure of the French and English armies, so that besides the mortification of staying in this country we shall be in a continual bustle and confusion.

20th Sept. I have had no opportunity of continuing till now, having been on board four days to regulate my own detachment, and mount a guard, for we had the forms and ceremonies of a court to go through. Here has been the Capt. Pascha of the Turks, the 3rd man of the Empire with a power of life and death over the sultain's subjects (without assigning a reason), and the Admiral of the Gallies with just such a train as fancy forms, upon reading the Arabian Knights [sic] entertainment. I never beheld such grandeur, and magnificent pomp. The Turkish Admiral's Cabin is said to have cost 20,000 pounds sterling in fitting out alone; I supposed myself in a mansion above. Our new Admiral has been exceedingly polite to me, asking me to dine and promises to introduce me to the great man of the Turks; also very kindly inviting me to be of his train in an excursion to grand Cairo, and the Pyramids up the Nile, where he intends going the instant all the French are embarked. You may suppose this to be the most gratifying to me, of all things, as I had little hopes of such an opportunity, it being 260 miles from here.

I imagine we shall set off about the 12th of October, that being the most favourable time of the Nile; so you may look for Rosetta on the Map and follow me up to Cairo and the Pyramids, as we shall go by boats, it being 186 miles from the Harbour of Rosetta to Cairo.

I must now inform you of my past time since I wrote to you in July, but I have so much to say that I fear I shall not find room.

When I wrote last, I was on the other side of Alexandria, it is only since the 20th Sept. I landed here, as the Army invested this side of the Town; on the 26 only and as the "Madras" was cruizing off here I again volunteered to join the Regiment for I was soon carried on board from the other side, having caught a violent fever and flux which nearly killed me. The "Madras" was then 20 miles off and I suffered much by being sent on board. To my good fortune I was sent to the beautiful Island of Cyprus about 80 leagues from Egypt to get water for the Fleet and did not return until the fall of Alexandria when, not contented with suffering so much as I did before, I could not help going again especially as I understood we were to storm the Town, and I wanted to see the nature of such a grand military operation; however the French had no inclination to be butchered for the Turks were to join in the attack and they never give quarter to age, and scarcely to sex.

After a few skirmishes in which I never saw such narrow escapes, such extraordinary hairbreadth chances that would scarcely be believed if told, and which indeed men would be foolish to tell at home as no one can form any idea of a field of battle unless they had been in one, the English advanced under the Walls of the Town driving the French in twice; at length a flag of truce was sent out,

The Ottoman Empire ruled Egypt through Cairo, with Britain's blessing, owing to its enmity with Russia and France. In return for promised support, Turkey allowed Britain to trade in the Levant, and secured overland routes to India which Napoleon had threatened in 1798 with his invasion of Egypt.

Cyprus was under Ottoman control at this time. Turkey was co-operating with Britain in its campaign against the French in Egypt, with the dim possibility of renewed Turkish suzerainty in Cairo. Cyprus received the Mediterranean fleet as allies.

when we all knew it was over with them, when at the end of three days 11,850 men surrendered to about 7,000 which is all that is on this side except Turks who we could not trust and who the English General from motives of humanity kept in the <u>rear</u>. They had lived upon Horseflesh for Months and many of the poor inhabitants died daily from famine, and thousands too ill to be removed. When we told the French of our intention to send the Turks in, as soon as a breach could be made in the Walls, they were motionless with terror.

On 26 August four batteries on each side of the town opened against the intrenched French.

I had the honour to march in with the Grenadiers, the sight was fine, two columns of the finest-looking fellows in the whole Army marched through the two gates on the East side and two other columns on the West side of the City, all the bands playing, drums and fifes, and making the air resound with the tune of "God Save the King" while every division displayed the <u>old English</u> Colours at the same time the French struck theirs.

The walls of Alexandria were covered with the Inhabitants and the Enemy. After this part of the business was over, we took a hasty view of the place, which corresponds very much with those accounts given by travellers. The Castles round the town (100 in number) are nearly down, but the French contrived to place a great number of Guns upon the tops of many of them, which cut up our troops very much.

We visited Pompey's Pillar, Cleopatra's Needle etc., the first day, since which we have been to visit Diana's Temple underground, supposed to have been sunk by some convulsion of the Earth, also a vast number of Catacombs and ruins, these places are about a Mile from the Town; I had the curiosity to go and see the very spot where St. Mark suffered martyrdom, this is however in the Town that was of old Alexandria, and over this spot is a Mosque of 1001 pillars. The Mosque of St. Athanasius is to be seen near this place.

Should we remain any time I mean to go into Syria, as it is not more than 48 hours sail and Jerusalem is only 30 miles from the landing place. So that I may have the satisfaction of rambling over a great part of the track our blessed Saviour went in former times: you have no idea how I love to explore, and pursue all the schemes my imagination points out. As I shall have but little time to write previous to my journey through a part of the Country, it is most likely you will not hear from me again till our arrival at Gibraltar or Malta when I shall inform you of whatever is curious at Cairo as it will amuse me in my voyage, at the same time I do myself the pleasure of writing to my dear Sisters. I expect to find myself rich on my return, as everything here is a hundred per cent cheaper than in England.

We live here sometimes like Princes, and at others worse than beggars, for instance, on shore, hard salt Beef and a little stinking rum and water a little saltish is the best fare on active service; but on board, and indeed since the war is over, on shore, the Arabs supply the Markets very amply so that we shall soon get fat again.

You would not know me at this time. I am as black as a West Indian, my face absolutely masked and my hands black and blistered, the heat is so intense that it melts one away. I cannot help being astonished when I think how we all live in such a climate and in spirits, thank God I never lose mine and they tell me I keep them all alive when on board. We shall not get much prize money for this place. I find that the Holland prize money is paid, and I trust the Copenhagen also.

When prize money was to be distributed to an absent crew, most officers had agents in place to collect it on their behalf, for a commission.

To Cyprus for Convalescence

I have spoken of our hardships here etc. I must now give you an account by way of conclusion, of the lovely island of Cyprus. Here all the luxury of the East is to be met with, and the whole of this heavenly spot is so diversified with the richness of nature that there is scarcely an object wanting to render it complete except our dear Country women, as few are to be met with in these parts. A few French and Italian Ladies resort to the Capital, but it is above 50 miles from where we landed.

I soon recovered my health upon arriving on this Island, and as a soldier was soon invited to the Turkish Governor's and the Consuls, who are Greeks, and one English Consul.

The Island is subject to the Turks, but the Inhabitants are of various Nations. No one is permitted to carry arms but the Turks, or even to be seen with them upon pain of death, the English of course excepted; the Turks have a Garrison also.

I know not for what reason, but the most marked attention was paid to me, while a Capt. in the Navy was scarcely noticed; I can only attribute [this] to my securing two Epaulets, which all foreigners pay the greatest attention to. I have had an Officer's guard turned out to me, while an Admiral has been neglected.

In this Island everyone lives out of doors, or rather under an Awning sloping from the top of the house, there being no rooms above the ground floor; in most parts mats and Carpets are spread upon the ground, and on benches with large Cushions, and they lounge away most part of the day, as few stir out [between] eight in the morning and five in the afternoon. Jessamins, Lemons and Oranges hang over your head whichever way you go.

I was invited with others to the Greek Consul's country house, about seven miles up the Country, we set off at four in the Morning upon Mules, and passed through so delightful a country that would surpass my powers of description. The house was more like a Palace than anything else, surrounded by every kind of Shrub and Fruit. I am sorry that I cannot enlarge upon the beauties of this Paradise, and the glorious time I spent here, but my paper will not admit; will only observe that the Natives never eat breakfast, but dine at eleven to noon, take Coffee immediately after, then sleep till five in the afternoon, then Coffee again and smoke after it; about eight they sit down to every luxury and go to bed directly afterwards. They always wash before and after meals, the slaves attending and pouring water over the hands, as they never dip a second time in the same water, or use a Towel twice.

Adieu my dearest Sisters
England is to be invaded, Fudge.
Your Affectionate
T.M. Wybourn

Dec. 20, 1801
H.M.S. "Madras"
Malta

My dearest Emily,

I have been prevented from writing by illness, which the miserable climate of Egypt subjects every one to, though thank God, I have not experienced the ill effects that many have.

You will scarcely believe that one regiment alone with whom I was doing duty have not more than one man in ten left, and when we left Egypt we had buried nearly three hundred men and fourteen Officers, and seventy men gone quite blind as the complaint of the Eye is a sad plague in Egypt. We have also 160 on the sick list; we are experiencing much misery from illness.

We are now in a charming climate, and can get out more in the day time, as the heat is not so great at Malta at this time of the year, but such a passage as we had was most alarming as we never expected to reach a port.

We were 21 days coming from Egypt, only about 800 miles; before we had been out four days we sprung a dangerous leak, which however did not alarm us much until we were overtaken by a storm, the most tremendous. It lasted many days, and our leak increased from one to four feet of water in an hour with all the pumps going, and I must tell you that the pumps of this Ship are calculated to throw out three tuns of water a minute; we at length stopped part of it, which was found by a miracle for the Capt. ordered a great quantity of shot to be removed to ease the Ship, when they discovered the leak, but alas, we got in sight of Malta, a more violent gale came, and actually drove us three days sail away, and to our dismay another leak sprung out. This storm happened in the middle of the night, everything was shook out of our Cabins, and the rolling of the Ship occasioned such a crash from one side to the other, that we thought she was foundering; what is most curious, the Turkish Admiral assured us we should never get past Candia [Crete] because we brought away the holy stones with many other curiosities from Egypt in the "Madras", that many attempts had been made to take some away, but the ships could never make a port, and that by great accident, the last ship that attempted it got back again to Egypt when after taking out the stones they had a prosperous voyage. You have no idea what an effect this had upon the superstitious, especially the Scotch, we had the Inspector General on board, who became melancholy with fear, and many others were praying, however we got safe in, and the ship is now going to be repaired before we sail to England, which will take three months, so that I shall have an opportunity of seeing enough of Malta.

*A*ccording to the British Museum, 'After the successful operations of Sir Ralph Abercromby in Egypt in the spring of 1801, a Treaty of Capitulation was drawn up (with the French) and by Article XVI the Rosetta Stone and several other large and important Egyptian antiquities were surrendered to General Hutchinson at the end of August in that year. Some of these he dispatched at once to England in H.M.S. "Admiral" and others in H.M.S. "Madras" [see Wybourn's list] but the Rosetta Stone did not leave Egypt till later in the year, [see *below] when Major-General Turner obtained possession of the stone from the French General Menou and embarked with it on H.M.S. "L'Egyptienne", arriving in Portsmouth in February 1802. It was given to the Society of Antiquities, then at the close of the year to the British Museum. It had been found in July 1799, not far from the town of Rashid ... Europeans call it Rosetta. The finder was a French Officer of Engineers named Bouchard who realised the importance of its inscriptions in 3 different scripts, one in Greek ... it was removed to Cairo for scholars to observe ...' –* British Museum booklet 1913 rev. 1950.

One of the items listed by Wybourn can only be the Rosetta Stone: 'A stone with 3 inscriptions, hieroglyphics, gobtic [Coptic] and Greek, black granite from Rosetta.' Despite what is written above, it seems that the stone was intended, at least, to be carried on the "Madras" along with the other antiquities. Wybourn certainly assumed that he had carried it as far as Malta, and there is perhaps room for further investigation into Turner's story. At the time Turner was actually a colonel, not a general, and there are discrepancies between his account and that of other witnesses.

All kinds of luxury even are cheap and plentiful so that we live well and as for amusements, this place is full of them, Balls etc., only paying 1s 6d at the Theatres. At Christmas the grand Carnivals come on – they are elegant and last long, but I need not describe them, as you have often no doubt read of them. The Churches are very superb and costly, nothing can be more magnificent than the appearance of this elegant place, all buildings are of free stone and the Town being built at the foot of a hill upwards, the houses are above another, is most strikingly beautiful. I must give you a more particular account some future day as I am not strong enough to venture upon much fatigue and there are, I think I may say, many hundred steps to ascend which keep me on board much at present.

I intended only a few lines to you my love, to convince you I am alive. I can have no news for you more than I suppose you are acquainted with. Peace, Peace, is echoed in all directions, we soldiers do not chime in with the same glee that others do who are not wishing for promotion, it appears to be a very dishonourable peace for the English Nation.

This must be Peace of Amiens, then being discussed.

We have wondered we have not heard from England and suppose our letters are gone on to Egypt as we had the mortification to find a ship gone a few days ago with letters, we came a different way. Pray write immediately all news, as we shall be here three months. Do you know I found the elegant handsome Bladon Ruspini a private in the 26th Dragoons? Call on Capt. [?] about the 26 pounds, give my affectionate love to Matilda, tell her I long to see her in England.

Adieu yours affectionately

T.M. Wybourn

Feb. 25, 1802
H.M.S "Madras"
Malta

We are so unfortunate as to be again ordered to Egypt with Admiral Sir R. Bickerton, the object of our sudden departure is a profound secret at present; how vexatious when we were fondly anticipating the pleasure of returning to England, to be ordered to the vilest of all vile places and at the hottest time of the year. I have often thought of you my dear Sisters when I have been melting with heat, and considered that you were at the same time perhaps muffled up in fur Tippets and snoosling your noses into your Muffs with your shoes full of snow. One consolation is we have nicely cheated the Winter, and shall arrive at home I hope, in the Summer, for should it be winter the change might be fatal.

I have spent a most charming time of it here, for the ship being turned bottom upwards to repair we provided ourselves with the best quarters we could get. The Purser and myself took a house ready furnished, with every accommodation on the banks of this beautiful harbour. From the Balcony on the top we had a view of the City of Viletta on the left, that of St. Angelo in front and the Town we live in called the Isola, or Island, harbours dividing the above places; on our rear, we had a most extensive view of the country with several little Villages and their magnificent Churches. For this said house, we only paid two dollars a month. I was much astonished at the cheapness, and the beauty of it, we were since informed they asked so much because we were <u>Englishmen</u>. I have before given you an account of the cheapness of provisions, but they are dear now as there are still 11,000 Men in the Town of Viletta only.

The Maltese adore the English, the poor creatures are in sad grief at the idea of our leaving them. I never met with more attention, indeed I may say affection, one family in particular really overwhelm me with kindness and absolutely cry if I do not sleep at their house every public night. There are two public nights a week at the great Theatre, and private balls and concerts from morning till night in some parts of the City. I have a most extensive acquaintance among them.

The men are not so jealous as the Italians are in general, but they are very watchful. We had a few Officers stilletoed, for being too attentive to the Ladies, who are forward and very partial to the

English. After these Villains commit a murder they have only to run to the Church, the doors of which are always open and they are exempt from punishment, but since the English have been here, it has been objected to on account of an Officer having been assassinated.

There are four Masquerades every night at this time of the year, and also two grand ones at the Theatre, admittance 8d. at the common, and 1s. at the grand one, operas are performed every night but Friday at the same price. The first seats in the Boxes are reserved for the British and a Guard always turned out to them. In three days the annual feast, or great Carnival will commence, it lasts four days, and then all amusements cease, as Lent begins. These people call themselves religious but in my opinion they abuse it, for on these four nights all Shops are shut, and one continual scene of riot and debauchery goes on, every person is masqued, men, women and Children; every house is open, the Streets illuminated and music and dancing in every part of the City.

I forgot to tell you I am making great progress in Italian, as I study very closely; should we return here, I shall be proficient. I am acquainted with a delightful family at Alexandria with whom I shall spend much time, which will improve me by conversing. We are very anxious for letters from England, we want to know whether it is peace, or war; we have not had a single letter since we left, so dread my anger should there not be any on the way for me. I am so fatigued and sleepy, I can hardly hold my pen, as I am just returned from visiting where I heard some of the sweetest music and Italian songs from such a lovely Girl, one of the Knight's daughters – they all dine with me tomorrow to see the ship before we sail, and I have stipulated that they bring their Guitars with them. As we have a band on board, I mean to treat them with English dances.

I am perfectly enchanted with the Italian music. I am sorry my paper is so short, I could dwell long on this charming theatre of gaiety; but I must conclude, as I have not written by this conveyance to my Uncle Wybourn, send him this letter and tell him I am very anxious for news from my Agent and the Admiralty. Tell all my friends that I do not forget them though I do not name them. I have sat for my likeness in oils; it is a poor performance as I could only sit an hour. Get it altered if you can, if not, burn it [*] as it is a vile daub as you will see. Adieu all dear friends.

Affectionately yours

T.M. Wybourn

* We did burn it when he came home; he was present and enjoyed it – Emily

April 20, 1802
H.M.S. "Madras"
Malta

My dear sister,

This day with the news of <u>Peace</u>, arrived your letter which I have been grumbling for the receipt of these six months, well knowing you must have written; I will not say which gave me the most pleasure. We have remained in the most shocking state of suspense, for nearly three months, as to <u>Peace</u> or <u>War</u> and only a week ago Vessels arrived from all parts with accounts the Definitive treaty was broken off; as we were preparing for war, to our astonishment <u>all at once</u> came the confirmation of Peace! However it is pretty certain, we shall be at War again soon, so that I cannot get home, and pray for a few old fellows to sum up their accounts as speedily as possible, or I may stand a chance of remaining a Lieut. for some time; under this hope, and a little philosophy, I may perhaps chance to pass a tolerably pleasant Peace ….

Among my numerous acquaintance in this Island there is one for whom were she but English, I should feel a something more than common esteem, for what is the whole world to our hearts, without <u>Love</u>? even if it does not last long. She is an Italian Countess, nothing less I assure you, but there is no difficulty in being introduced to a Princess in these parts. A lovely Girl indeed, possessed of all the charms and accomplishments a man can wish, with the manners, and that diffidence and modesty peculiar to our charming English women, and so unusual to every class here. I spend most of my time at their house, for it being Lent which these people observe most rigidly there are not amusements except a <u>conversatione</u>; this sweet Girl always leads her favourites from the group, to a music room, and enchants her hearers with the most beautiful Italian airs ….

I suppose you read my letters of December and February last when I also sent you a shocking daub of my sweet person, upon second thoughts I would have you destroy it as it was merely a hasty sketch. The reason I suffered it to go home, I may now tell you (for we are not likely to go to Egypt); we were in short ordered to that terrible place where the plague is raging very badly at present, and we were within two hours of sailing, I therefore really imagined I might not survive, and sat for my Picture in a hurry, thinking it would be acceptable to you.

A peace treaty was signed at Amiens in March 1802. Britain returned Menorca to Spain and was to have handed Malta to the Knights of St. John, under Russian supervision. France evacuated Egypt, Naples and the Papal States, but continued to threaten British interest in the Mediterranean.

Wybourn cannot move up the list until death or promotion or retirement removes some officers higher up.

I hope the day is not far distant when we may either live together, or near each other in the country, and [enjoy] domestic life, for with all the gaiety of my disposition as well as profession, with all the alluring phantoms attending it and my certainty of success to high rank at one time or another, yet I feel just now, as if I could give all up for domestic enjoyments; a beautiful passage I met with the other day has inspired me: "So the most determined traveller returns at length to his Country, and finds in his own cottage, in the arms of his Wife, in the society of his children, and in the labour necessary to maintain them, all the happiness which he sought in vain in the vast deserts of the World". I could not write to anyone but you in this manner, as they would laugh at me, nevertheless it is true.

Only think of my meeting Newton here and Major Barnes. They are going to Sicily and have offered me a passage with them which of course I shall accept most cheerfully as it will afford me an opportunity of visiting Mount Etna and all the other places worthy of notice there. I hope to be in England about June, so that if you go to visit our dear Caroline and family, I shall most probably be able to fetch you up to London as I shall get long leave after the fatigues and troubles of War. But I am sorry to learn we have made a <u>degrading peace</u> to our blessed Isle although it <u>will not lessen</u> our consequences or diminish the dread of our Enemies I am certain, and with respect to ourselves we may say with Hudibras:

> For the outnumbered, overthrown,
> And by the fate of War run down,
> Their duty never was defeated
> Nor from their oath and faith retreated
> For Loyalty is still the same
> Whether we win or lose the game
> True as the Dial to the Sun
> Althou' it be not shin'd upon.

You see I am determined to quote as well as yourself. These lines I am charmed with beyond everything, as happily expressive of Loyalty.

27<u>th</u>. I left off writing the other day, as I was in no humour to proceed, the weather for the first time having commenced bad, and Englishmen are always affected by the weather in all countries, we have not had two hours rain since we left England until now, when it rained for three days with most tremendous Thunder, such as in England we never experience. It is now Fine and we feel as if in another world.

I should not have finished this letter till I am determined what to do, but a Ship is ordered for England, and I may be gone from here before another sails, and I have hopes of leave to accompany Newton, in that case I shall have the inexpressible delight of visiting most of the Islands hereabouts & returning home through part of Germany and France, I wish I could know before this goes. I regret I have not some ancient history with me as I should like to trace the Heroes of old, the most astonishing of whom was Xerxes but his wonderful march is too well known to all. I have already been to the Island of Cyprus and Candia and perhaps on the very spot where Telemachus was entertained by the Goddess, and in my projected Tour shall first land as Ulysses did at a short distance from his own Island. You may be sure I shall amuse myself from morning till night on these subjects and continue my journal for amusement for future days.

You ask me if I had seen the tower, or window where Cleopatra drew Mark Anthony up. I had the satisfaction to go all over it as well as all other ruins, but I was not fortunate in having any history of Egypt with me so that I [could] not trace further than my memory would admit. I must hasten to conclude as the ship sails today.

Wybourn must be thinking of Xenophon, who after the Battle of Cunaxa in 401 BC, found himself in charge of 10,000 Greek mercenaries, cut off and leaderless, deep in the heart of the Persian Empire. He led them to safety across 1,000 miles of hostile territory on the famous March of the Ten Thousand. See Xenophon's work Anabasis.

This is now the first of May, and has brought lovely weather indeed, it is in the middle of Summer and the appearance of the whole country is charming beyond everything: from several heights we can see almost the whole Island which is covered with verdure and the Corn grows higher than in England; several plantations of cotton are interspersed over the Country and the Orange and Lemon Groves are in full blossom, and loaded with the richest fruit as there is a constant succession of that fruit from Nov. till August.

I was the other day upon the top of the tower on the Palace, the highest place in the Island, but to give you a description of all I saw would take a week. I can only just sketch to you the beauties of this curious, but very grand Island. In the first place turning to the Sea, which washes three sides of it, Sicily is discovered, this is 60 miles across, so you may conceive what clear serene weather we must have, and sometimes Barbary is seen – but to look towards Citta Veccia inland is the most wonderful, it appears that the whole country is a regular fortification, from the thousands of Walls about two feet high, made to keep the earth together, or to prevent its being washed away by the heavy rains which sometimes prevail and they are all of white stone; nearly thirty Villages are seen all the same stone, with a

The Barbary States were those of the coastal region of North Africa, bounded by the Atlantic, Mediterranean, Sahara and Egypt. Named after the Berbers of the region it was famed for a flourishing 'black economy' based on sponsored piracy in the Mediterranean, until European occupation in the 19th century.

multiplicity of suberb Churches etc., etc., we also see the height St. Paul preached upon, and the very Cavern where he was confined, which by the way I have been in and have a piece of the rock inside of it, which they say is a certain remedy for most diseases. I have not room to say a word of the Catacombs, and the wonderful Aqueduct which is seven miles long, and I do not know how many Arches erected at the expense of one of the Grand Masters, and supplies all Villetta with water for six Months in the year, and the rain the other six.

Because of the continuing threat from France, Britain had refused to hand Malta back to the Knights, and Captain Alexander Ball of H.M.S. "Alexander" continued as Governor.

I had nearly forgotten to mention my dear Caroline, for although she has never written me a line, nor I her, for some time, I am not inclined to think our affection for each other is the more diminished, I know indeed when a husband and Children are in the case, there is not much to spare. However I shall now wait till I can in person explain.

Remember me most kindly to them all,
Adieu my dear Sister
T.M. Wybourn

Sept. 15, 1802
H.M.S. "Madras"
Italy

My dear Matilda,

You will be surprised to find me in Italy instead of my being on my passage home, to the only happy spot in the universe; the more I see of other countries, the more my own is beloved and endeared to me. Never do I wish to leave it when once I see it again, which to my grief I am unable to say how soon that is likely to be, – I must now endeavour to collect myself a little and give you a categorical account of my time spent since April last, which I am ashamed to say is the date of my last letter.

We have just set sail from Naples for Messina, in Sicily, on our return to Malta, and though I am so weak as to scarcely [be] able to hold my pen, I will endeavour to sit quiet in my snug Cabin while we glide through this Paradise of a sea, still in sight of Mount Vesuvius, and the delightful Town of Naples with the adjacent picturesque country.

From the time I last wrote till the beginning of August not a single change had taken place, and indeed we scarcely believed <u>Peace</u> was certain; nothing could equal the suspense and anxiety of all classes from receiving no official accounts from home, and being told that the Garrison could not be sent home till the Troops from Naples arrived which were daily expected (but which <u>we</u> have only <u>now</u> brought under our convoy as protection from the Turks). Malta became intolerable from the heat, no one could appear after eight in the Morning until about six or seven in the Evening when a little breeze sets in from the Sea, the Inhabitants then enjoy themselves outside their Doors, and upon the tops of their houses, all of which are flat with Balconies from which you have enchanting views. They seldom go to bed before Morning and of course sleep all day.

In this distressing situation we were compelled to remain without a word of consolation from home, or even a newspaper to inform us what was going on in England, the Troops all sickly, many of each dying every day, and many of the Inhabitants falling off also, for August and Sept. are the two most dreaded months in the year, as the Sirou wind blows which brings millions of insects, and if anyone *The Sirocco* stands long in it, they are suffocated, it feels exactly as if one's head was before the mouth of an Oven, or rather furnace; everybody shuts their Doors and Windows, and do not go out as it affects the consti-tution. This plague sometimes lasts ten days together: judge what havoc it must occasion. Fortunately we had not experienced any violent effects of it before we sailed for this heaven [Italy], how lucky was it for me who was taken ill the day before only.

Nothing but the change of Climate has saved my life, and as it is, I have been in little less than Purgatory for five weeks. Never my dear Sister was I alarmed before, and although I have had several severe illnesses since I have been from England, yet all of them together was not to be compared to what I have now suffered, and the Surgeon such a brute, that had I not had more fortitude than many would have hastened my end, for he told me in the midst of my pain, and at the height of my complaint, he did not know what more to do for me and that he feared a mortification must take place before Morning. I at last got worse and actually made up my mind upon the matter, as I heard the surgeon direct his Mate to bleed me, and put me into a warm bath, adding we will see if that can cure him.

To the skill and attention of the Mate, a very attractive young man, I may attribute my recovery. He told me one day he would try a

Surgeons provided their own equipment and, until 1804, their own supply of medicines. The Sixpenny Office of the Navy Board funded the Naval Hospitals; seamen would give sixpence a month towards this health insurance; the Haslar in Portsmouth regularly treated some 2,000 patients in 84 wards. Of the 100,000 seamen who died between 1793 and 1815, only 1.5% died from combat; 65% died of disease.

desperate remedy at night, without consulting the Surgeon which he thought would give me ease and turn the disorder, he then had me into a bath again and next between blankets. I need not tell you the effect of all this, when cool he made me get up to have dry bedding, gave me Mercury and Camphor, applied a poultice over my stomach, also a strong opiate; at twelve he came into my cabin and strange to say I had no pain. I slept for four hours, the only sleep I had had in fourteen days and nights. I put myself entirely under this young man and you see my love, I am able to write though very weak.

What do you think was the cause of all my sufferings? Pleasure, as we made a party to go to the Island of Gozo, and wishing to see all that was curious, we went to the Fungus Rock, said to be the very spot Mentor threw Telemachus from after Calypso burnt his Vessel, for this Island is that alluded to as having been the residence of that Goddess. This journey proving farther than we thought, and being in the heat of the day, I immediately felt the effects of but kept up my spirits, and after much fever for a few days I thought I got better and we sailed from Malta and in a few days arrived at Syracuse, where I of course went on shore, and saw much worthy [of] notice, afterwards proceeded to Messina, when one day on shore I again overheated myself, and threw myself in a fever – from that came on inflammation of the bowels, from which I have had a narrow escape for life, but thank God now all is over but I am reduced to a shadow. I much regret my disappointment in not having strength to avail myself of this favourable opportunity of going to Rome, and to the top of Vesuvius: however, I recovered so far as to be able to spend three days in Naples before we left it; I must endeavour to give you some account of this sweet Country, but the Ship is getting a great deal of motion, and I am a little fatigued by writing, so must leave off till tomorrow. Addio, I am just going to have some Chicken broth, which you I know will be pleased to hear I have a good appetite for.

Malta, November 1st. What must be your surprise at the date hereof when above I have commenced on the 15th of Sept., in short, the night I left off there came on such a tremendous Storm that no power of language could describe. For eight hours we could not hear anyone speak, the lightning awfully vivid, every sail was blown away, no man could go aloft and we were at the mercy of the winds, and waves which ran mountains high; all night and next day we were in this dangerous state, with the ship filling with water, every bed wet through, & yet, even at this most alarming crisis it was hardly possible

See the Odyssey.

to help smiling at the ludicrous figures that every moment presented themselves; there were some families on board – we all pitied the poor Ladies, for to them it must have been not only horrifying but disagreeable. Everybody was up of course, and what with the noise of all the Carpenters at work securing the Guns from breaking loose, and all the sides of the ship creaking etc., etc., every plate, dish, Glasses etc., etc., broke and rolling from side to side, roast and boiled beefs, tubs of Anchovies, bottles of wine, and everything belonging to us swimming about. And here and there an Officer appearing in his dressing gown and nightcap reeling, and endeavouring to hold fast, a fine scene for Hogarth, it was impossible to restrain the risibility that this picture presented.

We were two days before we got into Malta, the Ship in a most deplorable state; it is thought we could not have lived two days more at sea. I am living on shore, still poorly, doctor attending. I bathe in the sea when allowed and take Goats milk in the Morning which agrees so well with me that I shall now be famously again. I ought to apologize for filling so much of my paper with my illness, but there is no news here, and we have not heard from England these eight months, or received a single paper, it is really infamous of Government. I recd my dear Emily's letter and yours which are the only two since I left England. Everything seems as mysterious as ever. The Troops know nothing of their destination, or the Admiral either. Rumours are flying about of War again and we know not what to think.

Malta has become quite insipid, no variety till the Carnivals commence which will not be till after Christmas, and not hearing from home, we feel as if Transported for Crime.

I am sorry my paper will not allow of my entering at length on the description of Naples and Sicily, but it would fill a volume, and you no doubt have read if from a more able pen than mine, by More, as well as <u>Homer</u>, therefore you may judge what I have seen when I tell you I have been to the famous Lake Vernus; Sulphor Terra; the Temple of Jupiter Venus and Diana; River Styx; Elysian Fields; Nero's prison; Sepulchre of Agrippina mother to Nero; also the Stygian Lake and the curiosities taken out of Herculaneum, Pompia [sic] etc., but I could not venture down into Herculaneum, as it is extremely cold.

One day we got into a Gig and drove a few miles from Naples through such a <u>Paradise</u>; we had to go through an immense Rock hollowed out by labour in the most astonishing way wide enough for two carriages and about half a mile long, there are in general lights to conduct passengers, but we had to explore our way, and the horses are so used to it they will go very safe; in the middle of this passage it became so cold that we buttoned up our coats.

When we got through, such a picturesque country presented itself, we drove four Miles through Vineyards all in full bearing. The Vines are planted in the same manner as our hops but much higher and arched over from pole to pole or to trees, the Grapes hung in such clusters it was beautiful to behold. We next got to the Grotto del Cane, this is situated by the side of a Lake said to be [?] where if a bird flys over it is immediate death. We took a Dog to this lake & laid him down, in one minute he was in convulsions, and in two, lifeless to appearance, afterwards by getting him to the Lake he recovered; a frog would remain one minute longer than the Dog, a Man would be senseless in half a minute. An officer, from curiosity, held his face to the ground for a moment which gave him a headache and pains in his head that he did not recover in ten days.

In Naples there is a street three miles long, at the end is the King's Palace, a most magnificent building like our Somerset House. The day before we came away there was a review of all the Neapolitan Troops by the King who was in the balcony of his Palace with all his family, they all passed by through this great street with colours flying and music playing, it was a very superb sight, they went about four miles out, the Royal Family followed and then [the review] commenced. The Evening concluded with fireworks and Illuminations. It is the only day in the year that the King so far honours his subjects.

The Operas I can say nothing of, they surpass everything of the kind, the dancers, or flyers, or Ariels, astonish us Englishmen. The King and family were at the house, no plaudits are allowed nor does the King take the least notice of his subjects either upon entering or retiring – he is a perfect brute, and very ignorant.

I left Naples with much regret, as it would take a month to see everything in that great Museum of Arts, Sciences and Antiquities.

You have read of Syracuse and Messina, we stopped at both these places and saw much, Dionysius' Ear is the most surprising. This is a Cavity cut out of solid rock in the form of a human Ear 84 feet high and 30 broad: at the top for <u>focus</u> is a small apartment hollowed out by that Tyrant, where he confined himself to overhear the debates and opinions of his Senate which sat below at the bottom of the Ear by his order, he put his own Ear to the focus, and could distinctly hear

Ferdinand I (1751–1825), King of Naples 1759–1806 and again 1815–1825 (in between Naples was under the domination of Napoleon), King of Sicily 1759–1825. The government was really controlled by his wife, Marie Caroline, friend of Lady Hamilton.

This must be a reference to Dionysius the Elder 430–367 BC, tyrant of Syracuse. Through his conquests in Italy and Sicily he made Syracuse the most powerful of the Greek states in the west and the greatest power on the Italian peninsula.

even the smallest Whisper, although at that great distance; accordingly he astonished them all by knowing their secrets and used to put to death those who were not in his interest. He likewise put to death all the workmen who made this wonderful Cavern. We fired a pistol at the mouth of the entrance and it made more noise than a clap of thunder, and to prove how easy it was to hear all that passed, from the top of it, we flicked a piece of paper only, and in about a minute heard the vibration at the very top as plain as could be.

Nov. 30th. I close this as a friend is going to England. I hope it will not be long before I embrace my much loved Sisters in England.

Adieu my dear sister

T.M. Wybourn

January 1, 1803
H.M.S. "Madras"
Messina

The New Year began with me rather unpleasantly in consequence of my giving my opinion in my usual unreserved manner, upon the person and conduct of a Lady whom I found afterwards was a favourite of a brother officer; it appeared rather serious at first, but friends took it up, and as my antagonist was a good-natured man all was soon amicably adjusted. They invited a party on board, some Messina Ladies, and the day passed off tolerably. In the Evening we went to the Opera, were delighted with the great vocal powers of Signora Colderalla and Agesta; we were <u>all</u> smitten by the beauty of the 2nd Actress Signorina Diomira Guarini.

Wybourn has narrowly escaped being "called out", or challenged to a duel, over a lady.

Sunday 2nd. Signor Salvo, a chief Greek and other Gentlemen of Messina dines with us.

Wednesday 12th. This being the birth day of Ferdinand King of Sicily, it was observed as a grand festival, no business transacted and all dressed in their best. After various amusements during the day, everybody of note went full dressed to the Opera and the house being illuminated had a most splendid effect. The women are very beautiful and being in their court dresses, as well as every nobleman, and all Magistrates, Senators etc. The Governor politely ordered seats to be placed in the front for our Officers, being the only English at present in Messina. Indeed the attention of all classes to us cannot fail [to] remind us of our deficiencies in acts of courtesy but we should be too perfect if that was added to our other excellent qualities as a nation.

Wednesday 18th. Being the anniversary of our Queen Charlotte's birth day, we had a grand Gala on board, dressed the Ship in colours, manned the yards, every sailor in white, at one o'clock fired 21 Great Guns, after which walked till dinner time when the Captain gave an entertainment to some of the inhabitants and our Officers – at dark beat to quarters, and every man having a musket they were divided into several parties and in the tops, at the word of command they all fired together which had a beautiful effect from the Shore where thousands of people were assembled as we were not 50 yards from the promenade; after the 2nd Volley the Ship was illuminated with blue lights, and after the 3rd Volley Sky Rockets were let off, after which several loyal tunes were played by our band, this being over, we all went to the Opera.

Monday 23rd. We are just returned from a most delightful excursion to the Faro about 12 Miles off, a point which divides Sicily from Calabria by a narrow strait about two miles wide; through this pass every Vessel is obliged to pass from the North to the South, which affords the inhabitants a most delightful scene. On the point stands a Light-house, surrounded by a few houses, in one of which lives a worthy old Priest (about 86) perfectly active, and as cheerful as a youth. He is much attached to the English, it was excessively entertaining to hear him converse, he has lived all his life on this spot, and has witnessed every eruption for the last 70 years, and had most wonderful escapes from Earthquakes. We disappointed him much, for his hospitality is equal to his good humour and he had brought out food and sweetmeats, wines etc. He said he was unhappy that his retired place afforded so few opportunities of seeing the only men in the world he most admired, and that when he did catch any of us he could not let us go without sharing a part of all he had with us.

However our dinner was nearly ready, so that we were under the necessity of excusing ourselves. The Gentleman with whom we were going to dine is a Merchant of Messina, speaks English, and all the modern languages, and is more the Englishman than any I have met with. We left our Ship in two boats, and after two hours rowing arrived at this little village with our Guns and Dogs and after enjoying the sport of Shooting a few hours on the borders of

Relicks brot down from Egypt & now in the British Museum by me, in the Madras, 50. guns.

1. An Egyptian Sarcophagus, with Hieroglyphics of [?] breech [?] from the Mosque of St Athanasius —
2. Do of black granite from Cairo
3. Do of Bazaltes, from Menouf.
4. The first of a Colosean Statue supposed to be Vulcan [?] red granite found in the ruins of Memphis —
5. Five fragments of Statues of Lion headed women black granite from the Ruins of Thebes.
6. A Mutilated figure of a man kneeling, black granite [?]
7. Two statues, Septimus Severus & Marcus Aurelius — white marble from the ruins in Alexandria.
8. A Stone with 3 Inscriptions, hieroglyphics gothic & Greek black granite from Rosetta.
9. A Statue of Lion headed woman sitting black granite from upper Egypt
10. Two small fragm[en]ts of lions head black granite [?] U.E.
11. A small figure kneeling, with hieroglyphics Do Do
12. Two fragments of Lion headed women Do Do
13. 2 fragments of a Sarcophagus Do Do
14. Two small obelisks bazaltes,
15. a Rams head, very large &c from Upper Egypt
16. a statue of a woman sitting on ye ground black Do U.E
17. a fragment of a Lion headed woman, black granite
18. a Stone with Hieroglyphics [?] of Memnon from [?]
    Chest of Oriental manuscripts from Cairo —

List of antiquities brought from Egypt in the *Madras*

The *Maidstone* Frigate paying off at Portsmouth, by G. Chambers, courtesy of the Parker Gallery

the Lakes, returned to dinner. We found an entertainment equal to a City feast, for our host had sent his servants with his boat the day before to have all ready for us. We sat down with keen appetites, but as Englishmen, were disappointed to see above 30 Dishes of all kinds of ornamental things upon silver frames, and everything as grand as a Lord Mayor could expect. After the first course came fowls, Turkey and meats which were highly acceptable, and we made an excellent dinner, when lo! came for the last course some of the finest fish I ever saw, which is the greatest variety in this country being very scarce, we were all vexed we could not eat more. What a ridiculous custom.

After dinner came a most elegant service of every fruit of the Country and choice wines, but their custom is to break up after the third or fourth Glass, not quite according with John Bull's notion. After Coffee we embarked, and with our flutes we played cheerful songs as we rowed in this beautifully serene evening until we reached the Ship. This is enjoying the winter.

August 7, 1803
Portsmouth

My dear Sisters,

We arrived here the day before yesterday from Gibraltar after a most miserable passage of 43 days; I take the earliest opportunity therefore to assure you of my health, and the happiness I enjoy in the thought of returning to my beloved country once more, and after staying a little while with those I love, to volunteer my utmost exertions in the common cause, which to all us (<u>Egyptians</u> and <u>Maltees</u>) was joyful news upon our arrival to learn every <u>Englishman</u> is engaged in: May we ever continue unanimous, and under the blessing of that Providence who has ever protected our happy Isle, destroy those disturbers of the World, the French.

We are in Quarantine but expect in consequence of our long Voyage to get Pratique in a day or two. I cannot therefore employ my time with more satisfaction than giving my dearest Sisters an account of my voyage which has been, however, either of little pleasure or profit. I feel so <u>cold</u> I can scarcely hold my pen, and we are literally half-

'Pratique' was the permission granted for a ship's company to deal with a port after quarantine, or on showing a clean bill of health to the port authorities. It was used especially in southern Europe

starved, with that and our short allowance together, for not a man of us in the fleet of nearly 100 sails, has had more than two thirds of the normal allowance either of meat or bread, the salt Beef I never could eat, and the bread was full of vermin and musty – but the greatest misfortune was want of water: we were allowed only <u>one</u> pint a day for these last five weeks, and this was so bad sometimes, as to oblige us to hold our <u>noses</u> while drinking, and had not the wind changed in our favour, as it did, and blew a violent Gale for eight days, God knows what we must have done. We only had provisions for a fortnight at <u>half</u> allowance, however we escaped famine, but then on the contrary we were wet through for the Ship I came home in was so small, that not a dry bed was seen for this part of the Voyage. I never was in a small ship before and I vow I never will again. We left Malta in this Ship, which is a <u>store</u> ship (but by name only) in May, about a month after the rear of the Egyptian Fleet, but I must tell you I obtained leave to come home for the benefit of my health, as <u>the "Madras" is left guard ship at Malta</u>, and the Admiral sent me home in this ship.

War resumed in 1803

We had a delightful passage down the Mediterranean to Gibraltar, and might have made prize money had we known it was War for we passed several French and Dutch Ships, who also knew nothing of the War; we were chased by an Englishman who made a variety of signals to us, but the Captain being desirous to make all haste home, would not stop to hear what he had to say; which he was most heartily sorry for since, as that ship knew of the War, so that the Capt. has lost prizes for his pains, when if he had stopped only 3 or 4 hours he might have taken those ships near us.

Upon our arrival at Gibraltar we were astonished as you may suppose at the news, and was thankful that we escaped the Enemy in a voyage of above 1,100 Miles – there we found all the Fleets that had sailed from Malta, and other parts, waiting for this convoy so that we were detained to take in more Guns and make a warlike appearance, also a detachment of the 20th Regiment. I visited the Rock, and went into Spain, and spent a most pleasant time of it.

We sailed with four ships of War and near 100 Transports and Merchantmen, a very valuable Fleet, and Regiments. The first two days we had a fair wind, but on the third it became adverse and continued so above a month, which drove us near the western Islands, and occasioned all the misery I have stated merely the outlines of, not to say a word of our anxiety. We also took a few trifling prizes, and one day being alone at some distance from the Fleet, before it was light, a Privateer was close to us thinking we were a Merchant Ship, everyone was at quarters in a minute and took a Musket with the Troops. We gave him a whole broadside with 32 pound cannonades and a shower of musketry before he imagined we had a gun on board, he was beside us so close that our Capt. spoke to him and ordered him to strike, by this time the other ships coming so that the action was over in less than half an hour and he was miserably treated by our shot; we made sail after some others.

We had another Gale but it drove us home at an amazing rate in eight days. Thus you have a history of our voyage, in brief, we only now wait with the utmost impatience to get on shore to refresh a little. I shall instantly set off for London and stay a few days before I arrange for future proceedings, as now is the time or never, for fortune and rank, the latter I am very near I think.

T.M. Wybourn

June 4, 1804
H.M.S. "Republic"
Aberdeen

My dear Sisters,

I fear you will think me remiss in delaying to write so long but as Capt. Lawson and myself are on the recruiting service we found something to do, and I have daily wished for the satisfaction of communicating our movements, and began my letter on 22 of May, and should have finished it, but thought (and with truth) I should have much to say after a short time, as we were hurried away to Capt. Lawson's Brother's to spend a week thirty miles from Edinburgh, besides I wished to know my destiny first, which turned out to be this place, which is a sweet country, everyone envied me. Our Colonel honoured me in the most distinguished manner, and although two of superior rank solicited this command, he gave me the preference; we were in Egypt together, he commanded our Battalion there.

Had I come here before I went to Lawson's, I might have been satisfied and thought it the garden of Scotland, but alas! I have seen such a place and such people that my heart and soul is in Lanarkshire, I need only refer you to the geographical account of that part and of the river Clyde from Hamilton by Lanark, and to Stirling. Of all the romantic wild and picturesque scenes, this certainly stands first: England, or <u>Italy</u> cannot boast such beauties. But as to entering into a description of the falls of water, woods, Groves, avenues through them over immense precipices looking down upon the rapid streams and all those stupendous works of pure nature it would be necessary for me to select the choicest authors, and borrow their elegance to do even faint merit to all I beheld. But upon the banks of the river Clyde stands a seat, the residence of a Mr. Lockhart, a particular friend of Capt. Lawson, and just a mile from his house is a nobleman's palace indeed, to appearance; the proprietor was a Capt. in the Army, he lives now on his Manor consisting of <u>5,000</u> acres of land besides 200 laid out in Shrubberies round his house and along the Clyde.

I almost fancied myself in heaven, for such is the genuine hospitality of the affluent in this country, that they fancy they cannot do enough, no superior rank or title is considered. All free, generous and profusely liberal, you will easily imagine I was soon at home with such people; his family consist of one son and four Daughters, the Mother possesses all the sweetness, elegance and accomplishments of our dearest Mother, she put me in mind of her; but unfortunately she has little of the Woman in her grandeur, which was foreign to our beloved parent, but this is excusable, when I tell you that she drives an elegant Coach and four with two outriders, 4 Servants in livery. The Scotch are ostentatious, and fond of show, they will live up to their income but never beyond it. The Son keeps his hounds, hunters, Guns, and a pleasure boat, and strange to say no one goes with him, in fact he has not an acquaintance to accompany him, no one but himself hunts in this part; he was much pleased with us – we went sailing about, fishing etc., etc., and he wished he could have such companions always. I like everything about this noble estate, but the confounded pomp and ceremony at meals: we have three courses, the service silver with four ridiculously dressed Valets watching every motion; were things more in the country style it would be a paradise.

I have said nothing of what I admired most, the Daughters, possessed of every accomplishment masters could afford – the eldest is the finest girl, and really inherits all her Mother's qualities. How fascinated was I, on the second visit, at being shown into a most spacious room with three Windows down to the ground, the middle one opening into a Lawn commanding a most delightful view. The Daughters at various amusements in the green house, at drawing, music etc., etc., the eldest a perfect mistress, the Grand Piano touched by her was a concert of itself, but how was I delighted when I beheld her at the Harp, she is a fine figure and accompanies it with her voice – everything was enchanting.

The old fellow was so enraptured at my admiration that he swore I was the only man he had ever met with who had a true taste for music, and when I looked at my watch I found I had been three hours listening. It was nine o'clock, at which time the old Gentleman retires. He gave me a hearty squeeze by the hand telling me there was a bed for me, and desired I would come as often as agreeable to me; but my raptures have led me through half my paper when I wished to have enlarged on an equally lovely place, tho' quite opposite to the one just described, this is general Hamilton's whose niece Capt. Lawson married.

This mansion, or rather Castle, for so it has been, is a mile on the other side of Capt. L's house, and here we met with true old style hospitality; the establishment was not so large or costly as the other, but far more to my taste. I cannot go into a description of this place, but if you remember the mysteries of Udolpho, it will come nearer than I can tell. It is the most gothic place I ever knew of, for as to have seen anything equal to this, or the other extreme in Mr. Lockhart's way, I never did I must confess. I thought my Father's at Guestling a Paradise, but it would not stand in a rubbish corner to what this is. I imagined everything romantic and wild, it was dreadful to look from the Turrets down precipices hundreds of feet, with a wood at the bottom scarcely discernible, with a torrent of a river which runs through the Wood with the trees covered with Rooks and Ravens: it was to me really awful to a degree. We went into rooms that the date can be traced 600 years, some part of the East wing is inaccessible.

This could be Lee Castle, built by the Lockhart family who had held the estate from the 12th century, or more probably it is nearby Corra Castle, where there is 'an amazing 100 foot drop to the river below'.

With respect to Capt. Lawson, I shall say little, as when you know the Brother you also know him, generous, and warm in friendship, his lovely Scotch Wife is all goodness. I feel the regard of a brother for her, as she was as a Sister to me, so many kind attentions, I always found a fire in my room with my shirt and cap airing. I staid a week longer than I ought to have done, they would have kept me till now, if the duty of my profession had not called me away. Alas! I am now 160 miles from them. I have not been able to say a word of my Voyage, it was a very delightful one, we arrived 18 of May at Edinburgh, the night after I left you in London; being about ten minutes too late for the Coaches I had a sad nocturnal ramble over Shooter's Hill.

The Vessel did not arrive at Gravesend till the next day, it being calm; my friend Lawson therefore took Coach, and came to Fothergills just in time to prevent my going on the water about 10 at night and waiting for the Vessel; if he had not come I should have been all night on the water in an open boat as it did not reach until 8 in the Morning. When we joined we found a pleasant party on board, except one thing, which caused me much Laughter, as well as my friends when I told it. A Lady from India, with three young Misses, the youngest was learning to read, and will you believe that they had the very same spelling book that I was so fond of when I was learning to read myself, and as I used to run after you & my Sisters and tease you in turn to hear me read the story of Tommy and Harry, with this old story I was dinned for four days, and although I used to delight in hearing it even after I was in bed and then before I got up, I was quite tired of it now and almost wonder at your patience.

> Affectionately Yours
> T.M. Wybourn

dinned: repeatedly assailed

9 March, 1805
H.M.S. "Repulse"
Gibraltar

The "Repulse" was a 3ʳᵈ rate ship of the line, probably 74 guns. Wybourn transferred from her to the Ambuscade *at Gibraltar, as she was then based not in the Mediterranean, but off the coast of North Spain.*

My dear Sisters,

We arrived at this astonishing Fortress, where we had the satisfaction to see the whole of the Convoy get past the Enemy's gun boats and Batteries unhurt, as these cowardly warriors skulk their shore to a point where it is scarcely possible for our Ships to avoid passing. About noon the day cleared up and presented a most glorious view of the Rock, with the surrounding country of Spain, and on the opposite side the coast of Barbary, and the stupendous Mountains, raising their stately tops far above the Clouds. I was extremely pleased at the sudden alteration of the weather as it afforded a sight highly gratifying to a number of Gentlemen on board who had never been here before. The devastation a most dreadful fever has made at this Garrison for many months past, prevented communication with the shore: a Capt in the Navy came to us and staid in his boat alongside. Gibraltar lost 5,000 in this dreadful malady, now happily terminated.

The Toulon Fleet are supposed to be on the point of sailing on some secret expedition: our Admiral is resolved to proceed to Toulon, where he expects to find the Gallant Lord Nelson, we accordingly set sail with a fine wind round the rock and close in with the Spanish shore. On the 12th the wind became quite adverse, it should seem as directed by Providence for our deliverance: saw a squadron of Danes who informed us the French fleet had ventured to sea, and Lord Nelson supposing them bound for Egypt again had gone thither, but that in the meantime a tremendous gale of wind had dispersed the Enemy, and they had put into various ports as they could, with the loss of one ship; that since which 6 line of battle ships of 74 Guns each had collected, and taking advantage of Admiral Nelson's absence, were then cruizing off Barcelona, so that as we were only a few hours sail from them, we should evidently have been taken had we not seen these Danes.

"Ambuscade" was the flagship of Rear Admiral Thomas Louis.

The Admiral now directed to run before the wind to the Barbary shore and proceed along it to Malta, as it blew a perfect storm. A heavy wave broke my Cabin Window so that everything was aflote: Clothes, Books, Boots, Shoes, etc., etc. I now experienced the advantage of sleeping in a Cot as it swung about under me, added to all the dreadful thunder and lightning which would not be believed in England, could I describe it. And the confusion on deck, bellowing through trumpets, to be heard aloft, would make many believe they were the last trumpets. The Admiral was much diverted at dinner by the recital of my Cabin disasters.

On the 17th we came in sight of Algiers, which is built of fine white stone extending above a mile in an ascent. As we approached nearer, the Country and the summer residences of the principal people afforded a delightful and Picturesque view – we observed by the Sun we were 600 miles from Malta, our clothes an encumbrance it is so very hot.

26 March 1805
Sardinia

After beating against a heavy gale of wind several days in sight of this Island without gaining any ground, the Admiral determined to run for shelter into a Bay we fortunately had under our lee; which proved extremely lucky for him who was so anxious to join Lord Nelson, and his own Ship, for we gained intelligence which rendered our going to Malta unnecessary.

Palma Bay is on the south west corner of Sardinia near Cagliari.

The name of this delightful spot is Palma Bay about 20 miles from the capital; it is very extensive and affords shelter on either side within for any number of Ships. Here we found several ships waiting for Admiral Nelson whom they daily expected to arrive, it being his rendezvous for supplying the fleet with all necessaries. It seems the Toulon fleet had escaped from port, and Lord Nelson thinking they had gone again to Egypt, had proceeded thither while the Enemy had returned to Toulon and other ports, having been dispersed in a storm much damaged and one ship foundered. To our great joy at Night we discovered the gallant hero staggering under a heavy press of sail, in order to gain the Port after a long voyage, and reduced to a small quantity of salt provisions, and less stinking water; such is the zeal of this unparalleled officer, he could not stop a moment at Egypt when he found the French had not arrived, or at any other port for refreshment, but dragged his half starved fleet back again, and looked into Toulon, where seeing the Enemy snug enough, he proceeded for this Bay where the Victuallers were ready for him, and notwithstanding the Ships (11 sail of the Line and some frigates) had not been in port for 2 years, no officer was allowed to go on shore, but everyone was employed in compleating for sea, and refitting ships.

In 4 days the whole was ready, except water, which was not so convenient to obtain here, we therefore all moved about 10 miles farther to a place called Pula Bay, without exception one of the most romantic & enchanting places I ever saw. Here we arrived on the 31st, and anchored in a sort of Cove, in one corner of the Bay, which is not less than 10 or 12 miles across. Cagliari is discovered at the very farther end of it, which has a very charming effect, the country between us and it, which borders this Bay has the appearance of a garden, and though so early to us in the year, is covered with a delightful verdure, and as fertile as a Paradise; who could avoid the contemplation that such enchanting scenery inspires?

On the evening we arrived it was delightfully calm and serene, just wind enough to steer the ships which were gliding round the point of a Promontory, and coming to anchor in succession so near the shore one might almost jump to it. Indeed the place had more the appearance of a land than an inlet of the sea. On this point is an ancient Tower, or rather the ruins of one, in which reside two or three miserable looking men who attend the light on the top of it, for the direction of Vessels, or fishing Boats; the Sun was setting full upon the ancient City of Cagliari which appeared in perspective as an immense pile of stately Buildings; innumerable vallies were seen, and many Villages scattered on the ascent of each Hill, which were bounded in the rear by tremendous Mountains covered with snow, whose summits tower far above the clouds: in short the scene was truly sublime. I confess I felt provoked that no-one appeared to enjoy it as I did, but they were all engaged, some in boats to fetch water, and others putting their ships to rights. Nelson himself did not set his foot on shore though close in to it, and three days here.

Monday April 1st 1805: everything being in readiness to receive the water, all the Boats proceeded on shore with Casks etc., and in a short time Tents were pitched, Guards stationed, Triangles erected and the whole shore looked like a Camp and a Fair united; hundreds of the Natives flocked down bringing quantities of provisions, Animals, Vegetables, fruit etc., which of course met with a most welcome reception from 12,000 men, with plenty of Money, and no means for two years before of spending it, so that these ships were all loaded with these luxuries; besides as many Bullocks as they could carry which Government supply, it being much cheaper than salt provisions, besides the benefit to the men.

Never was a place better adapted for watering a fleet: the boldness of the shore admits the Ships to approach within a few hundred yards and about a dozen paces from the sea shore is a delightful river, divided only by a bank from the sea, and empties itself into it; it is a running serpentine stream from the interior, of course very clear. The boats are ranged along close to shore, the casks rolled over to the river, and when filled by one party, are returned to the boats, hoisted in by the Triangles and rowed to the ships, and so return. The Tents pitched on shore are for the guards who attend these proceedings, and pass the day in a most delightful manner, as the shore, especially the banks of the river, is covered with flowers, in the midst of which they pitch a Tent, and their friends dine with them, their dinner dressed after the fashion of the Gipsies etc. In this manner is a fleet of 15 Ships completed with water for 12,000 Men for 4 Months and in the space of 2 days and some hours.

On the second day a friend or two accompanied me, took our Guns and made an excursion to a Village about 3 Miles off and seeing a

A 'Triangle' can be seen in the foreground on p.12.

decent house with stabling, Gardens etc., we concluded it was the residence of some one of consequence, and were not deceived, for as we were exploring the grounds with the assurance of an Englishman, a charming old Man, a perfect John Bull in appearance, with his two daughters approached, and soon convinced us of his attachment to our Country, commenced a conversation and observed that several Officers had honoured his house during the day, and hoped we would walk up (for they all live a mile above terra firma) and cool and refresh ourselves.

We soon found he was a Man of education and held some post of consequence at the capital, and that he had made an excursion for a few days to this, his Country seat and estate; he had for the first time indulged his Daughters with a jaunt, the Wife and rest of the family remaining at Cagliari. After regaling ourselves with various wines, fruits and sweetmeats of all kinds, the fine old Gentleman proposed a walk in the Gardens, which was readily accepted, and we were astonished at the beauties of the place, for the Garden, Orange and Lemon groves are all enclosed by high Walls, so that we could not discover appearance of those things until a huge Gate was unlocked. Those agreeable Girls condescended to cull the choicest fruits for us, after which we ascended the house and drank Lemonade.

He would fain have us stay Dinner, but we did not wish to risk a return by Night; we got down to the shore, and after lounging about from Tent to Tent till dark we went on board in order to rise by four o'clock and trudge with Dog and Gun. Towards Noon, and agreeably to my promise, I paid my worthy friend Signor Grondon a visit; he was rejoiced to see me, and finding I had a commission to purchase Sheep, sent a Man to the Mountain for some fat ones, but he returned with only one, which he insisted that I should accept and brought a cartload of fruits, among others sweet Lemon, a fruit quite uncommon to us: these he sent to the boat. Wines and Fruits were displayed in greater abundance than before, and above all a bottle of Ale, a very uncommon thing in this Country, was produced with a welcome which enhanced the value, for when he found I thought it a treat also, he was delighted. Walks etc., are again proposed, and this Old Gentleman took such a fancy to me he expressed himself much pleased at the satisfaction I discovered at such hospitality. And when he could not prevail on me to stay to dinner this day also, he sent for his Steward, and after desiring the Man to take notice of me, ordered him to consider me as perfectly master of his house in his absence, should the ship arrive again, which as there is no other place to water at we shall regularly do (as he well knows) three or four times a year. He observed, as his chief residence was in Town, he should feel hurt if I only considered his request as a compliment, [and] that should he at any time hear of our arrival he would ride over with part of his family and make us a visit; he took a most affectionate leave (by a kiss on each cheek, a favour I could not readily have excused) and loading me with more presents; I departed, not without remarking the difference between the genuine hospitality of foreigners in general with the surly selfish conduct, and even general brutality of my own countrymen to strangers. The only return I could make was some Brandy, Gin and some English wine, also cheese, all inestimable in this part of the World. I sent some tobacco with some powder for shooting too.

<u>Wednesday 3rd April 1805</u>: Admiral Louis and his retinue has just joined his own Ship, the "Canopus" of 80 Guns; this being a leisure day, and we expecting to sail, I paid a visit to the Admiral and dined with my former Messmates who expressed themselves happy to see me. I forgot to observe [that] yesterday being the Anniversary of the gallant Admiral Lord Nelson's action at Copenhagen, [he] commemorated the same by entertaining the Admirals, Captains, and others of the fleet on board the "Victory" of 100 Guns, when the day was spent in a manner which may easily be conceived for a Man who is beloved by all ranks and classes of his fleet, as much as he is admired by his King and Country; the whole fleet drank his health with three cheers.

It seems Wybourn may have dined with Nelson.

In the Evening we got under way intending to proceed off Toulon, and once more defy the common Enemy, with a Squadron far inferior in number. We had not proceeded far before we discovered a Frigate with a Mass of sail firing guns and signals flying which we knew to be no common alarm. We soon understood that the French fleet, knowing by their Spies etc., that the fleet was employed victualling, had put to sea; the anxious Admiral [Nelson] made only two signals (his usual way) that the Enemy's fleet were at sea, and to prepare for Battle. Then making all possible sail, everyone as well as he was able keeping up, for this extraordinary Man never confuses his fleet with evolutions at such times, and would not wait for a bad sailing ship, and if in sight of an enemy would get to them alone and keep it up till the rest joined.

As the Enemy had no intention to pay us a visit, but only to escape us with 14 or 15,000 Troops on board, it was difficult to decide which way to pursue them. A Council of War was therefore deemed necessary, all Commanders summoned on board the "Victory", the supposition was the Enemy would attempt Egypt. The Admiral stationed himself across from Sardinia to the Barbary shore, so that had they intended, they must have met our fleet. Next day we came close to the shore of Barbary, passed the Ancient, and at present beautiful City of Carthage, stood along shore, past Tunis, a most lovely sail indeed but no tidings and our anxiety was so great as to take off our attention which otherwise would have been highly gratified.

Palermo, April 9th. The Admiral [Nelson]distracted with vexation at gaining no intelligence of the Enemy pursued his rout after them towards the French Coast. We were dispatched to this place, the beauties of which as we approached is not to be described, but by a poet. Boats came off to us with Fruits, most acceptable.

16 April 1805
Sardinia

Contrary Winds has occasioned our not again joining Lord Nelson and we have been buffeting about from one end of this island to the other without being able to gain one port or the other, where we expect further instructions from Admiral Nelson.

The drum beat to quarters in the middle of the night, alarm occasioned by the appearance of a large ship, the "Phoebe" frigate, close to us. The usual ceremony of clearing for action, and after getting wet through, for it rained hard, beat a retreat. She gave us bad news, that the cursed French fleet passed Gibraltar 7 days ago, 21 sail of the line, 15,000 troops on board, and were gone first to Cadiz, and then with the Spanish fleets to proceed to Ireland, but the most general opinion is the East or West Indies.

This guess was correct: Admiral Villeneuve ran for the West Indies, hoping to give Nelson the slip before doubling back to invade Ireland.

We also learnt Bonaparte is to be crowned King of Italy, that 60,000 French troops are marching to Naples, and 80,000 Russians (our allies) towards France. This year is likely to prove full of great events. God send a happy issue to Old England. We parted company with the "Phoebe" who is gone in pursuit of Ld Nelson with the above news.

17th April, Wednesday: We bore away for Madalena, one of the numerous islands at the extreme end of Sardinia; from thence we proceeded round Corsica, called off Toulon to see if any other ships are ready for sea, then followed Lord Nelson to Gibraltar. Poor fellow, his mind is always so agitated when he thinks of the enemy that he is said to have behaved like a madman when he found they escaped him.

18th April: Chased a suspicious vessel, certainly a Spaniard, but as usual our Captain, who is fond of little else but taking the longitude of headlands & rocks, did not choose to follow it, but hove to at 8 o'clock. This would look like fear or something worse in a suspected person … This is so provoking to men anxious to make Prizes; this strange reasoning the other night would have lost us the ship, had the Bomb we fell in with been an Enemy, as she must have been on board of us before we could have been at Quarters.

Saturday 20th: From some unforeseen success, we last night made shift to reach in among Islands, and as it was late before we could reach our anchorage, resolved to bring to under Bear Island, so called from the Pinnacle of a huge Rock at the top of it exactly representing that Animal. The situation of this cluster of Islands are truly grotesque and beautiful, scarcely a ship's length between them and yet the navigation perfectly safe. Sometimes it appeared as if we were running plump upon the land, when a small opening would discover itself thro' which the ships passed with astonishing rapidity and opened a new scene of various Islands, and in five minutes, perhaps, we tacked and there stood other inlets imperceptible at the very approach; it was excessively pretty as well as extraordinary.

Sunday 21st: At daylight in the Morning we were near the Town of Madalena, a most romantic looking place, and built so intirely among Rocks and secured behind by inaccessible Mountains to secure them from the attack of the Turks, that there appeared no possibility of approach even in Boats – a small Fort is their only dependence, but they are so well fortified by Nature that they live in security.

While all the Boats were employed in getting provisions, water etc., I went on shore, was introduced by our Commissary to the Consul M. Brandi, who obliged us with a cask of Wine, at the astonishing moderate price at 1/1d per gallon, better wine by far than the Port we were drinking. We met with much hospitality, many invitations; we were no sooner in company before several of the family and relatives made their appearance from various parts of the Town – among others, were three lovely girls, Sisters called Laura, Josephina and Catherina, these dear girls behaved with much ease; it being a Saint's day they proposed taking us to Church and said with great good humour, if we would attend them there they would take us a walk afterwards: the two young Naval heroes with me felt perfectly abashed by this abrupt invitation and it was with difficulty I could persuade them to go; as I was their interpreter, I caused much mirth at their expense.

The "Niger" Frigate joined us after having conducted a large convoy to Malta from England, and had a most narrow escape from the French fleet having passed thro' them in the night; it seems a kind providence protected us and our <u>Commerce</u>, at the same time it permits those wretches the French to scourge the Earth, & O! how dreadfully.

Several rumours on shore that a fleet was in sight, we judged it to [be] Lord Nelson and got under way, the weather was most heavenly and we sailed thro' these romantic Islands to the straits of Bonifaccio, the wind being fair, we steered between Corsica and Sardinia and in the Evening was clear of all danger. Captain Durban dined with us, and we enjoyed our sallad from the shore.

<u>Wednesday 24th</u>: After three days' patience again arrived at Palma Bay, sent on shore for Letters and at length proceeded for Gibraltar in quest of Lord Nelson. Met the "Seahorse" Frigate who gave us fresh orders to proceed to Cagliari to join the "Phoebe" and wait for a convoy from Malta which we were to escort past Carthaginia where the Enemy's fleet lay; we have now the whole Mediterranean to ourselves.

<u>25th</u>: General exercise swords and pikes. In sight of Oran Bay, the last post the Spaniards held on the Barbary shore. The "Seahorse" arrived in a gale of wind from Gib. Made signal of news of importance, but no possibility of communication, the sea running mountain high.

<u>30th</u>: Capt. Stains came on board, informed us 6 sail of the line (Spanish) were looking for us. We are much concerned for our convoy being 100 sail of Ships, with but 4 frigates to protect them and only a few miles from the enemy. The Commodore immediately ran in for the coast of Barbary and communicated the news to Convoy. Capt. D sent us papers to the 11th mentioning the disgrace of Lord Melville (& Mr. Trotter) a man to be regretted, being a favourite of everyone.

<u>31st</u>: In the Evening the whole fleet was under sail and passed the Enemy's gun boats and batteries unhurt with a fine wind & cleared

Henry Dundas, 1st Viscount Melville, Baron Dundira (1742–1811), was a clever and successful politician who, under Pitt, rose to the peerage and the position of First Lord of the Admiralty. He was suspected of misappropriation of public money during his time as treasurer (1782–1800) but was acquitted by an 1802 commission of enquiry which reported in 1805. Melville never held office again.

The *Seahorse* off Palermo, by Nicholas Pocock, courtesy of the Parker Gallery

Gibraltar

the Straits. Our orders are to proceed off Cadiz. Accounts at Gib. that Admiral Sir R. Bickerton is there with Sir J. Craig & 16,000 Men going on an expedition.

Nelson left for the West Indies on 9 May, leaving Bickerton in charge.

May 27, 1805
H.M.S. "Ambuscade"

My dearest Sister [Emily]

I did not expect to find another opportunity of writing, when I sent my last the beginning of April, but circumstances have happened which have quite altered our destination for the present – we have heard of Lord Nelson, and that he pursued the French fleet to the West Indies, so that I have reason again to rejoice. We were ordered to remain in this sea – we are only three frigates and all of us have agreed jointly to share prizes, our two consorts are away, doing their best, and we hope to hear of their taking many ships. Nothing has occurred particular since my last, except that we have fell in with a convoy from Malta, and are to keep them company till they pass the Enemy's post, where are several ships, and I thought I could not employ my time more to my satisfaction, than by writing to you, as I rather imagine, it will be long ere I can have that pleasure again, for no one can yet guess how we are to be disposed of, or where to. This uncertain sort of life is far from being agreeable and my disappointment in the service occasions in me a general dissatisfaction and makes me more than ever determined to quit it, as soon as possible.

We have had boisterous & miserable weather upon the whole, tho' in this sweet climate, but it is mostly the case upon the eve of summer it comes all at once, and then has a succession of lovely weather – I have had a slight attack of the change of climate, but am now recovered, but fear I shall lose my faithfull servant after being together 7 or 8 years. He has been too much indulged by me at home, particularly on the recruiting service, and now this climate has laid hold of him. I have great hopes in our surgeon who is a clever man, and it affords me satisfaction to observe with what assiduity he attends him, as well as the attention of all the officers, who have the highest opinion of him; he lives as we do and the fresh Provisions, fowls etc., does him good. You know how I value him, indeed anyone must respect a man whose fidelity has been so long proved, then his wounds in the service and loyalty insures him, at least, the good wishes of us all. The poor fellow seems to feel his situation and appeals to me on the supposed severity of the Doctor.

I have little employment at present, except my Italian & then music, tho' I really must confess I have lost all relish for this latter amusement, & do not know why. I have perused lately your journals, etc., with the intention to select some of the beautiful passages you notice & thereby form some variety in mine, which from the sameness in a voyage must of necessity be composed of little else than a common Diurnal – however I can never take up one of your books but I am insensibly diverted from my purpose – O! what wd I give to be possessed of the elegant taste and judicious remarks you are so capable of making, but I can never hope even to form my mind or disposition for the charming and connected track you are so eminently distinguished for – those chaste sentiments (as well as practice) of Religion, a soldier is but ill calculated to succeed in – if you knew, my dear Emily, how really happy I feel and what inward Pride and exultation I enjoy in the thought of having such a sister, you might believe the correspondence and perusal of your charming books and letters will have the effect I know you desire.

But when, as today, I read some passages where you refer to former times, how can one be reconciled, how patiently submit? I have just finished that part of your Journal to our lamented brother – where you so pathetically regret our scattered state, how widely dispersed. Nor is it profitable to be otherwise than melancholy when one reflects, as you observe, our revered parents are no more – how I deplore their loss, and think, had they survived till I was at years of maturity, what affection, what a study it would have been to convince them of my sense of their worth (how I have arrived to my present state, and rank, without them, or any one earthly guide or assistance, I am at a loss to account, and this is my greatest consolation). Then our beloved sisters at a great distance from one another, and one with her family scarcely known to me, an only brother no more, and nearly the whole of our other relations extinct. When we compare this with the former part of our life when we were all together, is it not enough to awaken sensibility in the most obdurate heart, and you, my dearest Emily (which grieves me still more) seem alone, to be the most persecuted, and yet possessed of the most resignation. And I will not dwell any longer on this painfull part of our history – Let us hope those expectations we have hitherto so patiently awaited, are now nearly within our grasp. I indeed, have long expected to have been instrumental to the comforts of my beloved sisters, but the services of men (who are not otherwise independent) are but slowly rewarded by their country, while those who drive in a carriage to sollicit preferment will be considered as most deserving. Many of my former acquaintances who have served in the army no longer than myself are Majors, and I have but just obtained a Captaincy, altho' been constantly in actual service.

It was a continual source of complaint that Royal Marines could not win promotion in the field as Army officers could. But at last Wybourn has achieved his Captaincy.

I shall not close this till we arrive in Gibraltar which will be in a few days, when I hope not only to be more cheerful but have such satisfactory information as will render a letter more acceptable.

It is the finest weather in the world today – we are gliding along the Coast of Barbary, within a stone's throw – adieu.

In 1834 some Captains were retired to give promotion to Lieutenants RM of 26 to 29 years' standing!

June 1st: We are close to Gibraltar, what an escape we have had! We were 5 days in a parallel with Carthaginia – there are 6 ships of 90 & 74 guns each, waiting for our convoy and we have escaped them, tho' 100 ships nearly. We shall get in tonight. A frigate has just come from Gib. with this information – also that Sir Richard Bickerton (the Admiral I was with in Egypt) is at the Rock with 6000 troops, with General Craig (my uncle's landlord) supposed to be going to take Minorca. We are all in the highest spirits as we shall now have some real pursuit in view. Thus am I once more likely to tempt Dame Fortune to think of me. How strange that no Expeditions have taken place, that I have not been engaged in. Should I at last succeed in getting good booty, you are well assured with what eagerness I shall seek to return to my dear Country & Sisters & share it.

This is most unexpected, we had no idea of going to Gib. nor did we suppose any admiral was there. Now, my dearest Emily, I really think my stars will be propitious. Prospects certainly brighten and nothing but ipso facto Italian Sky is before me. I have fortunately an opportunity of sending this by a friend to my Uncle. Write my dear Matilda all the news, and assure her I would write but the expense of foreign postage is great and what I wrote to you is of course to her and if it would not be ridiculous I would address to both. Give my affectionate love and say I hope to be home before the year is near out – with Rank & Honours, not forgetting a good Prize. As I find the convoy is not likely to stop at the Rock, but proceed straight thro' I shall send this away as you will get it gratis, and when another opportunity happens I shall write at all events with all news, etc., etc.

I have besides much reason to apprehend my letters to everybody of April may be in this Convoy, as I sent them to Malta; if so you will get two at once. I have there told you about Lt. Lawson etc. – I hope to God it will reach you, or that you have received it long ago.

Should you hear or see L. tell him I wrote to him in April & by this Convoy – Assure him of my regard even as a brother.

I fear my former letters were severe, but heaven knows how far from my intention of causing him a moment's uneasiness.

Remember me kindly to all friends and your inmates at home, and do not fail to write the earliest opportunity with all the news, etc.

With constant prayers for your happyness

I remain, my dear Emily

Affectly,

TMW

1805
Cadiz

June 1st: Close in with the Batteries, had an excellent view of the beautiful Town & harbour with fortifications and went so near as to discover the faces of the inhabitants – what a galling insult to see two or three Frigates approaching their very houses, while they possess 4 sail of the line in their harbour, but the cowards dare not attack us, tho' we pay them this visit every Evening.

An American come out of Cadiz informed us that just before we came, a Galleon worth near a Million of money got in and did not know of the war: thus I am doomed to be unfortunate.

June 9th: A fleet under the command of Admiral Collingwood arrived from England, and ordered us frigates in all directions, after giving us provisions from the "Acaster" which was most acceptable, with some English sheep, [and] Port wine the officers spared us – as we had been some time on Salt Provisions.

Gibraltar 14th June: Found the greatest bustle and confusion, the Bay full of Shipping, Sir James Craig Expedition all embarked. Went on Shore, met many of my old acquaintances.

June 22nd: After paying visits went to Mrs. Coxes' the Lord Nelson

Tavern close to the landing place, here I met all the Naval blades enjoying themselves with Sigars, Grog etc., and the witty conversation of Miss Coxes who is certainly the prettiest girl about here, and tho' only 16 a very sensible good girl which is a wonderful thing in a situation of that sort, but as she has about 6, or 8,000 pounds she gives herself a few airs and is superior to all the little nonsense she would otherwise be subject to.

June 25th: The preparations of the enemy for an attack on our Shipping being ready, a council of war deemed it prudent to remove the Troops & Shipping to Tetuan Bay on the Barbary shore which was accordingly done, on the very day the enemy brought about 80 gun boats & five ships out, and would have attacked us at night, when to their mortification they saw the whole flotilla moving off – and the Men of War only left, who they did not choose to attempt.

June 20th: Got under way with Gen. Sir James Craig & Suite who were carried to the "Lively" frigate in company with the Expedition. [Adm.] Sir Richard Bickerton with 4 sail of the line escorted us past Carthaginia & while he blockaded the Enemy we proceeded with a delightful fair wind to Malta.

Malta 18th July. Nothing particular has occurred of late, when you see this journal I think you will smile to find I am again at Malta, but do not fear. Paid visits to old friends who were much pleased to see me again. Went with the surgeon to shew him the City particularly St. John's Church which is next to St. Peter's at Rome for beauty and grandeur, visited several Maltees and found my charmer (of old) the Marchioness De P. married, who received me with the greatest kindness nevertheless: Marriage in this country is but a bargain between families – the happy couple seldom see each other, and they are often unknown to one another. However I was pleased to see her style of living most comfortable, with a degree of domestic happiness in her house rarely found among Italians. In the Evening went to the Opera it being a Gala night – took my amiable Dulcinea to a Box, and was soon recognized by all the circles, of course had enough to engage my attention without even looking at the play; as nothing is more agreeable than meeting old friends after a long absence, compliments, visiting from Box to Box, a Cup of Coffee, sweetmeats, etc., etc., took up the whole time. Spent the evening with Major Weir & Delmont, at one proceeded to the Water side expecting to sail at daylight to Naples, on my way on board past the house of <u>Rendezvous</u>, alias the Ice and Lemonade shop, where I found some of the Lieuts. regaling.

Returned on board just before Garrison Gate was closed for the night.

Messina 25th July. After a delightful sail from Malta, anchored at this port, but the scoundrels, influenced by the French parties, refused us Pratique, however we got some Bullocks on board etc. The Neapolitan squadron at anchor near us, the Commodore very attentive, sending offered services, etc. In the Evening a grand fete was given by the 74th and we had all the beauty and fashion of this gay town who honoured us with their company; the Ship was elegantly fitted up for the occasion.

Nothing can be prettier than the Messina manner of fishing, which we were gratified with a sight of. Some hundreds of Boats rowing in all directions about the harbour, with a large lighted torch in each boat, which they lay over the side, this attracts the fish while a Man with a barbed prong strikes them as soon as they come near the edge of the boat – it was a dark night, which rendered the scene truly picturesque for the reflection of the multitudes of lights on the town & Shipping with the additional lights all over the Town, presented a most charming variety to the Eye. To us it was a most astonishing sight, at first we could not conceive what it meant, and judged it must have been a festival of some sort.

July 27th: At daylight this morning proceeded on our Voyage and once more passed the Gulph of Charibdis, in sight of Stromboli & the Lippary Islands, the former burning down to the very edge of the water. 31st: Still in sight of this Phenomenon, a small mountain in the shape of a sugar loaf, standing alone in the midst of the Ocean, & perpetually throwing up fire and lava, while a few scattered inhabitants on the opposite side of the Volcano seem to disregard the impending danger. It having been calm some days, we had a fine opportunity to contemplate these awful scenes.

Naples 1st August: Anchored in this heavenly Bay, the weather very hot. The Ships were soon surrounded by boats, bands of Music welcoming us & this being a compliment they always pay foreigners; the other boats brought Fruits & Vegetables in abundance, others were filled with the <u>fair sex</u> some their <u>own</u> mistresses, while others were brought by their <u>Mothers</u> & <u>brothers</u>, literally like sheep for market, infamous to a degree & reflects eternal disgrace on both the Government and the vile Brutes under it. Girls were thus forced by their Parents not 10 years old, but the lowest wretches in this climate will sacrifice everything for a trifling sum of money. No part of the

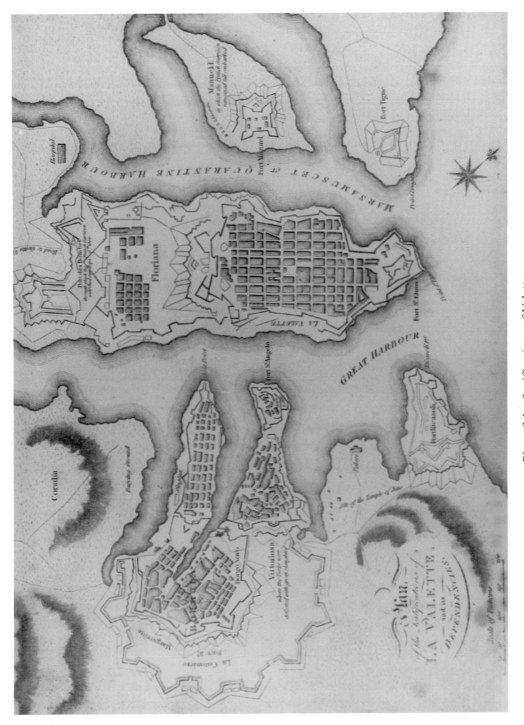

Plan of the fortifications of Valetta

Interior of St John's Church, Valetta, from a painting

world can possibly be so depraved as a Neapolitan, not excepting a Savage, the worst of whom value and protect their offspring.

We were exceedingly gratified by a perfect view of an Eruption of Vesuvius which burnt with astonishing violence, throwing up fire and stones to an amazing height: two rivers of Lava, or liquid fire running down the Mountain in torrents, for upwards of two miles destroying Villages, passing through Vineyards & occasioned great devastation, but so many signs are providentially given that every one removes from their dwelling and probably never return again. As I intend to pay a visit to the Crater I shall endeavour at a better description. The appearance of the Bay, Town and adjacent Villages and Country for Miles round occasioned by the illumination from the burning Mountain in a very dark night, while the ship is gliding thro' a calm serene sea to the Anchorage, is beyond my feeble powers at description, and must, I am sure be better conceived than described. I can only say I was up nearly the whole night absorbed in wonder & astonishment & could hardly believe myself [not] in the lower World.

Mt. Vesuvius underwent severe paroxysmal eruptions, ending its cyclic eruptive stages, in 1794 and 1822. The eruptions witnessed by Wybourn would have been minor in comparison to the extremes of those two dates. Scientific study of the volcano did not begin until the late 18th century.

As soon as we obtained Pratique, Mr. James the proconsul came on board and politely requested our company to his house. Some of us accompanied him on shore, we went to the Grotto del Cane, I do not describe it as most have read of its terrible effects. We returned home through Vineyards & Gardens and enjoyed a most heavenly ride, the Grotto of Pausillipa upon the top of which stands Virgil's Tomb, an extraordinary work of Art. Drank tea at the Consul's, was introduced to his niece Miss Newman, much sweetness and affability in her manners though so much secluded. Her Uncle being 74 years of age but with the activity of a young man having a multiplicity of business can attend very little to her … our intention is, to proceed at daylight to Pompia [sic] & Herculaneum etc.; was agreeably surprised at the old gentleman's proposal to join us and that his niece was also to be of the party. The poor girl was delighted as it is seldom her old Uncle attempts so fatiguing an excursion.

In the Evening a small party was made to promenard [sic] at St. Lucia, or vulgarly called the fish market – this is a place resembling our Bartholomew fair (but in a sweeter situation) hundreds of Booths are erected for near a Mile long in one Street the houses in front looking over them and commanding a full view of the Bay of Naples with Mount Vesuvius etc., etc. In these booths, and on benches and tables are display[ed] every kind of Fish, Fruits Sallads etc. The Nobility passing backwards and forwards some in carriages, others on foot thro' this dirty and filthy group. The nights are lovely here, and as light as day which afforded a most novel sight, thousands of people of the lower class regaling themselves with <u>fish suppers</u> in public, others smoking and drinking.

After walking till we were tired, and it was eleven o'clock, having feasted our eyes with a sight of most lovely and elegant Women while passing as in Kensington Garden, Miss Newman, to my surprise, proposed supping here but her Brother assured us of the impropriety, and we proceeded up a few steps to the Houses & entered a saloon where tables were laid for those who choose to sup. Looking along the row of houses, I perceived several other parties regaling themselves, there being no doors to these rooms, every body sitting in public and admiring Vesuvius which was raging dreadfully, while the Mob passing and repassing below, some with Guittars others singing etc., it put me in mind of some group I have of Hogarth's, it was exceedingly diverting to me. Our supper was now brought and according to the Charter of this place, it consisted of Fish only, but in such vari[e]ty that it would have puzzled the wisest of us to tell what they were or count the number of Dishes. I discovered however there were Soals, Smelts, Carp, Trout, Lobsters, Oysters with many more. We passed the time very pleasantly till midnight & then left the gay throng who kept it up as long as the Moon lasted. The season for this amusement is from 1 August till nearly the end of September.

<u>August 3rd</u>: We all got up at 5, had Coffee ready, and as the Consul's house was just by, I ran over to apprise them, found <u>Miss Newman</u> quite ready; I escorted her to the Albergo del Sole, our Tavern, where two Coaches & four waited and as the old gentleman was soon with us we proceeded on our journey, three Servants attending. It would be considered vulgar in the extreme to appear in a carriage unattended. We passed thro' the Town at full gallop, had a most delightful drive round the head of the Harbour, a distance of at least 5 Miles, entered Portici the residence of the Royal family during the summer. We intended to visit the Museum at this place before we proceeded onwards but was informed it would take some hours, as all the Curiosities, Antiquities etc., taken out of Herculaneum and Pompia are deposited here, so must take another day for that treat.

These two Cities were destroyed about 60 years after Christ, and not discovered till 57 years ago, but a Nobleman accidently digging a Well to his House, the workmen came directly upon the seats of the

Pompeii, Herculaneum and Stabiae were all destroyed by the eruption of Vesuvius in 79 AD. Pompeii and Herculaneum became important stops on the Grand Tour for English visitors, who were often guided by the amateur archaeologist and ambassador to the Neapolitan court, Sir William Hamilton. Tourists would also have been gratified to meet Sir William's second wife, the beautiful Emma, Lady Hamilton.

Theatre which led to the discovery. How it is possible, that a rich and extensive City should have remained swallowed up for nearly 1,700 years without some attempts to find it, is most wonderful. We proceeded to Pompia and arrived over fields of Lava, at that part of the City called the Barracks; the pillars, piazza, rooms and parade, are quite perfect, and the paintings in Stucco in as good preservation as if only done yesterday with even the names & various scribblings of the Soldiers in their Barrack rooms; adjoining this, are two Amphitheatres in perfect state. The Temple of Isis in which the oracles were delivered is complete as if newly built, all the Paintings, Mosaic pavement, Altar pieces & Priests' secret holes where the vagabonds pretended the Statues before them spoke, are entire. We were most highly gratified and wrote our names where many other Travellers had as a momento of our having visited these Antiquities, on the Marble & in conspicuous places.

We now advanced among ruins, and came out at a vineyard under which is a great part of the town, but supposed to be trifling Streets etc., & near the Barracks is a great Gate and part of a paved street which evidently corresponds with another Gate discovered about two miles on and to which we were now proceeding. Upon our arrival at this part of the City we were indeed surprised – we descended into a complete Street entirely cleared from the ashes and rubbish. The pavement was good with the perfect marks of wheels at least two or three inches deep. The houses on each side were for the most part perfect & the Paintings good, the Mosaic floors were beautiful, all the Gentlemen's houses had a Court yard in the center of which was a square fountain supposed as a refreshing luxury, all the chambers being on the ground floor surrounding the Water. What is remarkable, all the rooms at the present moment denote the uses they were appropriated to by the Emblematical Paintings in stucco on the walls, the Eating room was distinguished by all manner of Game, and dishes of various kind, fruits etc., etc. In the Dancing or Music room was all kind of Instruments then in use displayed, with groups of dancing Men & Women and Merry Andrews. Bed rooms likewise exhibited scenes which Miss Newman soon withdrew from, and which prove the depravity of that age was by far greater than the present, in short all the Palaces (for such all these little residences appear to have been) exhibited the remains of the greatest luxury and grandeur, but to relate all particulars of this place would fill volumes.

I may again attempt a description perhaps, but now must proceed

A Merry Andrew was a type of clown.

to the romantic residence of a most opulent wine merchant, for so it must have been from the appearances, but which we visited after dinner, so shall relate our proceedings and charming repast in a place where perhaps the noblest Romans have eat and drank in ancient times; where Cicero, Pliny and the great Caesar spent much of their time. This House and estate, is situated outside the great entrance of the city, and called the Country House. The view from this eminence is luxuriously beautiful, commanding the whole City of Naples, the Classic Fields and ground near Pozzoli & Baia across the Bay to a great distance. Below the house are miles of Vineyards, extending to the seaside while the whole of Portici, Terra del Greco etc., etc., are included in the view; behind this lovely residence are stupendous hills and mountains including Vesuvius, the Eye extending along the chain of Mountains to the edge of the Horizon.

In this enchanting ruin we resolved to dine – accordingly our servants assisted by our Ciceroni, or Guide, with a few wretched creatures who reside here, and who are very officious, formed a Table with the Stones and other Antiquities and our Ham, Fowls etc., soon made a splendid appearance on a nice cloth & notwithstanding all our guides, servants and the wretched assembled around, some from politeness, others from curiosity, we made a most sumptuous repast, and the poor eagerly devoured what was left while we visited the Cellars under ground, in those days appropriated as Vaults for Wine, and which was truly astonishing – they extended round the house and Garden, and as we were half an hour walking through it I suppose it must be full a mile.

Here we found hundreds of immense Jars which would hold 60 Gallons ranged in the nicest order close to the Walls on each side, and upon one another up to the roof. The Jars were completely cemented to the Wall and become immovable – the Wine was petrified. This Man was supposed to have been the richest in the Empire as a Tradesman, and indeed his palace and Gardens showed it, as well as the Sculpture deposited in the King's Museum at Portici, and paintings taken from the walls of the House. Had we not refreshed ourselves before we explored this ruin we should have been too much fatigued, as it took us two hours to go over this one residence, which was more time than the whole City (at least the part discovered and cleared) took. In half an hour we reached our carriages much tired, except the old Consul who really appeared the youngest of the party and proposed dragging us above a mile further, to observe some other Antiquities which, however pleasing to attend and support a Lady, I could not help wishing my gallantry had submitted to the other Beaux who of course had offered their services; we joyfully took our seats in the Carriages as soon as we reached them.

At five o'clock arrived at Naples and found ourselves ready for a famous dinner which was waiting us, and the Lady was the only one that did not partake thereof, as it was judged improper to request her company at a Tavern. I was sorry, as we sat down to all the luxuries of this gay City, with a dessert that would have been worthy of a king's table, but here is thought nothing of for the cheapness [of] the finest fruits; our dinner consisted of 5 or 6 removes, only a Dollar each including wine of the country. We soon joined Miss Newman to tea per promise; spent some time looking at her Drawings which were well executed, but her Music enchanted me, she played and sang many beautiful Italian songs accompanied by her Brother, a Mr. Billy Tribble who is quite the affected Italian and made himself highly ridiculous.

<u>August 4</u>: We left the Ship early, joined Miss N. walked to the Fish Market after we went to a puppet show, a ridiculous amusement, but exceedingly ingenious; returned at 11 when we sat down to a little elegant supper.

<u>Monday 5th Aug</u>: Spent most of this day in the company of this charming affable Girl [Miss Newman], she made me promise to breakfast 7 o'clock at parting last night. This put me to some exersion [sic] and I wonder at the old Gentleman choosing so early an hour for breakfast. About 2 o'clock we received orders to proceed to Malta with Despatches, to my mortification. I therefore took a parting farewell, and we made some whimsical agreements (in Italian) such as looking at the Moon etc., etc., and such nonsense as young people in the fullness of their hearts sometimes endulge in.

It is supposed that Sir James Craig who is expected at Naples in conjunction with the Russians will organize the Neapolitan Army, and then to proceed a diversion of the French, in favour of the Austrians and brave Germans, the whole Continent being now in a Blaze. Dined with Capt. Durban & Col. Smith, an excellent officer employed by Government to negotiate affairs of importance with the Court of Naples and to look over Sicily in order to judge of the disposition of the people towards the English, and what number of troops necessary to keep it etc., etc. He is going to Malta with us, on affairs we can know nothing about, at present. He appears to be a most keen shrewd Officer. I was highly entertained with his remarks and conversation. On the 9th we reached the Faro' of Messina, or what is called the Charybdes, here a French Privateer was reported to the Captain as being very near us, but strange to relate, he was too idle to get up, and too self-opinionated to believe it or some other cause, and said it could only be a Merchantman or Greek; two hours afterwards the Pilot Boat came to us, informed us it <u>was</u> & expressed surprise we let him escape.

10th: Blew a Gale of Wind, drove us furiously past Messina at the rate of 11 Miles an hour, soon came near Syracuse, but while passing Catania saw a complete action, and the men from the Masthead said it was 3 small Vessels engaged, but on the report our obstinate Commander [Captain Durban?] said it must be the Churches firing on some festival, and when from the deck we plainly saw the Action, he swore it was Turks firing a salute nor would he alter the course tho' it was in our way & we going at a great rate. We heard afterwards, that a Sloop of war of ours had fallen in with three French Privateers, and must have been taken, had not an English Privateer come to her assistance, when she engaged the Frenchmen one of whom blew up, and another ran ashore, the third they took, so that we lost 3 prizes, as well as might have lost our own sloop for want of giving that support a man of War is bound to do. We had the satisfaction however to see he was much Chagrined, and was finely laughed at on Shore, but he endeavours to impose upon us that he has Despatches of importance & could not stop – tho' we are all pretty well <u>convinced</u> he has more <u>substantial</u> reasons if he would confess it.

Saturday 11th: Arrived at Malta, passed my time as usual gossiping with my old acquaintance, dined with Major Wier and spent the evening at conversaziones.

Wednesday 15th [Aug.]: My birthday – by chance we had a large party on board. In the Evening went to the Opera in company with the ladies at 11 at night took a Boat and proceeded to a Water festival, very common at this time of year – some hundreds of pleasure Boats with Awnings assemble in the Bay within the Harbour, several Bands of Music, the Houses near the shore illuminated. Thus with refreshments, Music and singing passed away the time till day light – at 4 went on board.

Excavation of the Temple of Isis at Pompeii, engraving after Fabris

The Straits of Messina

las! We lose sight of Wybourn at this tantalising point, a mere nine weeks before the Battle of Trafalgar. Villeneuve, the French admiral, had sailed to the West Indies, trying to lure Nelson away from Europe, knowing that the British were desperately trying to bring them to open battle. The plan was then to return and attack England. But Nelson was close on his heels; this so worried Villeneuve that he disobeyed Napoleon's orders to wait for reinforcements, and headed straight back to Europe.

Threatened with dismissal by Napoleon, Villeneuve was obliged to put to sea once again, from Cadiz. On the 19th of October the 'Combined' Franco-Spanish Fleet headed for the Mediterranean, but early on the morning of 21st October, Villeneuve found an unexpected British presence off Cape Trafalgar, barring his way. Nelson had been waiting for him.

The Franco-Spanish fleet numbered 33 ships of the line, the British 27. After months of frustration, Nelson wanted to maul his enemy badly, and headed his line of battle, an unnecessary and unprecedented risk, although Admiral Collingwood led his own line in the "Royal Sovereign" and engaged the enemy at about noon, half an hour before "Victory". As "Victory" battered Villeneuve's flagship, "Bucentaire", she simultaneously engaged the "Redoutable". At about 1.30 pm a French marksman in the fighting-tops of "Redoutable" saw Nelson in his gleaming decorations walking "Victory"'s quarter-deck and brought him down with a single musket-ball; Nelson fell, shot through the spine. At roughly 5.30 the French 74-gun "Achille" blew up, effectively ending the battle. Nelson had died an hour earlier, well aware of his victory.

It is perhaps difficult to grasp how great a hero Nelson was to the nation; his triumph over the French could not have been more complete. Villeneuve and his entire staff had been captured when the "Bucentaire" had been taken and 17 of the enemy vessels had been seized; 449 British had been killed and 1,242 wounded. The Franco-Spanish, by contrast, had lost 7,000 killed and 3–4,000 had been taken prisoner. The destruction of the French at sea was complete and, the idea of invasion could never again be contemplated. Nelson had assured Britain's place as the greatest naval power in Europe.

January 1806
H.M.S. "Repulse"
Cadiz

My dear Emily,

We have been wandering about in all directions after the Enemy since I last wrote, & have at length reached this spot, the ever memorable Trafalgar is in sight, here we expect soon to receive some other orders. You may imagine how anxious we all are to go up the Mediterranean which is now become the seat of War, the Turks are going to war with us, their destruction is therefore certain. The French are everywhere routed where the English are opposed to them and we have reason to expect a speedy plunder of Constantinople. All the

The probability of a rift between Turkey and Russia, caused by France, induced the British to reconnoitre the Turkish forts in the Dardanelles in case an attack was called for.

Continent as you too well know e'er this, is in a Blaize, and we trust the rapacious enslaver of Nations is now like Renard – surrounded by death, and too far off his <u>Kennel</u> to crawl back into it. I was grieving (till lately) that my fate should be to ordain me to continue in the broils, and was going to write to you, to make use of your excellent pen to try if Lady Spencer could not be prevailed upon to get me some appointment at home; her son Earl Spencer dined with her lately at St. Albans, and would very likely oblige her, but I now shake off all ideas of ease & luxury and have made up my mind to renew the contest with redoubled efforts, nor would I retire if I could: a general spirit of enthusiasm appears to prevail alike in the breast of not only every Englishman but all those powers in alliance with us.

To my joy the other day I saw the well known characters on the back of your Letter as it was tumbled out of a large bag of letters from England; it was the more acceptable as the day before the general packet had arrived, and I perceived everyone happy round me by the receipt of letters, and had to deplore my hard fate not having received one line since I left England now many, many Months since. I thank you for all the information you intended for me, every part of which we had heard but too much of. An Expedition is planning of some kind, and as we are likely to be employed in it, I will give you a few lines as our departure will be sudden when it happens. I have but little to observe as to variety of scene, we have been 6 months on the Waters rambling about, and have been at this delightful spot cheating the Winter, and enjoying all the luxuries of a southern climate and with respect to communication with Spanish boats, have <u>fared well</u>.

Politics are indeed in a strange confused state, your sentiments were worthy of a sober politician. I need not say anything about it, as you and I probably received the same papers. I agree with you, that the ways of divine providence are unsearchable and for the best. I am pleased that Captain Lawson calls upon you, he told me that he should be most grateful to be able to render you any service, and to be considered in the light of a Brother in my absence from England, therefore you may command him as ours has been a long and tried friendship.

You wish to know how I have spent my Christmas: it passed in feasting – we invited the young officers to dinner both Christmas and New Year's day, to eat <u>mince pies</u> and <u>plum pudding</u> etc., and notwithstanding the frequent toasts, drunk to those we love and esteem, reminded us of our misfortune in being so far from them buffeting about a boisterous Ocean, and our enemies exulting no doubt at their own <u>skulking</u> comforts, as they view us every day, yet we pass our time tolerably pleasant.

Our quiet is at last interrupted, we are now all bustle, the "Repulse" is distinguished from all the Fleet, to accompany the gallant Wit [Admiral] J. Duckworth to the Mediterranean. I can give you no idea where we are going, but judge to Constantinople to adjust differences between the Russians and Turks, my <u>Medal</u> will perhaps ultimately turn out of service to me. Signals are just made to take leave of the Admiral, I fear I shall be too late to send this,

love to my Sisters
T.M. Wybourn

Wybourn had been given the Turkish Medal, perhaps at Alexandria.

Wybourn wrote a Memorandum, describing 'four Journal books, lost at the Post Office'. In Book 2 from 24 July 1806, he states that on 7 August he arrived at Plymouth, 'embarked on the "Repulse" – captured the "President" French frigate after 37 hours' chase', and in Book 4 from 13ᵗʰ May 1807 'dreadful account of the loss of the "Nautilus" sloop, on an uninhabited island, they eat each other for 6 days, 20 survived out of 126.' He had sent all the books 'on board the "Fervent" gun brig, Lt. Fullerton, directed to my sister at Chelsea', but the books were sent by Post instead of Coach, and lost.

March 4, 1807
Island of Tenedos [now Bozcaada]

My dearest Sisters,

I hasten to write you an account of my safety, by the same Vessel the Admiral's dispatches go by, in which you will read our fatal and disastrous proceedings, and in which your <u>fortunate</u> Brother was <u>once</u> killed but <u>lives</u> to tell you how providence (no <u>doubt</u> for your virtues & prayers, not his own merits) has spared him.

I know your affection for me, and that your anxiety must be on the rack should the melancholy account reach home before my letter, therefore in the midst of every confusion, and the groans of the wounded & dying – I proceed to give you some incoherent account of myself. <u>First</u> be assured I am <u>well</u> & untouched by the swift messengers of Fate, and should any account in any paper mention my being Shot, know it was another Captain of Marines & my particular friend that suffered, where I was engaged & was intended

Rear-admiral Sir Thomas Louis in the "Canopus", with the "Thunderer" and the "Standard", anchored off Tenedos on 21 December 1806. A Russian army entered Moldavia, threatening the Turks, and the situation worsened. "Canopus" and "Endymion" moved to Constantinople, where "Endymion" evacuated the British ambassador and a number of British merchants from the city. By mid-January Sir John Duckworth was ordered to attack the Dardanelles and bombard Constantinople until the Turks surrendered their fleet, consisting of 12 ships of the line and nine frigates, but he was not to open hostilities without the permission of the British ambassador, Mr. Arbuthnot. On the 19th of February, Duckworth took the squadron into the strait: "Canopus", "Repulse", "Royal George", "Windsor Castle", "Standard", "Pompée", "Thunderer", "Endymion" and "Active" and the two 'bombs' "Meteor" and "Lucifer". Wybourn himself, aboard the "Repulse", gives the best description of what fate befell the Turk that day.

to fall. I must lay my pen down for a few minutes, and collect my scattered thoughts, in order if possible to give you a detail, since I last wrote, for I was going to begin at the <u>last</u>, instead of the <u>first</u> part; indeed we are all <u>bewildered</u> and appear to be <u>dreaming</u>. Yesterday was <u>such</u> a day, when we passed the Jaws of Hell through a vortex of fire, & apparent inevitable destruction, that I cannot believe we were <u>actually there</u>, in short from the 19th of February (our first battle) till last night, we have been surrounded by Death, in every shape, and when I tell you we have lost three Captains out of 7 & by the various and melancholy manner of one drowned, one burnt, and the last shot by a rifleman on shore, you will conclude your poor brother has been boasting of his former dangers & exploits with but little reason in comparison – but here is a digression – I will go on after dinner.

2 o'clock, I have made an excellent dinner the first we have sat down to regular since the 16th of February. We left Cadiz 16th, remained at Gibraltar three days, had a most prosperous voyage and arrived at Palermo 25th of January and taking Sir Sidney Smith with us reached Malta the 1st of February. Of my engagements at all those places <u>you</u> need not be informed. Suffice it my time passed too happily amongst my old acquaintance to last long, the Admiral was impatient, the Maltees worked all <u>Sunday</u> to complete us, a thing they never do for any consideration, and we lost two hours in obtaining permission of their Bishop and his assurance of absolution as soon as it was over.

On the 7th we arrived at Milo, took Greek Pilots for the Archipelago and Dardenelles and arrived at Tenedos on the 10th. Thus you see I have hurried you to an immense distance in a <u>whisk</u>, in fact the winds were so favourable, and so strong, that we arrived here several weeks before we expected, so far our expedition seemed to prosper, and our fates propitious; we were now given to understand that we were to pass the Dardenelles or ancient Hellespont and anchor before the <u>very</u> Port of Constantinople. We were all <u>panic struck</u>, only 8 sail of the line and two Frigates and two bombs, to threaten the Capital of the greatest power on earth with 20 sail of the line, innumerable frigates, and small men of war in the Port, with an Army of upwards of 300,000 Men: their shipping we cared not for, as we knew all their Ships were not <u>ready</u>, and if they were, we could take them, as a Turk cannot fight if he sees a dead body by him (of this in its place) – we are now at Tenedos. A signal was made to prepare for battles as we should enter the Straits tomorrow at daylight, the wind shifted and here we remained (was ever anything so unlucky) till the 17th waiting for a fair wind, as the current is so strong against us we must all be knocked to atoms by their batteries & Castles did we not go by with a strong breeze.

You will perhaps imagine I will give you a sketch of all these Classic <u>Islands</u>, and that we are enjoying the beauties of these delightful places while laying in the very spot the Grecian fleet anchored before Troy (which City, at least the spot on which it stood, is close to us) but no such thing – neither myself, or I believe anyone else can <u>think</u>, or <u>speak</u> of one earthly thing, but our dangers, and the crippled wretched Fleet we are in – although the <u>mischief</u> (we hope) is passed.

I believe my beloved Sisters will not accuse me of boasting ridiculously by any service I have seen, and when they remember Holland and Egypt, will perhaps think I never spoke enough of myself – indeed I have seen many little skirmishes I have never heard of, but of this affair I must be <u>endulged</u>, and it will take up all my paper, and fifty times as much were I to tell of <u>every transaction</u> within this month. I shall trust to your candour in pardoning the vanity I feel, in having shared the glory of an <u>attempt</u> unparalled in the annals of <u>any</u> history, and which never can, or will be attempted again, and which no power, or indeed the world combined ever did think of before, namely that of passing the Dardanelles (when you look on the Map and measure 30 miles, little wider than a Canal in some parts) and consider we have to proceed against the current, it must appear incredible.

Never seen reported

<u>Mar. 14</u>[th]: Never was anything so unlucky, a gale of wind has blown directly against us since the 11th, the enemy in the meantime making all preparations. Our Ships in danger of breaking their Cables, and being cleared for action, we are perished with cold and wet, the climate here is as bad as in England.

He is now quoting from his Journal.

<u>Sunday 15</u>[th]: Our misery this night was nearly complete, how shall I relate the scene of horror, & consumation of <u>human wretchedness</u>. The noble "<u>Ajax</u>", the finest Ship among us of 80 Guns caught fire close to us, the wind blowing the smoke and flames towards us. Our Captain detained on board the Admiral three days by bad weather, and a dark gloomy night – had she blown up we must have been destroyed. She was on fire up to the very Mast head, all boats were sent from the Fleet and we got our Anchors up (with all speed as well as the Fleet). In short everything is easier conceived than <u>described</u>:

nearly half the people were saved, the ship was burning till 3 in the Morning when the Magazine blew up with a tremendous explosion; we were all out of the way of her, the loss is of considerable importance to us at this crisis. The name of the Ship occasioned many reflexions and the "Illiad" was the topic for some time; it is singular we should lose her, on the very <u>spot</u> where the mighty Grecian defended his own Vessels so obstinately. But I am delaying our proceedings – and a signal is this moment made for a Frigate to be sent away, so that I am afraid I shall not go to Constantinople & back before she goes.

<u>Friday 20th</u>: This day we arrived at Constantinople through a <u>vortex of fire</u>. I could never conceive much more experience. I often thought my dear Sisters I had seen service, but every shot I have seen for twelve years past, would not amount to half fired yesterday. We got under way by daylight on Thursday Morning, passed the two great Castles at the entrance, with but little loss and fought our way up till we came to the grand Key to the Capital 15 miles up – here we saw what even <u>Mars</u> himself might have trembled to behold, a narrow passage in the form of "S" dividing Europe from Asia, and so narrow one might fancy in approaching there was no inlet, – two immense Castles, situate on each point with Batteries on all sides, that threw shot from 40 to 60 pounds weight. After looking on this, I must not be thought a <u>Coward</u> if I declare I felt an unusual tremour at my <u>heart</u>, for I sincerely thought no power could <u>save</u> us.

To return was <u>impossible</u>, we <u>approached</u>, the gallant <u>Admiral Louis</u> led, we were <u>second</u>, to this I attribute our having escaped with less loss than any other Ship, 700 pieces of Cannon opened upon us, the Ships were cut to pieces in their Ropes, Masts, and rigging. The smoke so thick they could not see to fire with precision – their large stone shot therefore fell short, and passed over us, as second Ship – the first Ship was mawled dreadfully, and also the "Royal George" the 3rd Ship, the one received a shot which killed and wounded six men, and weighed 554 pounds, the other one of 640 pounds, I never heard of such a thing, and no doubt it would appear incredible at home. The two Castles are called "Abydos" & "Sestos", you will see where they stand in the Map. The strong wind we had soon cleared the first three ships of the danger, then, <u>what a sight</u> presented itself. Round the Castles were <u>Towns</u> two miles long: as the other ships and the two Bombs came through we had nothing to do for half an hour but look on; the slaughter on shore was beyond all calculation, the Houses flew in thousands of pieces, never was anything so dreadfully

Sir John Duckworth's flagship

102

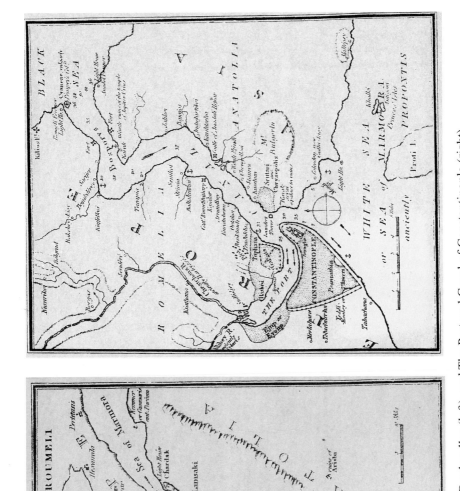

Charts: Strait of the Dardanelles (left), and The Port and Canal of Constantinople (right)

Sir John Duckworth's Passage of the Dardanelles, by Thomas Whitcombe

awful – as we looked on, we could not conceive that we had <u>passed</u> safe, tho' this was only half our work.

We now approached a point of <u>three fronts</u> and which had kept up a triangular fire with the Castles some time, the Channel led us inevitably to pass this enormous Battery also, when lo! as we turned a corner, we discovered ten men of War, with all broad sides turned to us & which we passed within a few yards of. What did the noble Sir Sidney [Smith] do, but run with two ships in between them <u>all</u>, and so astonished them, that our 3 first Ships passed with little damage from them. Our signal was now made to assist Sir Sidney, when we engaged a 64 and one point of the villainous Battery for one hour: now was the sport of the day at issue, thank God we were out of the reach of those frightful Castles and granite shot. The Turks took <u>panic</u> – they never think of quarter as they do not give it, they began to jump overboard. Cables were cut by our shot, the ships ran on shore, we now boarded & saved the people, and the day was our own. The Admiral had run with his squadron of about 6 Ships into a Bay out of danger – and we four ships took, and destroyed a squadron of 10. We made signals of victory, and the Admiral ordered all the prizes to be burnt. Alas! Money out of my pocket, but he had other objects, it was now 4 o'clock in the afternoon, we entered into action at half past 7 in the Morning – the Admiral repaired damages as quick as possible, so we proceeded on. The Turks covered the hills & country for miles round – we destroyed the Battery of above 50 Guns, took above 3,000 prisoners, and liberated them, to their <u>wonder</u> and <u>amazement</u> – and they perhaps, or even ourselves, never beheld a sight as grand as all their ships on fire, and blowing up one after another. We now joined the Admiral, and fought our way without much difficulty past Gallipoli, into the sea of Marmora, and were safe at eight o'clock for the present. Took something to eat, cracked our jokes and laid down for a Nap, but who could sleep? My brain was, and is now turned at the thought of our dangers and how we escaped.

I will not relate the transactions of several days' negotiations, parleying, and other disgraceful nonsense (for so it has turned out) we were all stark mad at it – only conceive, we arrived before the port of the Capital, there was not a gun hardly to oppose us, the Town was in an uproar & flags of truce came off, asked our terms and complied, will you believe that in their Harbour were 20 sail of the line, numbers of Frigates, in fact all their force. The population of the city 900,000

& 300,000 armed men, yet we with 7 ships frightened them. We asked their Fleet, peace, peace with Russia, dismission of the French; all foreign property confiscated to us; and the port of Alexandria in Egypt. They granted all in appearance – the Admiral was cajoled, and anchored the Fleet 7 miles off – lost his opportunity – the French party got the better of the Grand Signior – some hundreds of Guns brought down, the men of War put in a threatened posture: and in fine here we are at Tenedos again – ran the gauntlet under double disadvantages, are crippled beyond repairing at sea. Such a state as the "Repulse" is in never was heard of: we bore the brunt of the retreat. Their preparations were such, that had we remained one week longer before their City, we should never have got back.

The information we obtained from some prisoners I had taken at the Island of Prota, hastened our retreat – it had been calm 6 days, our Ships could not move of course, nearly a thousand Turks had crossed from the main to the Island we wanted water from, were making Batteries to prevent us; the "Repulse" was ordered to get under way – all boats manned and armed, to drag us <u>along</u> – the Marines to land, engage the enemy & destroy their works; towards the afternoon we arrived. They concentrated their force; we were all ready to land when the guns from the Ship alarmed the cowards, most of them took to their boats – our boats were sent after them, while I and 20 Men landed first, and after about an hour's engagement they retreated to a Monastery, fortified themselves, and bid us defiance, leaving their field pieces, ammunition, Tents, and even breakfast things behind them; these I took, sent the Cannon on board, burnt a Vessel, made a prize of the <u>Tents</u>, and brought off 11 prisoners. I only lost one man at first, but engaging the Monastery, we lost a Capt., a Lieut. & two wounded, 9 men killed and 30 wounded, & at last were obliged to leave the enemy in possession for they fired upon us from the Windows and there was no possibility of getting to <u>them</u> without battering Cannon.

Here I lost my friend Captain Kent. He occupied the spot I was reconnoitering the enemy at, and received a rifle ball through his temples. I am astonished how I escaped. As there is but one path up and I was on it some minutes, several balls came round me before I could tell from whence they came; a kind of providence has spared me however.

The information we obtained from the prisoners, was that at Constantinople the utmost preparations were making: 12,000

Volunteers to <u>board</u> us at <u>night</u>, all the Ships fitting to engage us, with nearly 1,000 Gun boats, fire ships & small things were coming upon us in torrents, in which above 100,000 men would be embarked. This news was confirmed next Morning – and we saw ten fireships coming to the outer Harbour and remained there till <u>Sunset</u> chall[en]ging the whole Fleet but they only looked at us.

March 3rd [?]: Passed the Dardanelles again, and our whole Fleet obliged to drop anchors to get sufficiently to rights to proceed to Malta. All particulars you will see in the papers (though perhaps not the truth). One shot on our return did us more damage than any, it came in near the Wheel, killed 11 Men & wounded 9, also mortally wounded one of my Subt. The best of the two, unfortunately. The Shot weighed upwards of 500lb, I have a piece of it to make into seals, it is granite; this, perhaps with a sword, Tent etc., is all I shall get, unless government allows us something for destroying their Flotilla. Thank God things are not worse. I cannot say I have not lost blood in this affair as from my hand I got a small wound from which a few drops only appeared. Remember not to give credit to reports for they have killed me <u>twice</u> in the fleet, and some fool might write home so. I conclude hoping to embrace my beloved, affectionate Sisters in the course of <u>this</u> year.

    Truly yours
    T.M. Wybourn

Sister Emily wrote:
Upon the terrific subject of the Expedition to the Dardanelles I cannot resist the pleasure of inserting part of a letter written to Major Wybourn from his amiable friend Captain Lawson; as it is not likely I can ever forget the excitement of the public, and the extreme pleasure and gratitude felt upon the receipt of these communications.

May 7, 1807
Half Moon Street
London

Dear Wybourn,
    Yesterday I received your terrible narrative of our Fleet passing the Dardanelles, which the whole Country had been on tip toe of

The squadron had passed through the Dardanelles and past Gallipoli in the west in order to get into the Sea of Marmora and attack Constantinople at the entrance to the Black Sea. They would then have passed from the Bosphorus back into the Sea of Marmora and out through the Dardanelles and Gallipoli on their return to the Mediterranean.

Britain's attack on the Dardanelles demonstrated that she was a far worse enemy than either the Russians or the French. In 1809 the Treaty of Canak or Chanak was signed, affirming that no warships of any power would enter the Dardanelles. Its secret provision offered the Ottomans British assistance in the event of a French declaration of war.

A captain of marines was called Major when on board, to avoid confusing him with the ship's Captain. He would also have become a major on demobilisation.

expectation for some weeks past of hearing from the Commander in Chief. I now congratulate you from my soul first for your escape, (secondly) that you can boast of having been engaged in one of the most awful hazardous and greatest undertakings ever recorded in history – Copenhagen, or the Nile affair I conceive to have been mere school boy play when compared with yours. I lost not a moment in forwarding it in person, to witness the joy it must give them, and received their commands for you, as I was determined not to lose an hour in replying to it, when behold I found them devouring the contents of one you had written them with all the affection and love of doating Sisters; we exchanged letters, which in effect are the same.

I read your account of the Hellish affair to Col. Berkely, our officer, who complimented you much upon your incomparable stile of narrating the business, and congratulates you upon your own good conduct and escape, and desired me to remember him kindly to you, for he recollects you perfectly. We all regret poor Kent's death here and think the Admiral rather censures his rashness too severely; indeed a liberal mind would have extolled his intrepidity and recommended his family to the protection of his grateful Country – but no such generous thought escaped the Admiral in his dispatches – Nicolls is spoken of very handsome in his letters, and I trust he will receive that honourable remuneration which he so highly merits – My God, I am surprised how any of you escaped – nothing but a kind Providence surely saved you – for I consider you to have fought under double disadvantages; if you had been made prisoners, those sanguinary Villains would not have given quarters.

I did nothing all day yesterday but think of the Dardanelles, and all night dream of you, Battles, Murders, Turks etc. I shall call on your Uncle [Wybourn] and see how he feels at his Nephew's heroism, success & escape.

I was very sorry to find your name was not mentioned in the Admiral's dispatches, it must [sic] have been very gratifying to your friends to see it honourably mentioned & of service to you in a future application for a Civil or Military employ you may hereafter think of. Col. Berkely wishes me to make an extract from your letter and send it to the Editor of some paper, particularly that part where you speak of having saved the Fleet by information from the Prisoners you took. But not to mention Names, but merely say it came from a Marine Officer of the Fleet. It will appear creditable to the Corps. Therefore believe I shall do it. Your sister desired me to say she has almost

i.e. it would have been

finished a very long letter for you, which she will send directly, therefore in all probability this & hers will arrive together. She was observing that a fine Boy of the Hesseltines wants a commission in our Corps & that she should request your endeavours to get him one – this I shall be attentive to, and indeed I feel pretty confident I shall succeed. I think them an amicable family, therefore shall have much pleasure in serving them. It was very droll that I should the day before I recd. your letter write your sister a note to say that I had heard from an officer just arrived from the Mediterranean that you was safe after a little warfare with the Turks and anticipated they would have it confirmed in your own handwriting in a few days.

In future recollect it is possible for my letters to Miscarry, or from your constantly moving about difficult to find you, therefore do not again make the rash resolution of not writing me till you hear from me. When abroad before you imagined I never wrote you but on your return my letters retraced you. My father & mother rejoice at your safety & desire their good wishes, etc. There is a report going about now that Boneparte is mortally wounded, but I fear its not true.

Richard Lawson

June 1807
H.M.S. "Repulse"
Palermo

My dearest Sisters,

At length an opportunity offers to send Letters to England, which we have been anxiously looking for this long time. I fear you will think it long since the date of my last; but I assure you no ship has sailed for England, and to send by <u>Land</u>, might cost 16 Shillings, which would exceed by, at least, 15 times the value of my scrawl, thus have I accounted for my silence, but what excuse can all my dear friends at home advance? Two letters are all I have received in ten months. I have scarcely anything new to communicate, except that the "Repulse" has been at anchor in this paradise on Earth nearly two months, and the officers & Ship's company been indulging in all the ease & luxury of perhaps the gayest Capital in the World.

To enumerate all the Princes, Consuls & Barons with whom I am acquainted, and have been <u>particularly</u> distinguished by, would take up too much of my paper & your time. The gayest Carriages and elegant Liveries have attended <u>my pleasure</u>, & no Conversazione, or public rout, have been given that the "Capitane Vibon" as they call me, was not invitedto – besides which, the Queen, has twice honoured me in the midst of her Court, with her gracioius attention, and even <u>Tate a tate</u> [sic] conversation. You may suppose I am a proficient in the Italian language. Latterly I have confined myself to the society of a few, whose attachment to the English have occasioned them to study our manners & customs more minutely than the generality of these frivolous vain Animals choose to do. I have formed a friendship for one who is in his heart a perfect Englishman: the third Son of the Prince of Patino: his Father's Palace is open to the English at all times, and the Princess, a charming young woman, (the 2nd wife) gives tea & Cards in our fashion, the only woman who does in Palermo; she is the most accomplished, as well as the richest Woman in the Island. She plays and sings, I could say most divinely: you will naturally judge therefore that I am more with this family than any other – in short I occupy the son's apartment as he sleeps in the Country for the benefit of the Air, and has insisted that I should not go on board at night, for you must know that the parties are very late at night: the charming Princess only excepted.

My friend's Establishment is very comfortable: he has a wing of the palace, about 20 servants, three Carriages, 12 Horses besides 2 English Hunters; we are constantly out together in one kind of carriage or another or on horseback; so you see your lucky Brother pops upon the good things of this life every now and then. Notwithstanding which you will think me ungrateful when I say I cannot divest myself of those constant wishes towards Old England, the most forcible magnet, nor any <u>earthly</u> allurements can wean my affection from the happiest of <u>all</u> places under Heaven.

The moment you receive this, I expect you, and my dear Matilda will write direct for me on board the "Repulse", Malta & by the time it arrives perhaps I may be there. We sail in a few days on a secret mission; our Captain has under his command two line of battle ships & five frigates & sloops. We go first to Smyrna, in the Archipelago. We are assured that our Cruize is likely to be a lucrative one; there is no harm in saying <u>God send</u>.

I must now just give you an outline of our rout [sic], since I wrote from the entrance of the Dardanelles; my Journal [lost in the post] which I have very faithfully kept among all difficulties I shall endeavour to send you by the first safe conveyance, and that will more fully acquaint you of all particulars – On 13th of March we sailed for Egypt, on the 15th anchored at Patmos for water, this renouned place where St. John wrote the Revelations. I have procured a relic, a Musel shell 20 inches long: the fish eaten by the Monks in the very Convent St. John was confined in. Sailed on the 18th and passed a vast number of beautiful Islands and steering between Rhodes & Candia so famous in history, arrived at Alexandria on the 22nd; little did I think I should ever see this place again.

Candia: modern Heraklion

On the 23rd anchored in the spot where the lamented Nelson fell, and also where the great Abercromby died. The recent disasters in Egypt, of which you are ere this acquainted we escaped a share in by being ordered on other service. We soon left the Deserts and on April 8th anchored in Syracuse, on the 16th at Malta, on the 22nd at Messina, and on the 27th at Palermo where we have been ever since, but are to depart in a day or two having had a pretty good spell after our hard services and perfectly recruited and ready for any other.

Nelson was wounded in the head at the Battle of the Nile, but, of course, did not die there.

Indeed, my Amiable Sister, the accounts you gave me of your Balls and continued dissipation, not a little startled me on the first perusal, until I arrived at the conclusion, knowing how little these things are to your taste. I cannot subscribe to the opinion that your faded charmes could stand in the way when you possess that which is so much more lasting Worth, and the charmes of the mind; As a man who knows something of the world, without being suspected of flattery, I must say I am astonished at the blindness, folly & ignorance of those (who have dallied in your train) to let such a treasure slip by them – I think I cannot close this tolerably long letter at a better time than when I have assured my modest Sister that there is at least one Man who knows how to appreciate her worth. Give my love to Matilda, tell her I am anxiously looking for letters. As for Caroline, I have little hope that she will keep up any kind of correspondence; Husband & Children are much in the way. She, I know, is ever anxious for my welfare, therefore pleased when you inform her of my safety & movements.

Caroline had 11 children!

    Your affectionate
    T.M. Wybourn

October 17, 1807
Sicily – off Syracuse

After Trafalgar, the weakest point of British Mediterranean strategy was Sicily. Britain could neither defend it properly nor afford to give it up entirely. It lay under constant threat from Italy and Toulon. The British maintained a tight blockade on Toulon, trying to keep the French squadron there from moving into the Mediterranean.

<u>Lines of Wordsworth</u>

I travell'd among unknown Men
    In Lands beyond the Sea;
Nor, England! did I know till then
    What Love I bore to thee.
'Tis past, that melancholy Dream!
    Nor will I quit thy Shore
A second time; for still I seem
    To love thee more and more, etc. etc.

I have not hitherto inserted Poetry in my journals, first because I experience much variety & were I to attempt to illustrate my Subjects it would swell my books too much, but the above has struck me so forcibly & are so applicable & congenial to my feelings, I could not resist them. The movements of our squadron are so mysterious that we are in continual doubts harassing the mind.

<u>Sunday 18th</u>: We are close in with this delightful shore, sometimes passing under the Prodigious Etna & then tacking, and going to the very mouth of the Port of Syracuse, yet the obstinate old Admiral [Collingwood] will not allow the necessary refreshment to the Crews. The first pages of my new Book will compass no other thing but grumbling & dissatisfaction, as I have been in a shocking bad humour; for which, as there are few reasons to be admitted, I must hope that the plea of ill health may plead a little in my favour.

One reason for my illness is, in a gale of wind I returned to my Cabin very sick, when my Cot (which to give me more room during the day) was fastened up to the Deck over my head – by some accident it came down, and the heavy wooden frame struck me violently on the head, & deprived me of sense for a considerable time. In short, bleeding & water grewel was my portion for many days in consequence, which not a little alarmed me, as I was translating Gilblas, from the Italian, & was impressed with all the horrors of <u>Doctor Sangrado</u>. Perhaps I was indebted to the thickness of the Scull, but nevertheless the Concussion at all events reached the brain, & set in such an uproar that headakes are yet occasional intruders on my

The Adventures of Gil Blas de Santillane *is a picaresque romance written in French by Le Sage, published between 1715 and 1735. Wybourn must have encountered an Italian translation.*

quiet. To mend the matter, I went riding to shew part of the Island to a young friend, when galloping along those stony roads to overtake the Mad young fellow, down came my Charger & over we both rolled together; not being bled at the time, but going to dine with a party I was previously engaged to, laid me up again.

<u>Sunday 26th October</u>: The Accession of our beloved and virtuous Monarch to the Throne of the only favoured (of Providence) nation in the world, at the present day, whilst all other great & Powerful Potentates are humbled to the dust by an Illegitimate Adventurer, how thankful to a just and powerful God – ought every Englishman to be. We maintain our Dignity amid the storms of Fate, defy the destroyer of Kingdoms, & perhaps may yet replace our allies on the footing they have fell from & convince them by our unanimity, and resolute Councils, that they might have avoided the degradation also, had they respected themselves in the first instance.

Will it be believed we are still off this point of Sicily, no change or the least news – no letters or papers to acquaint us with the particulars of the Copenhagen affair, which we have a glimpse of by French & Italian news or of Buones Ayres etc., etc., or in short one word of consolation.

Copenhagen affair – see below, pp 115, 116

It is reported 6,000 Men are embarked at Syracuse & preparations going on, but we cannot learn the truth, it is really too bad. The day spent as usual mustering men, Church, & Parade; after dinner they drank our good King's health, with the fervency with which he is beloved by us all – while poor me could only wish it, confined still to my Cabin & a <u>soup meagre</u>, with Toast & water, being my restriction. I will once more resolve to be more prudent hereafter.

<u>Catania. Monday 26th</u>: The Admiral seems to be gratifying his curiosity this delightful weather by standing close into the different Bays. This lovely City, famed in history & for its misfortunes from Etna's destructive fire, is in full view, it certainly is a most superb & Elegant pile of building – it was most magnificent in the time of the Romans, & its Edifices calculated to resist the attack of Time.

One of the greatest curiosities on the Island & which everybody goes to see, is the Villa of the Prince of Biscari, upon the celebrated torrent of Lava of 1669. Upon this black & impenetrable surface he has laid the plan of a Garden, built houses, planted trees in earth carried from other places and what is still more extraordinary has formed two large Ponds of fresh water supplied by springs that ouze through the Lava; it is said this Prince expends many thousands annually in whims of the like nature on the Lava.

Catania at present contains 40,000 persons & is the seat of the only University of Sicily & the See of a Bishop, whose considerable Revenues are derived principally from the sale of Snow on Mount Etna; one small portion on the North corner produces no less than 1,000 per annum. The Idle, Vile Monks have an incomes of 15,000 pounds a year, & their Monastery is a scene of elegance, of antiquities, gormandizing and all manner of Voluptuousness: a Convent stands just by and no doubt these sinners under the mask of Religion have a subterranean communication. I believe no scoundrels of Earth equal to these Priests & Monks, & if I have reason in a <u>small</u> degree to speak from <u>experience</u>, what must it be on a grand scale. So much for abuse, and for Catania.

Yet I do not know to leave this place without a quotation from Brydone, as he observes with truth, as I at this moment have occular demonstration of it: that the view of Etna from the sea is more complete & satisfactory than anywhere on this Island.

In the Voyage between Catania & Syracuse about 50 Miles, this striking object appears to great advantage, & exhibits a view which is uncommonly sublime. Here the Eye takes in a greater portion of the Circle, & observes with more distinctness how it rises equally on all sides from its immense base. Here it can at once trace the progress of Vegetation, from its utmost luxuriance to where it is checked by the two extremes of heat & Cold. The different Regions of Etna are distinctly marked out by their different colours, & productions. Every climate & every season, is at once exposed to the delighted Eye. Summer & Autumn, spring & Winter, succeed to each other in these enchanting Regions which are terminated by the fathomless abodes of unextinguishable Fire.

Admiral Collingwood had assumed command of the British Fleet in the Mediterranean after the death of Nelson. According to the history books, he was maintaining a blockade of Cadiz from 1806–9. According to Wybourn, he is racing around the Med.

<u>Wednesday 28th</u>: Yesterday Evening the Admiral [Collingwood] as if the D**** was at him, set all sail possible, and without <u>signal</u>, or other <u>notice</u>, <u>away</u> he went; we all followed of course, round Cape Passire & down the south east side of Sicily. Where we are going, or what to do, heaven & himself only knows, we expect to see Palermo tonight, should he go to the west of Sicily. He is the most extraordinary Commander I ever saw.

<u>Sunday November 1st</u>: Dreadful Gales with lightning & rain has annoyed us these three days past; fortunately this afternoon it became moderate which revived our spirits, we are now getting a little to

rights, & expect to see Sardinia tomorrow, for the Admiral as I suspected went off Palermo & served us just the same as at Syracuse, merely cruized off the Harbour & other ships left there for the protection of the City. Admiral Martin in the "Canopus" joined us, & away the old commander-in-chief set off, with six sail of the Line & the "Bittern" sloop, we suppose for Toulon. Captain Legge dined with us, he had no news or could conjecture what Admiral Collingwood was about. Our Ship is so very leaky after the Gales & being a weak Ship, that such another shaking would oblige a speedy return to England to repair, when if I remain in the same mind I am in at present, I will never go out again.

Monday 2nd: A charming day, visiting on board the different Ships, Captain Legge dines on board the Admiral; we hope he will get news, we are all rejoiced at the course we are steering, as it can be for no other place than Gibraltar or Cadiz.

Off Toulon. Sunday 8th: All our hopes have vanished respecting Cadiz, we arrived here in the midst of heavy Gales, and dreadful Storms, nor do we see any prospect of a relief. I must console myself with my studies. I am now reading the studies of Nature, by that elegant Author De St. Pierre translated by Dr. Hunter.

Thursday 10th: No one could sleep last night for dreadful Thunder and forked Lightening: never was daylight more welcome.

Towards noon it cleared away & was calm, when Boats communicated with the Admiral & we had the pleasing news of a Vessel in sight from England – no letter alas! A Steel's list however came, by which we see the Copenhagen & Monte Video affairs. The information from the Admiral is that the Toulon fleet consist of 6 sail of the Line & that they were out last week, chased off our Frigates & that five of their Frigates & a Sloop had escaped, supposed for Corfu. The Expedition talked of at Sicily has proceeded for England. We have made a prize of one of them. Accounts of the "Blenheim" with Sir Thomas Troubridge & all hands foundering is, I am grieved to say, confirmed. General Whitelock commanding in South America is to be tried by a Court Martial: a more disgraceful treaty never was even thought of, as he had made at Buenos Ayres with a plausible French intriguing General, who had been a Confectioner.

Wednesday 11th: The Captain sent us various papers up to the 8th of October, which was a great treat indeed. The full particulars of the Danish affairs were in them, stating that Copenhagen Capitulated on the 7th of September with all their Fleet, Stores & Ammunition etc.,

A Steel's List is the original 'Navy List' giving details of all those enlisted in the service. It must have been the best way to catch up with the developing careers of old comrades.

As protectors of the Spanish and Portuguese royal families, Britain could take advantage of new export markets despite the continental blockade. Brazil, Argentina and all Iberian colonies in Central and South America were

made available for Britain's economic growth.

The British landed troops at Copenhagen when the Danes threatened to join their land forces with the French. An expeditionary force under Wellington (still Sir Arthur Wellesley) defeated a Danish army on 29 August 1807. Fearing that Napoleon would seize Denmark and the Baltic approaches, Admiral Gambier attacked Copenhagen in September of that year, after Wellesley's victory in late August. Gambier captured the entire Danish fleet and all its stores.

In 1808 France attempted to occupy Portugal. Fearing the spectre of the Portuguese fleet in French hands, Rear Admiral Sir William Sydney Smith's squadron intervened and escorted the Portuguese royal family and navy to Brazil, out of Napoleon's clutches.

etc. fell into our hands – 114 Ships & Vessels of War & more naval stores than will fill all our fleet & their own. This must be a death blow to Boneparte, as it is certain he meant to seize that Country & employ all its force against us, as there was five times the quantity of stores more than was necessary for all the Danish fleet. It will also again check a Northern Confederacy &, by all the papers, Russia appears dissatisfied with the Peace of <u>Tilset</u>. And that Nobles have actually come forward offering to maintain 200,000 Men at their own Expense, so that hopes are still entertained the French may experience a <u>fraternal hug</u> from the Russian <u>Bears</u>, and with the spring great operations commence. Austria assumes a warlike appearance, & with the Brave Swedes, England could place 100,000 prime Troops in any part of Russia, or Pomerania, which will terrify the Corsican Adventurer. We are truly concerned at the wretched account from South America: the Commander must be shot or disgraced.

A large Naval promotion has taken place, a partial one in the Army & a considerable augmentation to the Royal Marine Corps.

Portugal it appears are preparing to send their Court & riches with other Volunteers to the Brazils, otherwise Bonaparte will soon surprise them. We send a large force to occupy Madeira, and two or three expeditions are on foot, this looks like Energy & Spirit & we hope the present ministers will continue to persevere in their good projects and try the strength & inclination of a Nation so powerful, but who has never yet been roused to extra activity.

<u>Sunday November 15th</u>: More Disasters! – The Admiral sent us close in shore to reconnoitre the Enemy on Friday & we have been liked drowned rats ever since. The heaviest sea, storms etc. have rendered us completely miserable & for my own part, I am surprised it has not killed me, being yet confined. This night I thought would have been our last, nor do I believe a Naval officer among the whole was <u>undismayed</u>.

The circumstance was this: about eight o'clock the officers came below & observed they never saw such lightning before & that the Thunder appeared close over our heads. I had just crept out of my Den, to have my bed made & was sitting at the Table talking of the dreadful cruize we have had for some weeks past – & in fact I was so [dispirited] by remaining alone solitary & alarmed for the Magazine, that I ventured out of my Cabin to enjoy company, such as it was, –

when a tremendous Sea struck the stern and made all stagger again thro' the Ship.

The Galley fire was put out by it, & everything displaced everywhere; the Men said the Ship trembled for ten minutes <u>fore</u> & <u>aft</u> & everyone thought a thunder bolt had struck us, but what was out situation in the Wardroom a minute after the shock – the wave burst in all our Windows, window frames, woodwork etc. and rushing into our Cabin, our Mess room and every place at once, filled us all with consternation & we really thought we were going down, the Crash was so great, which with the loud thunder, & all confusion, that no one had power to get away till washed into a heap together: Tables, Chairs, Musical Instruments, Backgammon boxes etc., etc., all swimming about, the water above our knees before it got vent, when it rushed impetuously out between decks & half drowned all the Sailors. Had any small Vessel been struck by such a Mountain of a Wave, it would have sunk in an instant. When we were acquainted with the nature of the Catastrophe – it afforded some mirth, the ludicrous figures we all cut when the Seamen came in to put all to rights, & see the extent of our mischief. We were of course wet thro' & thro' – & my two Subs, idle young men, were as <u>usual</u> sleeping on the <u>Window seats</u> – their situation may be easily imagined & when got on their legs (for they were washed away as a Cork would be in a Mill-sluice) astonishment & dismay was depicted in each countenance & "What's the matter, what's the matter?" was all they could say – for my part I could stay no longer, but instantly took off my clothes, made my Servant rub me with flannels and went to bed, had some <u>hot</u> wine, but little sleep.

<u>Monday 16th</u>: Thank God the Gale is over, & I have not felt the least effects from the sea bathing of yesterday. The Ship exhibits a pretty scene – a perfect wreck at our end, & no Glass to mend our Windows – 34 large panes of Glass was precipitated about the Ship in thousands of pieces & it will be a providence if the Men, who will go barefoot, do not lame themselves.

We are all busy getting Trunks, Linen etc. dry. The Sailors no doubt are enjoying the thoughts of <u>all</u> the <u>Officers</u> suffering <u>only</u>, and it is singular that we were all concentrated at the moment the disaster befell us, even our Chaplain (ill as he always is in bad weather) was a witness to it; he like myself hastened to bed astonished & alarmed beyond all description, indeed for 13 years in all climates & gales, the like accident never occur'd. It is considered by Seamen to be the most dangerous of any accident at Sea, as the Ship is of course broadest at the Stern, & the weight of a large wave generally presses her so much that she cannot right again, & goes to the bottom stern foremost. In going round the Cape ships are obliged to lay to, if caught in a Gale, for to Send, as it is called, before the wind, is certain ruin if the sea is high, the waves following faster than the ship can run; this was our case for there was too much wind to carry sail & the waves overreached us, tho' the Sea is not so high here, as at the Cape, nor did the Sea strike us very high up otherwise the Capt. whose Cabin is above ours must have been washed away.

So much for the comforts of a Sea Life – not anything else have I to speak of for every thing has been gloomy & every body sulky of late, & likely to continue so; if we get a few hours moderate weather, it but just affords us time to place our things to rights & talk a little together & then with the Gale we take up a Book or paper & sit in some snug corner to read & sulk. This sometimes happens the whole winter & off Brest or in the North Sea they enjoy 9 months of 12 blowing weather tho' not perhaps stormy & yet it is said by people who do not go to "Dear me, if I had as much time on my hands as you all must have at Sea I would <u>study</u> etc. etc." In short for myself, I am fit for no earthly thing in blowing weather & the <u>little</u> time we get with being in harbour etc. I am glad to get a little relaxation & comfort, consequently no time for studies in particular & no <u>inclination either</u>, so that I contend a sea life to be the most unprofitable of any except the <u>value</u> of our <u>Services</u> to the Country.

<u>Wednesday 18th</u>: Two Frigates joined us, the "Tigre" is to go home after proceeding to Malta for a Convoy.

A Son of Lord Spencer's came on board to see one of the Officers, I did not know who he was or should have shown him particular attention & informed him his <u>Father was my Patron</u>.

<u>Saturday 21st</u>: At length a change of scene is about to take place. It is said the Expedition is gone to take Minorca, but most probably to Cadiz or Lisbon. Our chaplain has obtained leave to quit the service and is gone on board the "Tigre" for a passage home. Various business transacted in the fleet, it is said we are to proceed under Admiral Martin's command to Palermo & old Admiral Collingwood with the other Ships go off to Cadiz, God be praised.

<u>Sunday 22nd</u>: Last night the Admiral made all sail from this vile & miserable Station, one [comfort] is, we cannot be worse, go where we may & a few days will determine what is to be done next. No

Wybourne as a young man, from a miniature

Divine Service on Board a British Frigate, by Augustus Earle

Church today having lost our parson. I am now taking Bark, hope another week will set me up. Capt. Legge dined with us & I again took my seat at the public Table. We are going at the rate of 9 miles an hour. I am getting very angry at receiving no Letters from England, the last from my Sisters dated May.

Our share for the "President" (French frigate) amounts to 26 pounds, 11 more than I calculated upon, I wish we could take one every Month.

Thursday 26th: Most lovely weather. I walked the Deck the first time since I left Malta. It is incredible what a difference we experience in comparatively a few miles. Off Toulon we were continually wet, cold & miserable with great Coats, here, in sight of Sicily it is so hot a single sheet is enough at night & in the day it is impossible to continue in the Sun. We all appear in new life & renovated with the blessing of Summer. Employed fitting up my sofa with the Turkish coverlid taken at the Dardanelles, wrote letters etc.

Saturday 28th Nov: The "Tigre" parted company for Malta. Lord Collingwood it seems is waiting here for the "Bittern" Sloop dispatched the other day to Palermo; we are close in with the Island of Maritimo, & west of Sicily. Delightful weather still favours us, we are looking for news, letters etc. with great impatience. Yesterday we received information that some trifling allowance would be made by Government for the Turkish Expedition. Completed my Italian Book & read some romances in that language.

Sunday 29th: A visible Eclipse of the Sun, also the Comet seen for many months past. The Eclipse brought on windy & rainy weather & the wind having changed to the East, it is impossible for us to pass Maritimo on our way to Syracuse, where it is said we are to winter. Capt. Legge dined with us, I presided the first time since my illness, no Parade owing to the bad state of the weather tho' warm & comfortable.

Not Halley's Comet, last seen in 1758 and not due until 1834.

Wednesday 2nd Dec: Five days have we been waiting for a fair wind, but no change in the weather except a Sirocco wind so dangerous in this part of the world; we are all unwell & can hardly breathe, pains in the breast, sore throats & headaches are the symptoms with Rheumatism. A few years ago the greater part of the population of Malta & Gozo died owing to the wind lasting ten days. A report made by the Master & Purser to the Captain of a number of Water Casks being rotten & unserviceable; this will no doubt send us to Malta, which we are much wishing for in order to pass a pleasant

Christmas, but more especially as our Caterer reports our stocks of Sheep to be consumed, & the Pigs two in number only so that a most deplorable prospect presents itself should the wind remain contrary.

Syracuse

At length we reached this port; & our Signal was made to lead in, which we did in great style, & anchored close to the landing place; no news whatever: the Expedition [of] General Moore was 7,000 men, but not heard of yet. We expect to remain a long time here, as the Ships are all in a bad state. Yesterday went on shore after passing the whole morning on board the "Canopus" & dining there made several arrangements about the Mess, ordered stock etc., etc.

<u>Tuesday 8th</u>: Called on my friend Lewis, who kindly offered me the use of his Horses, this is a great comfort, as riding is so essential to my health: met several acquaintances & paid various visits. The Admiral & all the grandees visited the Governor & Senate under discharge of artillery. A grand festival or Saint's day at Syracuse with a Fair, which lasts ten days, the place was never more gay.

<u>Wednesday 9th</u>: Rode out, made a purchase of some excellent Wine, returned on board to dinner, some officers of the "Canopus" dined with us. The Mayor, Governor & Senate with many followers returned the Admiral's visit & lunched on board, Trumpets sounding, Bands playing & Cannon firing the whole time. Found myself very unwell & retired early.

<u>Thursday 10th</u>: A very wet day, a general Court Marchal [sic] held on board the "Canopus", to try two officers for Embezzlement on board a Prize, & the Captain of the "Glatton" for <u>Tyranny</u> & <u>Oppression</u> etc. The usual routine of Business going on in the fleet, all bustle, confusion & hurry to get Water, provisions, repair Ships, set rigging to rights, painting etc., etc. This generally lasts for some days; the poor Sailors, fagged to death from daylight till after dark & frequently all night, & when all is complete <u>they</u> are the <u>only</u> Class not permitted to enjoy a few hours on shore; so much for the brave fellows who are so <u>conspicuous</u> in their Country's cause – how these undaunted men submit is a matter of astonishment. Several Men of

To hold a court martial at sea was often difficult because five captains were needed to adjudicate. This delayed matters until enough ships were gathered to provide the five officers and, once begun, a trial could delay the departures of a tactical squadron.

War & Transports arrived – also the "Glatton" – the harbour is full of Shipping, provisions very dear.

<u>Sunday 13th Dec</u>: Employed for the Mess purchasing stock, & riding about the Country to find it. It is the most delightful weather in the world & has quite renovated me. Went early on shore to see a grand procession of St. Lucia who is carry'd in great pomp to a Convent without the Town, and suffered to remain there eight days tho' a solid mass of Silver as large as Life. Took two of our young Honourables to see it, & provided them with Horses; was much pleased with the singing at High Mass, where <u>Madam</u> was deposited. Dined on board, in the evening went again on Shore to the Opera, the Admiral and all Grandees there.

<u>Thursday 15th</u>: The Nobles & Senate gave a superb Ball to the Admiral & Captains, Officers etc., etc. A more elegant affair never was witnessed even in the City of London: above 300 sat down to Supper & the dancing was kept up with great spirit before & after. I can never forget the particular & distinguished manner in which my old acquaintance Baron Bosco received & treated me; he is the first Nobleman in Syracuse, of whom I have spoken before while in the "Ambuscade" & when we returned from the Dardanelles. I had hitherto avoided his Palace for two material reasons: first my health would not permit me to enter into the dissipations of so gay a house & I had everything to apprehend from the attractions of his family, which, if I dared, I would call Angels. Secondly, the Admiral, Grandees, the Turkish Governor & Suite etc., etc., all were daily inmates of this hospitable house, which is ever open to Foreigners & Galas made every night for them; I therefore had determined to avoid a renewal of their acquaintance. But they all recognized me immediately & the noble Baron scarcely left me a moment, & tho' his daughters were engaged with Lords & Generals, he insisted upon their favouring me for one Dance, & his Sister the Marchioness of Sortina actually declined a Sicilian Nobleman in order to compliment me with the very first dance. Such distinguished attention in the face of all our great men, who really for the most part were left unnoticed, was not a little flattering to me & as it may be easily imagined was galling to several who repeatedly asked me, how I became such a favourite. My reply was, that in Sicily all Gentlemen were considered upon equality whether Titled or otherwise & that if I could take any merit from such pointed friendship, I could attribute it to my knowledge of their language only. This was understood especially by

There was also a deputy judge advocate to record the proceedings, and the paraphernalia was kept to a minimum: a bible, a copy of the Articles of War, pen, paper and ink. The captains acted as both judge and jury. Until 1815 there were no books of precedent or procedure to which they could refer, and none of them would necessarily have had any legal training. Certain offences were punishable by death, but captains were practical men of great experience and judged each case more by the spirit of the law than the letter. There were some traditions involved: if charged with a serious offence, an officer would surrender his sword to the court. For the reading of the verdict, some court presidents would lay the sword with the hilt towards the accused if acquitted, the point if found guilty.

my own Commander, who is as proud as Lucifer. My valued Baron & his lovely family – 21 in number (Sons & Daughters) which <u>prove</u> (according to Scripture) his worth & goodness, have made me promise not to absent myself in future. If I have occupied so much of my paper in Panegyric it is a tribute of <u>gratitude</u> I owe to them.

<u>Wednesday 16th December</u>: Paid a visit to the "Canopus" – found a large party of De Rolles Regiment & the 31st; songs & high glee till nine when we all went on Shore, called on Madam, a lovely opera singer, who entertained us very graciously, afterwards proceeded to the Baron's till 11 o'clock.

<u>Tuesday 22nd</u>: I never spent a more delightful day; a <u>Picnic</u> was proposed by several Ships, & the 31st Regiment & about 30 of us partook of the sport of the Day: a large Tent was pitched about 5 Miles off the River's head, a wild retired spot – & a sumptuous entertainment was provided. Every one pursued his plan of amusement till 2 o'clock, the hour named to Dine – some went up in Boats & remained in a Bason fishing, the Water as clear as Chrystal about 20 feet deep & the Papyrus Tree grows in it & multitudes of fish, the appearance on the whole most gratifying. The Bason is very small & the channel leading to the sea only wide enough to admit a Boat which must likewise be lifted from the Sea into the river. Many amused themselves shooting & others lounging round the Tent reading & superintending the display of eatables etc., etc. I, with two others rode out, & was much delighted with a beautiful romantic Road – At two major Leigh of the 31st came in from Shooting & the Gun was fired as a warning to those at a distance that operations would soon commence. We all did great justice to our Collation, & drank out 20 bottles of Wine 3 dozen of Porter & two Noyau; of course we were merry enough, & some famous Songs contributed to our hilarity. Our sports were somewhat dampt by hearing two Guns fired from the Admiral, and a Lieut. declared he saw preparations making for sailing. In short a few went away, who were most anxious & the rest resolved not to give it a further thought, as we expect to winter at Syracuse. So far from going to sea – it was after dark that we got into Town, I went shopping, afterwards to the Baron's whose lovely Sister was the means of my winning 14 Dollars at Faro. Went on board late.

The dollar was a silver coin common across Europe, derived from the German word thaler. *It was also the name used by English-speakers for the Spanish 'piece of eight', or* peso, *circulating in Spanish and English colonies in the West Indies.*

<u>Wednesday 23rd</u>: I was surprised upon getting up this morning to find our whole Fleet at Sea and was informed that the Admiral would have sailed yesterday had there been wind enough – of course we

should all have been left behind. Advice was brought that the French fleet was near Malta; this started the Admiral in a hurry.

Thursday 24th: Began to clear for Action; the Admiral seems to have good information of the Enemy for he made the signal to prepare for Battle. We are therefore in a miserable Plight once more, our Cabins knocked down, all windows out & loose Canvas Screens blowing about, a pretty prospect for us for the Winter, should we not fall in with the enemy immediately.

Friday 25th: We all hoped to have spent this sacred day snug & comfortably, but the fortunes of war forbids. I dined with the Captain – we drank to a merry Christmas – but it is the French alone that can get us in spirits. We entertained a party of Mids & gave them a good Xmas dinner. In the Evening two Vessels joined by which I had the happiness of receiving letters from my dear Emily & Lawson. They also bring intelligence that the French fleet of 16 Ships passed at the back of Malta on Tuesday, & we sailed on Wednesday at daylight, so that we are before them a day or two; should they be bound to Corfu a short period must bring us together, we are just going to pack up & send all below except one shirt & a change – God send us success & victory.

The command of 'clear for action' cleared the gun-decks to give officers a clear line of sight on the ship and allow the guns free movement. Any obstruction was taken below to the holds, including personal possessions, furniture, livestock or even bulkheads. This meant that officers' cabins would also be cleared, the canvas walls of which were rolled up and tied, their cots put aside. If a ship came to battle unexpectedly, or was unused to make such preparations efficiently, items would simply be thrown overboard.

1808
Off Cephalonia & Zante

January 1st: The New Year was ushered in with a perfect Summer's heavenly day – We are still in hopes of meeting the Enemy. Spent a cheerful day with a large party of Mids, etc.

Wednesday 6th: We are still in with these ancient & beautiful Islands guarding narrowly the only avenue to Corfu & do not despair of seeing the Enemy soon; several Vessels appeared in sight, we were all in a bustle in consequence but they proved English, and were looking for the Admiral. We therefore hope for News; the weather is now bad & Easterly wind; wrote to my Sister Emily. No news of the Enemy, a Gale of wind is coming on & we suppose we must return into Port.

Syracuse

Saturday 9th Jan: As we expected an Easterly Gale which is always tremendous in these Seas drove us to Sicily at the rate of 11 Miles an hour, and we are again in this snug Port just in time to avoid a hurricane. We now learn that the fleet seen were all Swedes who not understanding our signals & seldom coming into these parts alarmed our lookout frigates & cruizers, who thus occasioned our hurry scurry & miserable plight in clearing for action.

<u>Sunday 10th</u>: Accounts from Lisbon of the <u>Emigration</u> of the Court. Went on shore, took a pleasant walk amongst the Antiquities, dined afterwards with Major Leith of 31st, and met many I knew; [enjoyed] the hospitality & politeness of this distinguished Regiment. Before dinner there was a grand Parade of the whole Garrison, as usual every Sunday, this is General Stewart's hobby – but an abominable annoyance to the Troops. It is however a pretty show to standers-by and the Sicilians are delighted with it. After dinner we adjourned to the noble Baron's whose Palace is only opposite to the 31st Mess. It was his public night for Music, so that all the grandees of Syracuse and the fashion & beauty of the Place were there & our Admiral, Captains & Officers of the Fleet had assembled. The Musicians were numerous & the pieces of music new and <u>enchanting</u>. Certainly the Italian music is superior to any. Wills, who had sung some excellent songs at the 31st was prevailed on to exhibit his powers before an Italian Audience; he was evidently embarrassed & although he sings a scientific English Song, they did not show much satisfaction in hearing him.

The Baron's youngest Sister, the Marchioness, was present & captivated all hearts. She was the first acquaintance almost I made in Syracuse, four or five years ago, & our apparent intimacy occasioned me <u>many</u> compliments on the <u>supposed</u> progress I had made, everyone envying me my happiness for I was her humble <u>slave</u> the whole Evening. Her husband is the reverse of her, no one could accuse him of possessing one spark of Nobility but she has got one of the first titles by the match & I lament to say, that often makes amends for the want of much else.

A 'Bey' was an Ottoman governor of a province.

The Turkish Governor of Alexandria & the Bey of Tripoli with their Suite were present as usual & seemed delighted. I took an opportunity of asking the venerable Governor (who speaks good Italian) what he thought of the women mixing so much with the Men & who had so much <u>Liberty</u>. He smiled & said we were happy people.

The Bey of Tripoli has lately brought over his whole Harem (being deposed in his own Country) consisting of some score of women, Circassians & Persians, but as we had not seen them, I ventured to say as they saw so much good humour amongst our <u>parties</u> it was a pity he did not permit <u>them</u> to mix with us. He shook his head & said <u>Mahomet</u> would not permit. At a late hour we retired, everyone highly gratified with the Evening's amusement tho' I cannot but regret (according to our ideas of the thing) that they prefer <u>Sunday</u> for their Galas & routs.

<u>Monday 11th Jan</u>: A large party dined with me & luckily a friend sent me a Bag of Game, consisting of two Hares, a brace of Partridges & a luse [?] of Woodcocks, which was a great show off. Went on shore with Lewis & Brisset, afterwards to the Baron's played Faro & gossiped with the charming Marchioness & the Misses Bosco, between whom I had the felicity to sit.

<u>Tuesday 12th</u>: This being the King of Sicily's birthday the Ceremonies, Pomp, Court & Churches etc. created such a bustle in the Town as exceeded everything I had before witnessed of the kind here. High Mass was performed by the Bishop in the great Church, everybody in court dresses, Carriages driving about, Bells deafening, Cannon firing etc., etc. Drums beating, both English & Sicilian, marching to all the alarm posts of the Garrison, Great Guns and small arms, fireworks, more praying, bells, Music & Confusion occupied the whole day which closed with a brilliant Opera. From there we proceeded to the old Governor's where a superb entertainment was given, & at 1 o'clock went on board quite tired.

<u>Wednesday 13th Jan</u>: The old fractious Admiral ever on the fidget is hurr[y]ing us to be ready for Sea. Received a letter from my dear Matilda.

<u>Thursday 14th</u>: We sailed in the night & no one can conjecture where we are going or what to do. At War with <u>all the World</u> we cannot do <u>wrong</u>. The weather is very unpleasant. The Gulph of Venice appears to be our course.

<u>Sunday 17th</u>: It yesterday blew as heavy a gale of Wind as was ever known. For the first time since I have been at sea we were obliged to put up what is termed Deadlights, these are huge Shutters fastened up outside all the Windows, to prevent the prodigious Seas from breaking in, as was the case of Toulon. The "Malta" lost her maintop mast and received other damage, we had several Sails blown away, nor is it ascertained what mischief is done to the Fleet. Every one

cries out against the old <u>sea</u> monster, for he delights in these sort of Cruizes, instead of running quiet in Port during the Winter Months, to save wear & tear of the Ships. Yesterday alone must have cost Government some thousands of pounds, which might, & ought to have been saved. This Morning it became more moderate & we proceeded to dry our Cabins & put things a little to rights. Capt. Legge dined with us & in the Evening it was quite calm & I enjoyed a walk on deck which was to me quite renovating having been in bed all day yesterday, sea-sick.

<u>Thursday 21st Jan</u>: We this day met the "Standard" (64) & two Frigates, who are watching Corfu; The Russian squadron of 14 Men of War chased them a few days ago, but did not follow far – we stood close in with Corfu, & afterwards supplied those ships with provisions & Water, & left them to their fate, which in my opinion, is to be <u>taken</u> very soon, as it would be impossible to engage so great a force & they may not be able to run away if caught close in a Bay.

<u>Friday 22nd</u>: We were sent in chace [sic] & examined a ship with English Colours up which proved to be carrying the Russian Ambassador to Trieste from Malta, in consequence of our rupture with them. The Officer who boarded her brings intelligence of a supposed change of affairs in the Continent & it is rumoured, Austria & Russia will soon throw off the Mask & with Prussia attack the common disturber of Europe. God send this may be true. I think it probable, & that success would attend them if Unanimous.

<u>Wednesday 27th</u>: General exercise of Great Guns & small arms. I was not able to attend my Men, being indisposed but I heard them fire extremely well & highly to their credit. A Frigate joined us from Malta & brings us intelligence that the <u>Turks</u> have solicited our friendship & assistance; they had better have thought of this a little <u>sooner,</u> as I hear any thing we can do for them will be too late, as their Empire is undermined by their <u>Faithful allies</u> the <u>French</u>. All our Letters & papers by the last packet are most unfortunately gone to Corfu after us, which place we left a day or two ago for <u>Syracuse</u>. A Pilot came on board from Malta for us, which looks as if some service was going on. The "Leda" Frigate in the Baltic it is said captured a Russian Ship of the Line, and Capt. Honeyman lost a Leg. This will be considered a most gallant business, & I think will <u>convince</u> Russia how little they are likely to gain by a <u>War</u> with us. It is now certain that the Court & principal Inhabitants of Portugal have gone to the Brazils with all their <u>Treasure</u>, their <u>Fleet</u>, & everything valuable in

The Treaty of Tilsit, (July 1807), was hard on both Prussia and Russia – Prussia had been reduced dramatically in size and forced to close its Baltic trade ports. Furthermore, the newly created Grand Duchy of Warsaw, ruled by Napoleon's ally the King of Saxony, was menacingly situated between Prussia and Russia. Russia found that alliance to the Continental System (part of the terms of the treaty which meant a complete embargo of British trade), badly damaged Russian trade as well. Russia later opened her ports to neutral shipping in 1810.

Lisbon, after blowing up the Castles, Forts Etc. This a masterpiece of Deception upon master <u>Bone</u>.

The Prince <u>pretended</u> to shut his Ports against us, & even issued a Proclamation to his Subjects of his <u>determination</u> to assist the Corsican with all his Naval force, & other means <u>against</u> us. This enabled him to fit out his whole fleet, remove things on board & carry on appearances without suspicion of the <u>real cause</u> for it – when he left them in the Lurch & of course mute with astonishment. This is the way all other powers should have acted, playing with him in his own underhand way – then he would never have been certain how to act, or who to believe. Such was the secrecy of the proceedings that even <u>our</u> Papers <u>abused</u> the poor Portuguese for being so easily duped instead of making <u>friends</u> with us & the <u>French</u> papers were exulting at our supposed mortification. Three of our Ships of the Line have accompanied the run-aways. I should like to see the Paris accounts of this grand manouvre [sic] of the smallest State of Europe against the Victorious Usurper.

<u>Wednesday 3rd Feb</u>: We are once more safe anchored in this delightful bay – the Ship is placed in such a direction, that as I sit on my Sofa, I can see the noble Mountain Etna, towering above the City of Syracuse & all the Hills between it & us, the Clouds floating along far beneath the top of it, when there are <u>any</u>, for I can safely say there is not one hour in the 24 for weeks together in this heavenly corner of Sicily, that a cloud is to be seen.

<u>Saturday 6th</u>: Called with Capt. Vallack on Mr. Dennison who has a charming House & situation. He is related to Mr. Leakay a man of great speculation, settled on the borders of poor Nelson's Estate & has already laid out 30,000 pounds in Agricultural improvements, which will soon return him immense profit, & should the Island become ours, will employ all the Poor in the neighbourhood, who are the most miserable beings at present, owing to the neglect of the King & the power of the Barons. Went early on board after a ride.

<u>Monday 8th Feb</u>: Employed this day at Mess accounts as the Surgeon thinks I must repair to Malta for the recovery of my health.

The Admiral sent his <u>own</u> Surgeon to see me, not from any <u>politeness</u> but to report my real state of health, as he has an objection to officers going to sick quarters & pays little regard to Capts. or Surgeon's accounts unless his own, as the old brute imagines every one pretends illness in order to get home, & his general conduct is to frustrate the wishes of every class, if possible. I cannot judge what the opinion of the Surgeon is, but he seems to admit that I am in a bad way & should go home, altho' he must meet the Admiral's wishes if possible, which is, that any man may be cured on board as well as on shore. This is a maxim no Surgeon will allow yet the Sea Monster will have his own way, & I may in all probability be left to the chance of what <u>Nature</u> may do for me.

Wrote to Matilda in the hope now of an opportunity of sending it.

February 1808
Syracuse

My dearest Matilda,

Yours dated October last came by Packet in due course and proves to be the only certain conveyance, as I have had no communication from you, these 14 Months; all Emily's have, I believe, come to hand up to No 9, & I have been made happy by the rect. of them & my friend Lawson's letters in tolerable regularity. It is the chief consolation of us poor transported Slaves to look for letters upon the arrival of any strange Ship.

I cannot express how much I <u>envy</u> you, & <u>all</u> those in England, who can see the papers, & hear the <u>News</u>: since our communication with the Frigate of 21st of last Month, we are so excited, that it is impossible to express our <u>impatience</u> for <u>news</u>; this anxiety, in such eventful times will I hope plead our excuse. Your kind solicitude & anxious prayers for my welfare & return claims my sincere affection & gratitude & as I have before said, & must still think, that such virtues, as my amiable Sisters possess, will surely have <u>influence</u> with the Almighty disposer of us all, when the ungracious & irreverend life I am of necessity compelled to lead, against my better judgement perhaps, might not entitle me to expect for myself, indeed I ought not to attribute my <u>numerous</u> escapes to any cause else; although, the <u>Enemy</u> has not so many Terrors as the Climate, which of late has proved very formidable to me, in various shapes & I must soon beat my retreat, or be <u>subdued</u>. I must also thank you, my kind and considerate Sister, for not making a greater use of my Carteblanche, for, as you justly conclude, we must of necessity be poor; as our pay is small, added to which, they are always altering our

<u>Dress</u>, (an unnecessary expense) & the appearance we are obliged to make by being so much in the first company, is not done for a trifle.

I sent four Books of Journal directed to you the 16th of last October by T. Fullerton. I hope you have received them as an atonement for my long silence – they contain a full, true & particular account of all my Peregrinations, which may entertain you – get Covers for them.

The lost journals

Do not be alarmed at my observation respecting my health, as thank God, I am getting quite strong again, & can hold out I think another year if necessary, before I return, for Syracuse has <u>commenced</u> my restoration which I hope very shortly to <u>complete</u>. I have also some worthy acquaintance in the Artillery & Engineers, whose Houses & Horses are as my own, & it has done me more good than anything, riding out every day gently breakfasting upon <u>New Milk</u> (with the society of the English regiments) but the restless old Admiral [Collingwood] does not remain long at a time in Port. He should be <u>transformed</u> into a Fish, or a Sea Monster, for his delight is in gales of Wind & buffeting about – worrying all the other Admirals, Captains & Crews to death.

You are to know that our rides are, not as in <u>England</u> at this time of the year amidst snows & Frosts, but delightful verdure, shady Lanes & Groves of Oranges, the Trees at this moment in full bearing blossom, green & ripe fruit on the very same Tree, such is the Orange & Lemon at this period. It is Winter at <u>Sea</u> but Summer in Sicily.

I am glad that my Uncle Wybourn has a renewal of that very pretty Villa (Stone Bridge) as he enjoys it so much, I do not know any road out of London so retired and even romantic as it is, than he and our dear lamented Brother John together laid it out & planted so that every Tree & Shrub is endeared to him & I have seen the tear in his eyes when he has been pointing out those parts John laid out. I must leave you abruptly my dear <u>Mat</u> as news at last is arrived from England, & we shall have no Eyes, or Ears for <u>anything</u> until we have <u>devoured</u> it, that it may be propitious.

My love to Emily and God bless you
T.M. Wybourn

The News just arrived is of Peace nigh at hand, we cannot believe our Eyesight; it is said the French & Russians have sent to London to negociate a Peace, & requested <u>our</u> terms – that we sent a spirited answer rejecting all overtures, & desiring they would send the basis of <u>their</u> Terms that <u>England</u> might judge of the probability of their faith. In consequence Buonaparte has sent such an answer as leaves but little doubt that we must accept, & bets are laid that Preliminaries are signed e'er this, we are all quite happy upon the <u>mere</u> probability of such an event. In the mean time the Usurper follows up his leveling system & the sincere friends, the Spaniards are become a Province of France, or, at least have a French King – the brother of <u>Bone</u> has given up the Kingdom of Holland which Talleyrand now reigns in, & the peaceable poor King of Spain is deposed by the late King of Holland & is offered <u>Portugal</u> as an indemnity for the loss of his ancient rights.

Five sail of French Line & four Frigates have escaped from Brest & gone to South America, it is supposed two squadrons of ours are after them & were only 40 hours sail behind, so that a good account may shortly be expected of them, they were full of Troops.

<u>Thursday 11th</u>: A Vessel arrived from England, in 22 days, brings intelligence that nearly 30 Men of War & 10,000 Troops are arrived at Gibraltar on their passage up here. Accounts from all parts of the Continent confirm the misery of <u>every State</u>, & the prospect of Revolution in Russia & several Northern States, which are in a starving wretched situation: no bread to be had or common necessaries of life. At Paris, much discontent prevails & the <u>Conqueror</u>, it is affirmed, dare not stay more than one night in his <u>Good City</u>. If all these accounts are true, it would be a pity to make peace, as they would soon begin to cut each others throats, & most likely sacrifice the author of all their evils & the Villain is actuated by these fears to offer Peace, when he would break out upon us again as soon as his internal arrangements were made. Never was a more noble, energetic answer ever recorded on History as the King's to the Russian Manifesto, it ought to be printed in Gold and made conspicuous to all the powers of Europe.

Sent Home on Sick Leave

Wednesday 17th: In consequence of my health declining very much I was persuaded by the Surgeon to write the Commander in Chief relative to the survey etc., when to my surprise I received the most flattering & handsome answer possible, assuring me he had not been inattentive to my Case, and only waited an opportunity to meet my wishes.

Thursday 18th: News arrived that Scylla is taken by Siege – there were 4,000 French Troops against 200 English & after the Castle was battered down they affected a retreat by Boats sent from Messina, without the loss of a man, altho' 12 pieces of Cannon & 4,000 Soldiers were opposed to them; they however lost 45 Men killed & wounded before they retreated & the French lost as many as 700. The Castle of Scylla stands upon a Rock exactlly opposite to the Faro of Messina & cannot be approached while a Gun is standing, but they had dismounted every Cannon by continual bombardment & it was no use remaining there longer.

Friday 19th: I packed up everything & went on board the "Glatton" for passage to Malta. Received the congratulations of several friends, made a few purchases & returned to the "Repulse" to dinner – my friend Lewis dined with me. Dr. Grey visited me, & I am happy to find he is going to Malta in the same Ship. Dr. Halfpenny our Surgeon has behaved in the most friendly manner to me for which I must ever esteem him, he has not only been most attentive during my illness, but has arranged my getting home & has written a handsome letter to Doctor Allen at Malta, on whom much depends, also has given me a Certificate of his opinion of my Case, which will prove of infinite service to me hereafter in the event of their attempting to force me abroad.

Tuesday 23rd: Sent my Servant with the remainder of my things on board the "Glatton", dined on board the "Canopus" where I am at all times received as a Brother by them all. In the Evening went on board the "Repulse", eat Shrimps & once more took a parting glass, Mr. Huchings and Weymouth made me a present of two Amber Smelling Bottles. I gave my Sofa to one, Curtains to another, Backgammon table to a third etc., etc., and at 10 o'clock took a final leave of all my kind Messmates, returned to the "Glatton" & had the good fortune to be complimented with the state Cabin.

On "Weymouth" Store ship
Malta

<u>Thursday 25th</u>: In the Morning I called on board the "Weymouth" intending to look at the accommodations for passengers to England, Price 30 Guineas.

<u>Sunday 28th</u>: Arrived the "Bittern" with News that the Russians chased the "Standard" & our Frigates from Corfu. All Malta very gay – the first day of the Carnival the Streets crowded with Thousands of Masks; went home at five & remained, notwithstanding all temptation of Carnival, Opera & illuminations etc. a proof I am really ill.

<u>Monday 29th</u>: The Town in a complete mad uproar, every street crowded with characters extremely novel & entertaining; some Transports arrived full of Troops, upon coming on shore they must have imagined the place to have been Enchanted, as some scores of Bands of Music were playing in various Streets, all the town dressed in colours, the Windows crowded with <u>beauty</u> and the Streets with <u>Ugliness</u> & fun. Called on my late sweet favourite, now Mrs. Robinson. At 5 accompanied Dr. Hornsley to Dr. Gray's the Physician to the Fleet; called on Mr. Forrester our Minister late at Corfu, afterwards dined with Trounce on board the "Weymouth" met Lawson with Master Attendant of Malta.

<u>Thursday 3rd</u>: The Anniversary of the dreadful passage of the Dardanelles. Capt. Renolds, Dr. Moncrief, Hornsley & Truman dined & spent the Evening – long stories & good wine, Grog etc. kept them to a very late, or rather a very <u>early</u> hour, but I <u>prudently</u> stole away to rest early. I rode out much today.

<u>Thursday 10th</u>: Up at 5 in consequence of Guns firing & signals for sailing. Went on board when the Commander of the Ship politely offered me his Boat to remain on Shore with, till the Convoy all got out. This enabled me to complete all my arrangements, got Cash & Dollars changed for Gold, having settled all my affairs, had a comfortable ablution, took a little Brandy, & set off for a long pull on board – found it very pleasant rowing being a very fine day. But the poor fellows were all fagged as it was 3 hours before we reached the Ship.

<u>Saturday 19th</u>: Nothing occurred during our passage hitherto, till yesterday when a Sloop of War passed us with the intelligence that

the Spanish Fleet & two French Frigates were out, in order to inter-
cept our Convoy. Capt. Capel our Commodore therefore immediately
ordered us to run for the coast of Barbary & keep close to the Shore.

Sunday 20th: A violent gale of Wind sprang up quite contrary, the
signal was made to anchor in the Bay of Bajuah, being completely   *Modern Bejaia in Algeria*
sheltered from easterly Winds. We led the way in, & were rejoicing at
the smooth calm water in the Harbour, when the Commodore fired
a Gun, to enforce the Convoy to carry all Sail, which our Commander
foolishly repeated tho' close in with the Castle & Forts of the place.

Instantly confusion was visible in all parts – it was growing Dark,
alarm Guns were fired on Shore & in a few minutes we repented our
rashness, for the Batteries opened a heavy fire upon us, & we could
not get out of the way, it being calm & under the high Hills; large fires
were now making on every hill, to call the Military I suppose;
hundreds of Lamps, Lanterns & Torches were seen leading up the
Road, to the now visible tremendous Fortifications, which had they
been manned in time would have blown us out of the Water. Our
Capt. was much perplexed, quite at a loss what to do, we recommended him to hoist English Colours, which had very improperly
been omitted – & to send on shore, with a White Flag; this was done,
& the fine old Gunner volunteered to go in the boat.

They saw the Boat coming & were perhaps doubtful how to act,
it was now past sunset & the Convoy coming fast in tho' fired on at
every moment, no signal could be made to retreat & we hourly
expected the whole of the Batteries would open & destroy us. At last
we saw the Boat fired at by Musketry & a field piece, yet the brave old
fellow persevered till he got under the Walls, & spoke to them but they
neither understood him nor did they know the nature of a flag of
truce. They however gave him to understand he must go off & that in
loud & threatening language & even pointed a gun at the Boat. Away
he went, when a second shower of musketry assailed his Ears.

He brought intelligence that immense preparations were making:
Matches all lighted & a general confusion amongst them – the
"Endymion" now came in & was fired at from the Fort, when our
Capt. went on board & informed him of what had passed. A light
breeze enabled us to keep under sail, & it was agreed to get out of
their way without loss of time & such of the Convoy as had anchored
very prudently, or from fear, got them up again & followed our
example; all were clear out before Morning & perhaps it was fortunate
it was so, for either they were resolved to let all the Ships anchor &

when daylight appeared to bombard the Fleet, or else they had not ammunition enough that night to enable them to begin upon us for some time. We, however, put them all to the rout; they must have supposed us French, or else were resolved not to afford us protection, as no English Ship could ever have been in there before, & it is certain no one dreamt of their having such Castles & Forts there, as it appeared a wild uninhabited place as we approached, until we got round a point of the Rock.

Friday 25th: From the time we quitted the Harbour till this day, we have been buffeting about in the Gale, only 12 Ships are in sight, it is now fine weather again & the Frigate is gone in search of the lost Ships. A large Convoy from England to Malta passed through us which afforded a pretty sight – but they have a fair wind & we the reverse so that we <u>envy</u> them. It is a perfect calm, we saw several Turtle which come up to the surface of the Water & sleep in the Sun – we caught three. A great luxury at <u>all</u> times, but more especially at sea.

April 1st: In sight of Algiers, still creeping on slowly, light airs but favourable. The Ladies have been amusing themselves by making <u>Fools</u> of us, as many as they could. The little Italian, our late Consul at Turkey, was made a complete <u>butt</u> of.

Gibraltar

Did not get on shore being late, & too idle to dress, played Cards & was amused by the accidents occasioned by the Bay being full of ships many of which were hugging each other & making work for all hands for the night.

Monday 11th: Lunched at Dr. Bolton's, gossiped about all day & among other things was entrapped by our female passengers for the pleasant amusement called Shopping.

Friday 15th: Our Convoy has been detained some days owing to an account of the French fleet being in the Neighbourhood, but on this day (Good Friday) we sailed, after receiving several passengers in addition, making a motley group of 15 & being so singularly different from each other, I mean to amuse myself by setting down their names with the Countries they are of, or resident in.

First we have an old French Capt. (in the English service) 74 years of age, 56 of which he has passed in our service & is rewarded by being placed on a Capts. half-pay, his name I cannot speak or even pronounce, he is a Baron. Next Mr. Plunket a German Irishman, an ugly brute, with a pretty Wife (of a great family) – he is said to have been a common soldier. Next to him stands Mr. Summerer an Italian, born in Constantinople; of course he is a Turk, he was our Consul in Moldavia. Mr. Barnwell a Spaniard of English Parents, a Merchant; Mr. Lampacy, a Guernsey Man, but a Portuguese Consul for England. Then follow Mr. Hurst of the Guards, a Bond street Butter-fly – Capt. Dwyer an Irishman in a Veteran Battalion – Mr. Hamley a West Countryman – Mr. Owen a Welch family – Mr. Trounce a North Countryman, Mr. Fringham a Scotch Welchman, a parson. A young lady who shuts herself up all day in her Cabin except at Meals & then sits the picture of despair with such a curious stomach, that it certainly must be a natural deformity. Mrs. Dwyer far <u>advanced</u>. Mrs. Plunket, the German wife, a little Wasp & firebrand of the party who has set us all by the ears more than once – & lastly I believe the only <u>thorough bred</u> Englishman – myself. This is our number at Table every day to dinner & anyone may judge of the amusement such a Medley affords. Take the bulk of them together I really do not believe them worth the trouble I have taken to describe them.

<u>Wednesday May 4th</u>: At last the Wind has sprung up quite fair for old England. At night we were all suddenly disturbed by the cries of an Infant & its Mother at the same time, whose Cabin was in the centre of us all, when lo! the young innocent-looking <u>Miss</u> Hunter was announced the Mother of a fine <u>Boy</u>; no creature suspected her, every one thought her a fine Girl, well-behaved, Modest etc. These are the incidents we travellers are liable to. Variety they say, is charming, I have ever thought it so, therefore I must be mum, let it appear in what shape it may.

<u>Thursday 12th</u>: At length we have got within sight of the British Channel, spoke to a fishing boat & got some excellent fish which was a great treat. For two days, towards Evening it became calm and an Enemy's Privateer has the Impudence to come into the Convoy & during the fog took one of them. We heard Guns firing astern & at last the Commodore sent a King's Cutter, who has joined us, to see what was the matter, when he made signal for an enemy. The boats of the Commodore were then sent & fortunately recaptured the Vessel while the Cutter went after the Privateer – only one man was mortally wounded; the Boats were away all night.

<u>Monday 16th May</u>: We are now close to the Isle of Wight after

several days grumbling at the Commodore who, it appears, has actually been trifling with the Convoy in the hope of being able to put into Plymouth where his Wife is, everyone says he ought to have been at Portsmouth even last Thursday. Our hopes are now dampt again by a thick fog, so that if it does not clear away we cannot attempt to go into harbour with so many ships, so that it may be some days yet before we land.

May 29, 1809
H.M.S. "Blake"
Off Flushing

My dear Caroline,

I have been puzzling my brains to recollect whether I have written to you since you returned home, for I received a letter from Emily who says you are surprized you have not heard from me, in fact I am so wretched & vexed from a variety of circumstances, part of which you know, that my senses are absorbed, tho' perhaps it is a query whether I possess any. After leaving you in London, I proceeded to Deal, but all of this you know from my letter to Emily, which I wrote in very bad spirits, for after enjoying myself the last twelve months at headquarters & among my friends in England, how could I feel otherwise than a school boy would have done after a long Vacation to return to discipline & perhaps hard blows; besides which I have now no pleasing anticipations to soothe me after Gales, Storms & clearing for action etc., no snug ports to run into afterwards & to be greeted by friends who perhaps never expected to see me again. However time, which blunts the edge of all afflictions, with the influence of fine weather came to my relief and after a very delightful sail we anchored off Flushing, & are now catching the Enemy's Fish, & eating them before their faces, & are very sanguine we shall soon catch Men, an Expedition being talked of, though for my own part, to you I may candidly confess I had rather be feeding Poultry; but a truce to grumbling & discontent.

Your letter made me smile, to picture you surrounded by your dear Children, teaching Music, your Boys may one day thank you, as the flute is a pretty instrument, but how do you endure their practising? I recollect when you & Matilda were learning, our dear Mother used to send you into the Laundry, at the bottom of our large Garden. O happy days never to return. We yesterday received all our letters & papers, you cannot imagine how gratifying; as we are not a great way from the Downs it is an indulgence I shall often experience. You will smile when I tell you that yesterday also brought us a fine joint of Veal & Asparagus Sallad etc. upon which we regaled, not forgetting to drink the kind donor's health although unknown.

So you see we are not out of the reach of the land of the living. All <u>my</u> music is set aside, <u>my flute</u> & Flageolet full of cobwebs & the Italian Quitar unstrung, I am sorry to say I am as perfectly out of tune as they are and the prospect before us is not of a flattering nature. I think I can say I <u>never</u> had such gloomy presages at any other time. I expect a <u>preachment</u> from you on the receipt of this, but I do not fear, as a letter from Camden [Birmingham] will not fail to be acceptable, contain what it may.

Wybourn has experienced conditions in Holland before!

Tell my dear Ellen I am drawing from those [crayons] she was so kind to give me, but my colours are bad. With regards to Mr. Shipton and love to all your dear Boys & Girls.

    I am my dear Sister Affectionately

Yours

T.M. Wybourn

*T*he Expedition to the Dutch island of Walcheren was an attempt to remove the threat of Antwerp and mirror the Austrian offensive against France in the Danube valley. It involved some 44,000 men and 235 ships in an amphibious assault on Walcheren in the Scheldt estuary. It was a complete disaster, owing to poor planning, ineffectual leadership, bad weather and illness. In Wybourn's career it seems the only other occasion he encountered such appalling military ineptitude was in the War of 1812 with America – see later. Command of the military was given to the Earl of Chatham, eldest son of Pitt the Elder, for which he was quite unsuited. He later blamed failure on Sir Richard Strachan, who was in charge of the navy. The situation gave rise to the poem:

> Great Chatham, with his sabre drawn,
> Was waiting for Sir Richard Strachan,
> Sir Richard, longing to be at 'em,
> Was waiting for the Earl of Chatham.

August 15, 1809
H.M.S. "Blake"
River Scheldt [Holland]

My dearest Sisters

In the midst of dreadful scenes, & just as we are nevertheless preparing to get something to eat, & to <u>drink</u> to our <u>success</u> (<u>& my birthday</u>), I contrive leisure, not only to assure you of my safety, but to account for my silence, till <u>all</u> was over. No moment have we had either to reflect what was to be done or who was to do it. We have been at quarters many days, all Trunks etc. below & in short for many weeks past, we have been most unsettled & in a miserable plight.

I almost wish at this instant I had <u>returned</u> to England when I might, for though I have escaped what I positively thought certain destruction <u>yesterday</u>, still I forsee such improfitable & harassing Warfare before me that ill accords with my feeling; in saying this, <u>you</u> will be aware it is with <u>sincerity</u>, & that experience and much hard & <u>unrewarded</u> services, has rather <u>disgusted</u> than <u>intimidated</u> me.

I am afraid you will think me remiss in delaying to write, but what could I say satisfactorily? I do not indeed know when I last wrote, or what about, at any rate I was certain some severe service was at hand & I rather chose to await it than inform you of our proximity to it, tho' I am in general too faithful an historian to omit these things. However, my loves, I am <u>well</u> & past all dangers <u>so far</u>, the papers will point out (I fear before this will reach you) the alarming situation <u>our temerity</u> placed us in; we are now repairing in some degree our damages, though still in range of Shells from the other side. And before we go further up I must give you a sketch of our action, & assure you how much & <u>often</u> you were in my thoughts. My poor fellows suffered most from our exposed situation.

We had witnessed the <u>greatest</u> distresses of the unhappy Inhabitants several days, the Bombardment was awful & the Shells & newly invented rockets fired the City in several places, yet the Villain of a French General would not surrender, altho' above 1,000 of his Troops were buried in the ruins & perhaps many thousands of poor Women & children, for the Town is on a peninsular, & no cover for anyone. It was found the Army could not succeed in storming the Town of Flushing, which is inaccessible on the Land side, & Sir R. Strachan formed the desperate resolution of attacking by Sea (he is the bravest fellow in the world). We had lain just out of reach of Shot since the 11th & yesterday the signal was given to prepare for battle, at Sea; we & the other Flagship got within Pistol shot of the Walls – the havoc we made was <u>shocking</u>, when to our consternation we both struck the Ground, all the other Ships passed by further off, seeing the danger; for three hours & a half we were thus left to ourselves, the batteries cutting us to pieces and no alternative but to wait the Tide rising. <u>We</u> all thought there could be no possibility of escaping. We on the poop, which is the roof of the Capt's Cabin, were in such a line with the Guns, that it is amazing <u>any</u> of us escaped; almost the first shot killed my best Sergeant, a fine fellow, it took off both <u>thighs</u>, left <u>Arm</u> & right <u>hand</u>, the poor fellow called out to me, but I could not bear to look at him. Fortunately he died in half an hour, under amputation, 5 more men wounded by the same shot & you may judge what were our expectations; when this took place five minutes after we began I confess I never was more alarmed. The "Blake" is much damaged, <u>Providence alone</u> spared our Lives. It is thought bad enough to <u>pass</u> by Batteries, fear seldom occurs in equal battles, but when a Ship is under stone Walls, & in a position not to get one Gun to bear on the Enemy, it is the worst of forlorn hope. The Troops & all our Fleet were spectators of the danger the <u>two Admirals only</u> were in; every one gave us credit, but thought we were <u>lost</u>.

H.M.S. San Domingo

By the blessing of God, we lost but 13 men killed & wounded. The Shot actually flew about us at all angles, & it is a miracle how so many could pass among us with so little effect; 150 shot struck the Ship in the main Mast and the other masts & rigging cut to pieces – one shot carried 30 of my Muskets with it & shivered them to atoms.

We have learnt since, that so destructive was our fire before we got aground that the French could not stand at their Guns – the "Blake" killed 87 at the first Volley. But when they saw our situation, & that we could not fire, they rattled and peppered us finely. About an hour before we floated, we got about 7 Guns (out of 46) to bear, & these, with the "San Domingo's" <u>few</u> guns who had swung towards the Shore, kept them in check – & by half past one, we made sail from this Perilous position, <u>happy enough</u>. At 2 o'clock General Monet sent out a flag of Truce, observing he could not stand against the Ships. And this day (a memorable one for me) the Fortress surrendered with 7,000 French Prisoners.

My dearest Sisters will rejoice to <u>hear</u> I was <u>twice</u> wounded tho' no <u>blood</u> drawn; a splinter that killed my sargeant struck my leg, &

about the end of the action the breath was fairly knocked out of my body by a heavy blow in the side, which sent me reeling against the Admiral, who took me by the Arm & said: "Never mind!"

You see I have no other subject but War, in short our thoughts, dreams & converse is of nothing else. The sight from first to last was truly grand & awful, but to reflect a moment on the great scale of destruction we are employed upon, is horrid. Before the landing was effected we had 800 Ships full of Engines of Death. The Fleet reached along the shore, as far as the Eye could reach, while the Towns, Cities, Villages, & Ships & Batteries in our port seemed to defy the assault. The scene would make the greatest Coward brave, while the miseries of thousands, the destruction of Towns, plunder, rapine & confusion, are not considered. People at home by their fireside read of these things, they wonder & admire the onset, pity follows for the wretched-ness of families, poor Women & Children houseless, yet anxiously wait the next Gazette to read of more devastation, while we, the Executioners, must witness the facts & not allow time to pity or protect, but proceed from place to place following up the Glory of our Country. By heavens! A man who drives the Plough at home is the happier man.

August 17th: Private letters were not allowed to go with the public Dispatches, therefore I went on shore to witness the marching out of the Garrison, & the Triumphal entry of the Conquerors. It was the most magnificent sight imaginable – 16,000 English Troops were drawn up in different lines, reaching 2 and a half miles, the French then marched through them with Guns & Colours, drums beating & Bayonets fixed & laid down their arms in a field at the extremity. Our fine-looking fellows then marched in playing "God Save the King" & "the Grenadiers". The walls and parapets crowded with the wretched Inhabitants rejoicing to see us.

Bitter irony here

I went over the City, not a house was entire; the Streets one pile of rubbish, but no description can be adequate to the miseries we were informed of; it was no uncommon thing to see even little Infants with their legs & arms knocked off & among the multitude of horrible sights was one I think unparalleled. A whole family took shelter in a Cellar they thought secure, when one of those infernal rockets found its way into it, & shocking to relate 20 Women and Children were burnt & blown up together. Upwards of 100 people were buried a day after we ceased firing & 3 days were allowed before the Troops went in, but I will not dwell longer on these scenes.

We went on to the beautiful City of Middleburgh, 5 Miles off, the capital of Walcheren. I think I never saw a more splendid, or handsome Town. This had capitulated without firing a shot; here we felt as if in London – elegant Taverns & Billiard Tables, Carriages, with beautiful horses to hire – we went 3 Miles in one & paid 6d. This Morning we came on board, & as we are called the efficient squadron, we are immediately to proceed up the Scheldt. Our Troops are got as far as Batog, the farther end of South Beveland. Fort Lillo is our next object, & afterwards Antwerp, but I am of the opinion that neither the <u>one</u> nor the other can be got at, the River is so narrow.

If this plan fails, we then go to Helvort Sluys, afterwards to the Texel where, if we succeed in getting the Fleet, our object will be completed. I hope they will wisely leave the Continent before we are disgraced.

When I can write to you again I know not – we shall be out of reach of all communication I fear, so God bless you till I can return from these remote parts. A few days before we drew near to Flushing a packet arrived & I was most agreeably surprised to receive letters from Nelthorp, Weeden & my friend Lawson, with your postscript; never was I more happy than at <u>such a moment</u>, as I had thought it most unlikely, they came in time to cheer my spirits, just as we are going again to scenes of danger.

A Vessel is just going to Yarmouth so will send this, & fear I shall not have time to write to anybody else, so tell Uncle I am well. I shall sit up tonight to write to Caroline & Nelthorp, as I can give my letters to somebody to forward for me, we proceed early in the Morning towards Lillo.

So my dear Sisters & friends, Adieu, <u>how</u>, <u>when</u>, or <u>where</u> I may have the happiness of hearing from anyone, I know not.

Remember there is "a little <u>Cherub</u> that sits up aloft" so do not be too anxious – I saw no curiosities, except one, worth bringing away and that is the City of Middleburg inimitably executed by a Lady with pen and Ink.

Once more Adieu, your Affectionate,
T.M. Wybourn

1809
H.M.S. "Blake"
River Scheldt

My dear Caroline,

Providence has once more spared me, during a conflict with the Enemy, more dreadful than any I have before witnessed from our <u>inability</u> to retaliate, for Soldiers & Sailors seldom think of their danger when mutually engaged. The papers have doubtless informed you of the predicament the "Blake" was in by getting aground under the Batteries of Flushing on the 14th. Brave as is our <u>Naval</u> Commander, yet such an injudicious plan of attack never was made, or so badly executed except by us, who seeing the Commander-in-Chief in a dangerous situation went at all hazards to his support & had nearly sacrificed the "Blake".

I have been going to write to you, my dear Sister, ever since I received my Mary's prettily written letter, with your postscript, but really from that time to this, nothing but anxiety, expectation & confusion has attended us. I can only say with regard to my health, that severe fatigue & embarking before I was quite well, has occasioned me great inconvenience, having no place to sleep except in a draught of air. We have been on the <u>alert</u> so long & at quarters the whole time. I had permission to return to England just as we were going to commence this business but I feared it would be construed into a <u>disrellish</u> to meet the dangers before us. There is a certain something that leads us on, in these <u>National</u> (& what I once thought) <u>Glorious enterprizes</u> which in cooler moments & to a reflecting mind, (when there is <u>time</u> for it), appears horrible & contrary to humanity. You know how often I have of late wished to quit these scenes – tho' I have never <u>flinched</u> I trust from my <u>duty</u>, or from <u>danger</u>, notwithstanding my share has been larger & 14 Years <u>unrewarded</u> Services are reasons alone to be tired of these things. Besides how can one help sympathizing with the wretched sufferers who are sacrificed to ambition?

When we arrived at the point of Operations, you have no Idea of my <u>sensations</u> – the Magnitude of the preparations never before heard of – 800 Ships reaching as far as the Eye can see – along the Coast, loaded with Combustibles & destruction, while before us appeared the Towns, Forts, strong Citadels, & batteries with a numerous fleet protected by nearly 200 Gun boats, all their Colours

H.M.S. *Blake*, courtesy of the Parker Gallery

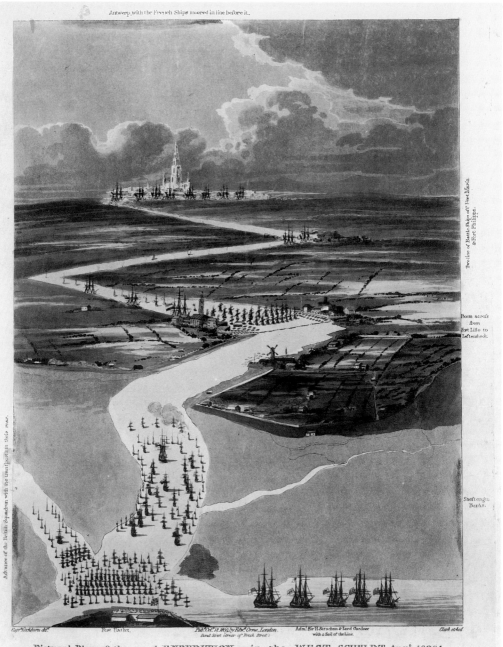

Antwerp, with the French Ships moored in line before it.

Two line of Battle Ships of Fort Maria & Fort Philippa.

Boom across from Fort Lillo to Leftenhoek.

Saeftengu Banks.

Advance of the British Squadron with the Transport in their rear.

Capt Cockburn del.   Fort Bathz.   Pub. Oct. 12 1809, by Edw Orme, London. Bond Street corner of Brook Street.   Adm. Sir H. Strachan & Lord Gardner with a Sail of the Line.   Clark etched.

Pictural Plan of the grand EXPEDITION, in the WEST SCHELDT, Aug. 1809; shewing the difficulty of approach to Antwerp.

Pictorial plan of the Grand Expedition in the West Scheldt

flying & seeming to bid Defiance. The sight would have enflamed the heart of a <u>Coward</u>. Then, on the other hand, the approaching <u>desolation</u> a flotilla of this awful & tremendous extent carries with it, of Towns, Villages, helpless families & Children, it must in spite of everything force the sympathetic sigh, & make one wish to turn the sword into a ploughshare.

The account of the landing you of course saw in the papers; the siege of Flushing lasted several days, the appearance in the night was most beautiful and I may say magnificently <u>terrible</u>.

We hurried from these <u>scenes</u> to divert the mind, & visited the beautiful City of Middleburgh & were much gratified, so magnificent, clean & gay, no appearance of <u>War</u> – everyone seemed contented & at ease. I regretted we were confined to time, but we are ordered to Antwerp, which if we <u>can</u> get so far, must undergo the fate of unhappy Flushing. We then went on board & sailed for this vile place not far from Fort Lillo, the first point of attack. Here we are surrounded by the Enemy & in a little nook, despairing of success. The Enemy in great force & should we <u>advance</u> they can <u>inundate</u> the <u>Army</u> & they are erecting Batteries all the way down on our left to prevent our <u>retreat</u>, so what our <u>wise heads, with sleepy Chatham, propose</u>, is yet a Mystery.

It is certainly provoking to see Antwerp, all their Fleet & immense Flotilla, just above us, & not be able to get at them, when it is beyond a doubt, that had <u>we dashed</u> up here at <u>first</u> & left Flushing invested (as it was) there were not 5,000 Men to oppose us. The only thing we can do is to sink vessels & stores at the narrow passage just by Fort Lillo which may for a time shut up the Scheldt to large Ships & block those up that are there. We have 400 Ships in this <u>corner</u> at <u>least</u>, some of them obliged to lay in reach of shot, how they will get back safe I cannot see. Thus will fifty thousand Men, at an Enormous Expense to the Country, have been <u>trifling</u> at <u>Flushing</u> to capture a handful of <u>Men</u> & a place little better than a fishing town, when such fine desperate fellows, instead of laying 16 days in the Trenches & <u>wet ditches</u> might absolutely have eaten their way (both man and beast) to Antwerp in the <u>first week</u>. Now General Hope says it will cost us 10,000 to attempt anything more. Besides, the Troops are falling off by sickness – many thousands have been laying 3 weeks in Beveland, in a <u>Marsh</u>, waiting for the <u>Gallant Chief</u> who was investing little Flushing with 21,000 troops, & living himself in beautiful Middleburgh eating <u>Turtle</u>.

This Letter is but a journal of <u>War</u> affairs – in short I have nothing else to entertain you with. We have no news, I have not received a letter since I have been in the Scheldt, & our senses are absorbed with the various services we are so uncomfortably employed in. I have been in all the Expeditions & was always pleasantly engaged after the first onset, but here is no variety, no duty on Shore yet, or anything but painful suspense & uncertainty. My next hope will be to inform you of their intention to abandon this fine Expedition, which I now regret I remained in, but now all is I hope over. I might have been sorry if I had and think as I ever do, that all is for the best. Remember me to Mr. S, love to Boys & Girls, accept the same from your

Her husband, Joseph Shipton

    Affectionate Brother
    T. Marmaduke Wybourn

After two years' silence, we rejoin Wybourn in the Baltic, where it seems he has passed enough time to construct a garden and grow vegetables.

Jan. 8, 1812
His Maj. Ship "Ardent"
Nore

My dear Sister [Caroline Shipton],

You will no doubt be gratified at seeing the date of this, if you have read the deplorable misfortunes that have befallen the Baltic Fleet. The Almighty alone conducted us safely into Port, for we had no hope of being successful. We left Wingo Sound on the 28th Dec., having been nearly frozen up. Alas! My garden, also made by such labour,

In Denmark

to the astonishment and surprise of the natives who with much seeming pleasure followed all our movements, for we had to fetch our soil from a distance, so I leave you to judge the number of men we employed – our garden flourished so that we had the luxury of fresh vegetables.

We attempted to sail many days, but it blew a hurricane and we reached to within 50 miles of our beloved shores, when adverse winds drove us to the coast of Holland, and for three days we were in a truly melancholy state of anxiety and distress. We passed wrecks every day and lament that the "Hero" of 74 guns had stranded and sad to relate not a soul survived.

The "St. George" of 98 guns and 800 men with the "Defiance" are not yet heard of, and the whole coast of Holland was covered with the poor convoy – 130 Vessels sailed from the Baltic and among them many transports, four of which had ordinance on board and stores to the amount of a million of money – I suppose there was hardly ever a more severe gale of wind experienced at sea, and judge how alarmed we must have been knowing we were in the very spot where the "York" of 64 guns was lost a few years ago, and not an individual saved. Last year the "Minotaur" 74 guns was lost in the same place, and out of 640 men only 130 were saved. This year, a woeful addition. How we got off the Coast is a miracle, but judge of our sudden transitions – on 31st Dec. we came close to Harwich, on the 1st, 2nd & 3rd of Jan. we were in a hurricane and up night and day – no sun to be seen, to get an observation to judge where we were. Suddenly, the wind changing a few points, we were on the Northumberland Coast, and a clear day enabled us to proceed for Leith – On the 6th a most lovely day and we reached within 6 miles of Leith, when the same storms drove us 40 miles to sea in two hours, but the wind was fair for the place. The rapidity of the passage is incredible, the Pilots declare we came 17 miles an hour on the average and now, thank God, we are getting a little comfortable, and anticipating the happiness of once more setting foot on English ground, although the long faces occasioned by the sympathizing stories of so many hundred brave fellows' loss must damp the joys, even of those who are but too much accustomed to witness distress in its most horrid shapes.

Thus my dear Sister I fill my paper with nothing but a nauticle [sic] narrative, the worst I fear however is to come as we left two more convoys on the road.

I have written to Emily, who will expect to see me, we are yet uncertain what may be our Orders. Love to my Brother [in law], and kiss all the dear children for me. I am, my dear Caroline, your affectionate Bro.,
T.M. Wybourn

The journal continues:

Journal No. 2

1812
Woolwich Barracks

*Cicisbeo: 'the name
formerly given in Italy to
the recognized gallant of
a married woman'
(O.E.D.)*

15th June: The round of gaiety as concluded in my last book, [lost] is likely soon to finish. Capt Thompson has embarked & Captain Richards, having a <u>Love</u> affair on hand, renders him too <u>unwell</u> for active service, so that I stand first for foreign service.

Thursday 18th: Caroline & Ellen gone to the anniversary at St. Paul's Cathedral & both having been brought up in the rigid paths of strickt religion, they must be exceedingly gratified with the solemnity of the occasion. I being engaged to attend Miss Watts to the Exhibition, called upon her at 10.0, but she attracted more notice than the paintings, which much flattered my vanity as being her Cicisbeo; she was dressed sweetly. My sister & Ellen came late. The company was numerous and fashionable, being the height of the season; a heavy shower and no carriages kept us late, so that upon attending my charming friend home, at nearly 6:00, I was obliged to accept a tete a tete dinner with her, Mr. Watts being engaged out, but this excellent creature manages her father's house though not yet 20. At 8:00 left this dear good-tempered girl & paid my respects at Craigs Court, afterwards passed an hour at his coffee-house & returned to supper.

20th: Went to the Opera, after being all day disengaged, a great row, much to the disgrace of so fashionable a resort, the subject relative to disappointment in some favourite actress. Slept at the Rainbow.

Monday 22nd: After passing the whole day at Mr. Lyall's in Craven Street, got up at 6 this morning, popped into a coach and arrived at Woolwich just in time for parade, being Captain for this week's duty. On my way to Barracks met Major Nickcolls [sic] endeavouring to break in two wild colts to the tandem, who had run away with him & broke the harness, overset the gig and other mischief. At 6 o'clock arrived at home, found Capt. Richards with a large party of ladies and friends but all my spirits fled when I was told I was that day in orders to embark & must proceed to the Downs with all dispatch – this was more inconvenient as I had made no preparation, expecting Richards would be ready to go, it being his turn, nor was there any prospect of such an order so soon, but my friend pleaded so fair an excuse, I could not be angry & amongst the assembly I soon discovered the object, who it seems has consented to admit his address, tho' but a very recent acquaintance. Mr. Ackroyd, Major Coombe and myself remained to drink a bottle, while the rest of the party went to the Parade, we soon joined them, and all the young ones being paired off, I was honoured by the company of Mrs. Boynton, mother of my friend's flame, a charming & sensible lady. A threatening storm soon drove us home & I made every effort to rally from that despondency an order to leave my dear Country always brings upon me – we had some of the Musicians in & made up a little dance, but all I could do was to assist the ladies with negus, cakes, etc. I soon discovered that the amiable Miss B. would perhaps have made me more happy than my friend may promise to be – not conceiving them at all calculated for each other – however as I have never yet fitted out for a matrimonial voyage, these ideas are but imaginary. At a late hour at night the carriages were ordered & our charming party drove off to Blackheath.

Friday 26th: Settled all accounts and made preparation to join the "Marlborough" at Deal.

1st July, Wed: Found a letter from Mrs. Boynton saying my great coat should be sent; propose paying my respects when I go to town. Miserable wet day, dined at the Mess and provided all necessary for my departure.

Sat. 3rd: Went to Woolwich. Emily came, extremely cold in the evening, large party came to Tea.

Sun: Came to town, saw my dear Caroline off.

Mon: Took farewell dinner at the Mess, a very large party, staid till one.

Tues: Sent my servant and baggage forward, dressed very gaily intending to call on some ladies at Blackheath, but not finding Richards could not recollect their address.

Joined the "Marlborough" at Deal

14th July: After travelling all night, bathed in the sea, made an excellent breakfast, introduced myself to Capt. Scott, Commander of the "Marlborough", by him introduced to the Lt. (Shed), afterwards made several calls among my old acquaintances.

Wed. 15th: Went on board & paid my respects.

<u>16th</u>: Visited my old & very respected acquaintance Mr. Catfield & after passing an hour or two with his good-tempered daughter Mary, who was a child when I last saw her, we made a party of gentlemen to Mungay [?] Fair, and had much rural sport, put in for prizes & gave our chances to the Village lasses, at the mountebank's, made conquest of one of his rope dancers who invitationed me to make a party for her benefit on the 20th.

<u>18th</u>: Ordered wine from Mr. Rickfords & received balance of £60. Went shopping and on board at 12. Got under way at 4 on our voyage off Flushing. Capt. Coley & self dined with Capt. Scott, who I found a most gentlemanly man.

<u>Sunday 19th</u>: At an anchor with the Fleet under Admiral Young off Flushing, wrote my friend Fothergill – lovely weather – great parade with guards, drumming & saluting, found a miserable Mess, economy stretched to the utmost & rather dry associates but this appears more so, having just left so opposite a Life.

<u>Monday 27th July</u>: Employed the last week regulating my Company, writing letters & <u>grumbling</u> – they say our papers & letters arrived from England, the communication being frequent, a letter informed me Richards was appointed to our Battalions going to the south, so that [tho'] he was too unwell to embark in his turn, it seems he was fit for service where fatigue is double, and of course he has deprived me of my birth right.

<u>Tues</u>: Our ship with 5 others ordered to take the advance.

Hovely Bay – <u>Thursday 30th July</u>: Arrived at this anchorage near Harwich, in order to wait for the Spring tides to go over to the Texel, where the Dutch have 9 sail of the line ready for sea.

<u>Friday</u>: Slept at the White Hart, found the Landlady, as is commonly the case, the oracle of the town & was besides a deep politician. Her old husband, being drunk & put to bed long before, I sat & chatted till 1 o'clock.

<u>2nd August</u>: Up at 6, my friend Hamilton's Packet appointed to sail this day, he gave me a passage and put me on board in his way, his amiable wife & eldest daughter were up & provided an excellent breakfast, whilst pleasure & affection appeared in their faces. The Gottenburgh Packets generally make about 12 voyages in the year & it is a very lucrative employment. H. is with £20,000 accumulated in that employ. Sent him a cask of port wine/duty free – met another packet coming in: great news from the armies, 15,000 French & 100 pieces of cannon taken. Peace between Russia, Sweden & England,

Wellington had taken the French-held Spanish fortresses of Ciudad Rodrigo and Badajoz, then defeated '40,000 Frenchmen in 40 minutes' at Salamanca, entering Madrid on 12 August.

Lord Wellington driving the French before him in Spain.

4th: Got under way for the Texel, calm all day, commenced the Caterership.

5th: The fleet in sight, after dinner stood close in with the Dutch shore.

9th: Nothing extra – remained these few days fishing on the banks and watching the Dutch fleet. They are 9 Sail ready for sea, we only 5. Caught turbot 16lbs. weight & also of an enormous size. At night we left the station the seas not being high enough for the enemy to get [out?]. Captain Scott visited Admiral Young, we thus learnt of the great battle fought by Lord Wellington with Mormont in which the latter lost 12,000 men. Peace supposed between America & us (I do not believe it) – the Russians repulsed all Bonaparte's army 3 times.

10th: Arrived at night, off Harwich again.

11th: Anchored in our former place, heard of a large naval Promotion which makes our Captain an Admiral.

Thursday 13th: Crossed the ferry in Billingsley's galley, walked to Walton 5 miles, no horse or gig to be had & Woodbridge 7 miles further; after trudging a mile or two came to a village with 3 cottages & a wheelwright's to whom I made my distress known & he generously offered me a little Galloway & his own son went forward to bring it back. While it was getting ready he took me into a pretty neat house & told me the history of the neighbours, while we regaled with home brewed ale & nice new bread & cheese, but was much surprized to see a young Lady bring the ale, whom at first sight I imagined to be high-born & perhaps making a morning call among her poor neighbours. She was neatly dressed as tho' her wedding day & hair fashionably braided up with a wreath of artificial flowers, pretty gypsy hat & silk shoes, with a countenance of an angel & about 16. I could not help admiring her, which the old man saw & said this was his daughter. I held out my hand to her which she innocently took & asked her several questions. I soon perceived the old fellow took more pleasure in seeing her admired than in having educated her; what a pity such loveliness should be so [unprotected?] in a rural, nay very rustic village in the neighbourhood of extensive Cavalry Barracks.

15th: My birthday commenced & finished with great mirth, gaiety & happiness, tho' no previous plan. A large party of 14 ladies & several gentlemen came on board to see the ship. I escorted them & having put dinner back an hour & increased it to double the quantity, made them all stay, to their inexpressible delight, not one of them having seen a military or naval society before & when they saw a room full of servants with 25 or 30 covers as bright as silver, with tables covered with plate & china, they stared in wonder at each other. We made the Men very <u>happy</u>, before they parted & the ladies were gratified with a dance on the quarter deck, our excellent Band was also a great treat. These people live about 7 miles from the coast in a very remote part of the country & overwhelmed us with invitations to go & see them & shoot, eat & sleep at their estates. One of them who I promised to call on, a gentleman evidently superior to the rest, so certainly conspicuous is good breeding, this was a Mr. Wood of Milton. The confirmation of Captain Scott's promotion arrived, which afforded additional reason for extraordinary <u>hilarity</u>, the day passed off to the satisfaction of everyone & the party went off by moonlight, escorted by several officers to bring the boats back.

18th Aug. Tues: Two days past at sea, anchored in the fleet, all bustle & confusion. As we foresaw, the new Admiral ordered to Portsmouth & the "Marlborough" to refit for Admiral Cockburn & suite to Command at Cadiz. Admiral Scott to hoist his flag in the "Chatham". Officers & Baggage moving on board for passage to Downs. Provisions supplied from us to various ships, boats out of no. flying about & lastly glorious news – <u>Mormont's army destroyed in Spain</u>, Russians successful everywhere, the Spaniards also, and affairs still to be settled with America. At 8 got underway, lots of Captains & Lieutenants came on board, promoted. The "Marlborough's" old luck, a foul wind.

<u>Monday 24th August</u>: After baffling winds anchored at Spithead.

25th: Exchange of men & officers; Shed left us, the sailors gave him three cheers. Captain Scott came on board with the Admiral, Captain (Ross) and the former shed tears upon making a speech to the men – a proposition from Admiral Cockburn to me, to exchange with Captain Lee, his friend, I <u>refused</u>.

<u>Thursday 26th</u>: A large party on board – 11 Lieutenants, all the new officers, a fine set of fellows.

Napoleon invaded Russia in the spring of 1812. The Russians retreated, adopting a scorched earth policy and hit and run tactics, as used 130 years later against the Germans. Their first real success was at the Battle of Borodino on 7 September. It was a savage but indecisive engagement on the approaches to Moscow, ably commanded by the Russian Marshal Kutuzov, but insufficient to stop the French moving into the capital.

Portsmouth

11th: Various visits on board & shore, taking leave & making purchases etc. Dined on board; the ship paid & full of Jews, like so many sharks devouring all <u>Jack's</u> hard wages by a show of baubles & other useless trash. A strict watch at night to prevent riot, drunkness or other irregularity, usual on payday. My subaltern, Lieutenant Barry, on all these occasions shews himself a valuable officer & sets a bright example to the other, who is an ignorant & worthless idle fellow.

Refugee Jews from Europe, in search of a living, had taken over much of the trade with sailors at the major ports..

Sept.13th, Sunday: The admiral being expected & the ship now ready for sea, we expect soon to bid adieu to old England for Cadiz, the gayest place in Europe. Two Spanish familys accompany the admiral, who had taken refuge in England, expecting the French would have taken Cadiz. The flag hoisted & a salute of 15 guns.

16th: Met Captain Lee, who takes a passage with us, the admiral having obtained for him a Lieutenant Colonelcy in the Spanish regiments, together with his Pay & Rank in our service. Captain Ross & Mr. Secretary Glover went on board & dined with me, everybody now on board.

Friday 18th Sept: The wind being fair, dropped to St. Helen's. Lord Melville, the First Lord of the Admiralty & Mr. Croker, the Secretary, came on board to visit Admiral Cockburn, a salute & Captain's guard turned out to him – a farmer-looking man & Mr. C. no better.

19th Sat: Was introduced to the Spanish ladies at Admiral Cockburn's table, Mrs. Barron & her two lovely daughters, & Mrs. Wm. Barron with her daughter, a Mr. Kelly, a kind of superintendant, or perhaps a <u>Confidential</u> friend of Mr. B. at Cadiz & who was sent to England on purpose to escort those 5 ladies, although they spoke English as well as a native & all otherwise appeared as English ladies. In the evening I had the Honor of a long walk with Margaret, the eldest daughter, a most captivating agreeable girl.

Sunday: The admiral with the ladies this day went into lodgings, to wait a fair wind. The officers made a large party to a Picnic on shore & chose the extensive grounds of <u>Judge Grose</u> to eat in. After depositing our basket in a shady alcove above a mile from the house & without the regular grounds, we strolled towards the elegant mansion to ask leave …, but in our way & whilst admiring a beautiful

Temple intended as a summerhouse, the old fellow came hobbling along & said sarcastically: "Oh, I am afraid I intrude." By chance one of our party knew the man & stept forth to apologise for <u>our</u> intrusion; this was not enough & he said he never allowed parties to eat on his grounds at all events, nor on a Sunday for his gardener to shew them.

We then observed to him that he must see we were officers & therefore not to be classed with those "Sunday folks", as he termed them, from Portsmo' & the neighbourhood, who might be unpleasant intruders from encouragement, & as we were about to sail for Spain we hoped he would make this an exception. He very reluctantly yielded one point to see the grounds, but would not listen a moment, the brute, to our refreshing ourselves with the contents of our basket, whatever our craving might be. He then left us tho' near his house, without the compliment of walking in, which in his secluded state & advanced age one would have thought to be natural, for a change of scene, & the old miserable fellow has a son at Cadiz, the very place we told him we were going to, of who we thought he might speak.

He promised to send his gardener & after waiting a considerable time & not seeing or hearing from him, we gratified our curiosity as far as decency admitted & returned to our magazine, which by this time we felt strong inclinations to behold the contents of, & therefore called a council whether that spot could possibly be considered as part of the pleasure grounds, as being in a rough & unfrequented place, close to the rocks without & hardly confined by anything except brambles; it was carryed in favor of our encamping there.

But behold, the suspicious sulky old lawgiver attacked us when least of all prepared to resist, all manner of apparatus for dinner, bottles & glasses scattered about, servants very busy drawing corks, & were greedily cutting up chicken & ham & devouring it, so that upon the very onset of an orator most wanted, all mouths were full & for the most part they all retreated shamefully, admitting the error, they voted as none.

Myself & two others remained, when the old Boy sat down on a root of a tree (for he had not taken so long a walk for ages before) & discharged a volley of unmannerly abuse, ordering the servants to clear all away & hurrying us to begone, saying in answer to all our explanations & doubts as to this part ever being visited, if included in his estate, etc., – that no gentleman would have been guilty of this after what he had said below – this was too much & I now rallied &

told him I no longer valued his wishes or threats & observed that his petulant & fractious temper led him to act unlike a <u>gentleman</u>, at which in a loud tone & jumping up, his honor touched, he asked if I meant to say he was not a <u>gentleman</u> – he asked my name & address etc.

After satisfying him with these I exploded as far as to say that seeing we could do no harm where we were & that no possible interruption or even a sight of us was possible from his residence, that I did think his conduct rude & his interferance unnecessary & as most of our party came back, I ordered the servants to put the wine out again & glasses which in their fear of the old fool they had put away & telling him I was resolved after such violence on his part, not to move an inch if even left alone till I finished as much of my meal as I chose; & filling out a glass & affecting more gentleness, presented it to him, saying if he pleased we might now part friends; this he instantly declined & threatened as he had my name & that of two or three others, to write Lord Melville concerning it; we then continued till the bottles were finished & asking if he had any commands for <u>his son</u>, we politely bid him good evening.

It seems the old Judge is the <u>Terror</u> of all the adjacent neighbourhood, who have often been prompted to make little excursions to this most heavenly spot, for which we have determined upon our arrival in England to terrify him with a party who will be amply avenged, & teach him moderation is best.

<u>Monday, Sept. 21</u>st: Very busy with carpenters putting my cabin in order & securing things for voyage. Tues. – ditto.

<u>Set sail to Cadiz</u>

<u>Wed.23</u>rd: At daylight a fair wind, the Admiral & Captain, Sec & ladies all came on in a hurry, cleared the Isle of White [sic] by 7 in the morning. The convoy all past within hail, the admiral spoke to them all; it was a beautiful sight & highly gratifying to our female friends. In the evening played whist.

<u>24</u>th: The admiral is very fond of Parade & shew, 60 men therefore to parade every morning; trooped the guard, the Band playing "God Save the King". The sweet Spanish girls came out to see us & were much amused. I never had so fine a body of men before.

<u>25</u>th: Anchored in Torbay, the wind not serving to go on. General Hay came on board to pay respects.

<u>26</u>th: Great fuss of parade in seamen & soldiers, I relieved guard

with 100 men under arms, bright muskets to be used. Night & day a gale of wind.

Monday: Attempted to sail – the convoy could not get out, two or three lost on the Berry head. We had a narrow escape, being under the cliff & the abilities of our Master saved us by carrying sail beyond what was approved.

Tues: Laid to all day, expecting the remainder of the convoy, but they could not get out.

Wed: Made sail off Plymouth. Pilot came off, promised to send us vegetables & papers.

Sat. 2nd Oct: A fine breeze down Channel, a Privateer boarded one of our convoy, in our sight, but could not carry her off.

Sunday: At evening saw the privateer chased down to us by two small men of war; after hour's chase captured her, found her a beautiful vessel mounting 15 guns & had 90 men on board. The chase & action afforded high amusement.

Mon: All the ladies sick, miserable weather. My charming friend undertook to teach me Spanish, if I could teach her Italian.

Tues: Good fun taking care of our plates at Table, sad weather.

Wed. Oct. 6th: Much rolling about & several valuable things broken. The ladies had chairs on deck & we took lessons all the morning.

Thurs: A fine reviving day & wind quite fair. Got into a scrape by offering to teach Kitty Italian, the cousin of my dear Margaret – the Spanish disposition is of a most jealous nature & tho' nothing particular is intended on either side, or even expected, yet the Etiquette is never to shew attention to more than one at a time, or forfeit both. My fair friend is the particular favourite of the admiral, yet she aims at universal conquest, while any gentleman she honors with her notice, must not look, hardly, at any other lady, without losing her esteem.

Sun. 11th: The time past very agreeably, lovely weather, lessons by day & in the evening Spanish dances, the admiral very accommodating & quite familiar with every one. Came in sight of the Spanish coast.

Thurs. 15th: Passed close to Lisbon to send part of the convoy in. Enjoyed a fine prospect of the mountains, convents & villas. An unfortunate accident happened to a young man in the agent's ship, having fell & broke both thighs & nearly cut in two, by which we lost our assistant surgeon who went into Lisbon with him, to our regret, Mr. Cruikshank.

Friday 16th: Dined with the admiral & was very unhappy at the marked displeasure of sweet Margaret who would neither speak to or sit by me.

Cadiz

17th: Came in sight of Cadiz; all joy & gaiety, the ladies at sight of their native place, & the officers expecting honor & promotion. Saluted Admiral Legge, my old captain in the "Repulse" in passing to Constantinople, thro' the tremendous Dardanelles – boats out of nowhere came out to meet us, congratulations etc., etc. Women went away, the wardroom full of people, friends & curiosity for news attracted them, the weather broiling hot.

Mon: Visited Cadiz, highly gratified with that superb city; called on our fair passengers & was graciously received by Mr. Barron to whom I was introduced, the dear girls appeared quite happy. Could not stay to dinner, having a large party on board.

Wed: Another large party on board, Mr. [?] Commander of a gun-boat voted an honorary member of our Mess. The French were quiet and the City free from danger after a long siege & tremendous bombardment.

Thurs: Went on board the "Revenge", paid my respects to Admiral Legge & dined with all my old friends.

Sunday Nov. 1st: In the evening went on shore, called on Madam Bocconis, a lady of the highest fashion to whom we were introduced, dancing & music in which her three elegant daughters greatly shone – staid till 1 o'clock. The early part of this evening visited the Navarier; this magnificent saloon is open every night as a kind of coffee room in which is an orchestry of music & tables calculated to contain perhaps 2,000 persons, the whole lighted up with the elegant chandeliers & festoons of variegated lamps, ladies & gentlemen indiscriminately visit there & listen to the music, nothing is to pay, except you call for refreshments.

12th: Dined with my friend Lindsay and a large party at the English Hotel; he gave us an elegant but ridiculously expensive dinner. Passed the evening at the "Navarier" – adventure with a Turk, whom I was obliged ultimately to protect & see home, he got so tipsy

Wellington fell back in a defensive campaign to Portugal, from which he sprang his final offensive against the French, bringing victory at Vittoria in a sweep across Spain to the Pyrenees.

& quarrelsome & the Spanish stiletto would have been in him if I had not taken care of him. Lost my silver snuff box here.

<u>Thursday 13th</u>: Captain Barrie of the "Grampus", 50 guns, gave a general Ball, near 200 ladies & officers partook of an elegant supper & danced till 5 in the morning.

<u>14th</u>: On board all day, not up till 12 & very much knocked up & fatigued.

<u>Nov. 15th</u>: Great doubts of Lord Wellington's success, reports that the people of Seville are alarmed that the French return; preparations for defence going on.

<u>25th Friday</u>: Sudden order from England arrived for us to proceed immediately to America: war to be carried on with energy & the Admiral [Cockburn] very well calculated to harrass them. Wet thro' all day marketting. Sparks so good as to accompany me. Sent off everything for voyage (being caterer).

<u>Tues. evening</u>: Had a fine run of 200 miles since yesterday, lovely weather, captured this day a large American ship "Eliza" of Philadelphia worth £15,000. Dined with the admiral, read the History of the Whig Club in evening.

<u>28th</u>: Spoke an English ship, got papers to the 7th. The Russians destroying the French by thousands.

Madeira

<u>Sat. 12th December</u>. At length anchored after 12 days' perse-verance, but had nearly bid adieu to this place without getting what we wanted, for we were nearly in the same predicament as on Thurs. The anchor would not hold again & the admiral lost all patience, abus'd Capt., Master & 1st Lieut. etc. & ordered the anchor & cable to be cut away (several hundreds of pounds worth) and once more stood out to sea & he would have proceeded on our voyage, but Dame Fortune, seeing we were in earnest, wd. play us no farther tricks, but suffered us to anchor in peace, for good. I immediately went on shore, being very curious to see this favourite place & fearing another gale. The two gentlemen, happy to escape, almost broke their necks getting into the boat & I thought it a fortunate circumstance they accom-panied me for I found them of the first house in Madeira, (Mr. Wardrobe), were friends of our admiral & one of them, Mr Gambier

is nephew to Lord Gambier, the psalm-singing <u>Hero</u> of Copenhagen, at that very <u>just</u> & <u>honourable</u> attack, & massacre. They immediately asked me to a late dinner & said a <u>Bed</u> was at my service during our stay here. This I thought exceedingly polite, but soon found the general hospitality of this opulent island, or rather of the English merchants, never suffered a stranger to remain an hour at an inn, if an officer, but that all vie with each other, who shall shew most attention, public tables open every day & beds always ready whether the generous host is at home or not.

Do we detect irony here?

But I must here notice <u>one exception</u>, as a perpetual momento in case it should ever be in my power to acknowledge it, a Mr. Veitch, our English Consul, a surly & most consequential Brute, universally detested in the Island. His situation in the Island is very lucrative, beside which he has an immense trade & residence like a Palace. I had occasion to call upon him the moment I landed, at the Admiral's request, & I wondered Mr. Gambier would not walk up or go in, but at parting assured me <u>he wd wait</u> dinner for me – well he knew the man; in short, the Consul received me in a cold ante-room, taking care a fine-liveried servant with wax-lights should attend & after various impertinent questions as to our misfortune, etc., he suffered me to retire without asking me to take a glass of wine – to add to his rudeness, the dining-room was frequently displayed, at which several people were regaling with choice wines & fruit. I delighted my friends at the <u>superior</u> mansion I now adjourned to, with a description of my Consul, & it spread afterwards through the Town.

My reception at the house of Wardrobe & Co. made me ample amends, & some of the very best Madeira wine the world affords was produced, as also Malmsey after coffee. In the evening we adjourned to a noble building erected by the English merchants at an enormous expence, it being Club night.

To describe this house does not come within my powers as it wd be necessary to be fully conversant in architecture to point out all its beauties, but as far as I can I will shew its convenience & how much obliged all strangers as well as the ladies & natives of Madeira ought to be to so public-spirited a Body – all the accommodations are upon one floor, after ascending a fine stone staircase – the main body of the whole building. Inside is of an octagon form, a brilliant assembly room composing the centre, from four elegant arches as many ante-rooms are seen, one for card tables, other for the Ladies' dresses, cloaks, etc., other for gentlemen & the last a beautiful finished Supper room. The remaining parts of the floor are for the Bar, servant's rooms & closets. The pier glasses down to the ground reflect from every part a view of the whole while the doors are open & present a brilliant scene as the fancy can imagine, not to say a word of its heavenly effect when on a public Ball night all the chandeliers, reflectors & lamps are displayed, while the most lovely women of Spain, Portugal & England are gliding in the midst of this illumination, multiplied by the numerous glasses.

Balls are given once a month, at other times this space is made a reading room of, where all papers, magazines and new publications are brought by every conveyance to the island. A Whist Club once a week & a Beef stake [sic] Club once a fortnight. The whole of this establishment, with servants, Librarian, suppers & in a word every expence attending it is defrayed by the English merchants, alone, all their entertainment given gratis – & strangers of the army & navy a free admission to all the benefits thereof. I suppose no Colony or Garrison in the known world are equal to this liberal body of men, their houses, carriages, horses, alike are offer'd.

Friday 17th Dec: In the evening weighed the anchor & kept looking through our glasses as long as we could see & it was easy to discover the particular houses up the sides of the mountain & even the ladies looking thro' their spying glasses, on the Terrace, at our ship. After dark & going very fast we nearly ran over a small ship – she was a Spaniard from Vigo, bound to Porto Rico – chased another which proved English.

Friday 25th Dec.: Asked one half of the midshipmen to dine with us being Xmas Day, cards & supper, a famous Devil for supper, Punch & Grog, parted at a late hour.

Wednesday 30th: Nothing extra these few days, the wind has enabled us to run 1,450 miles without stopping, ceased & rain with unpleasant weather succeeded. Painted the ship inside and out, dined with the Admiral, long discussion of West Indies & shore trade.

Thursday 31st Dec.: The last day of the old year, we as usual saw out & the new one in. Three large bowls of Punch crowned the night. We were at this moment in the very remotest part of the Ocean & as far from any land as a ship can be placed.

Atlantic Ocean

January 1st 1813 – Friday: The day commenced with lovely weather, & a fair wind. We have now traversed an immense expanse of water, upwards of 2,000 miles without seeing an individual object on the surface of the sea. Gave a very grand Gala & kept it up as on Xmas Day, as no idea of a [?] dinner, after so long a voyage can be imagined. I will merely enumerate the articles, as I myself gave the steward, and which, as we shortly expect to see Bermuda, we launched out in, certainly extravagantly: – excellent soup, salt fish, saddle mutton, round of beef, leg of roast pork, Giblet pie, a curry, a couple of boiled fowls, a ham, couple of roast ducks, a turkey, raspberry pudding, plum duff, pumpkin pie & the remainder of our old Port wine (11 years) with excellent Madeira & sherry – nor do I believe a London tavern cd. have dressed a better dinner. Conviviality & harmony subsisted till one o'clock, songs, glees, etc., the remaining half of the Mids dined with us.

Bermuda

12th Jan: Nothing material occurred some days past, amusement & employment as usual. At length anchored at this miserable place, & commenced refitting "Marlboro" which was un-seaworthy, the Cmdr. in Chief being in the Chesapeake.

14th: Went on shore, the sail being thro' a very narrow channel called the ferry, which separates St. George's town & the Garrison from the remainder of the island. The scene, as to picturesque, is certainly beautiful from the no. of little fertile islands, creeks and inlets to pass, but what appears verdure is upon nearer approach only the cedar trees, not a blade of wholesome grass is to be seen. The town is a wretched place & it seems is only frequented by such English as are contented to make money at any sacrifice. The natives are black, & possess a no. of slaves whom they use cruelly & work hard, as this is the Rendevous for the fleet & an Admiralty Court for condemning Prizes, of course will be overflowed by Jews, agents of other Robbers of the property of the Captors, who, risking their lives, health & Prime in the service of their Country, must find their Prizes here, for condemnation & sale, so that as there is no competition in the place, scarcely the Interest of the real value of captures, will be divided to

War with America had broken out, and the Royal Navy had suffered a series of humiliating defeats. Admiral Sir John Warren had commanded his Halifax squadron poorly, with no vigorous offensives. Individual frigate actions had shown that the better-built American ships could be defeated only by a concentration of stronger British force in American waters. Cockburn, an old acquaintance of Warren's, was ordered to join him at Bermuda and take a squadron into the American heartland. The "Marlborough" left Cadiz on 23 November, arriving in Bermuda in mid-January, 1913.

The amounts of prize money were decided at courts across the globe: in Britain, Malta, Gibraltar, Barbados, Calcutta and Madras. The courts were often corrupt, (witness Wybourn's comments on Bermuda) and sometimes deliberately prolonged proceedings to force a victorious ship to set sail before its money had been paid out. At some, 'court costs' came surprisingly close to full prize value.

the right owners. Met Mr. Ford who is in the "Cleopatra" frigate & Mr. Parkhurst the purser who is bro'-in-law to Lt. Scott of the "Marlboro". Was introduced to Capt. Steel of the 102nd Regt. doing duty at this vile place, a singular & eccentric Hibernian, but generous to a degree. He with a few others have their wives with them, which forms a little society. Just before we arrived the fever carried off almost half the Europeans & many are yet ill.

15th January: Being desirous to bid for some sheep brought from America, which looked tolerable, from their thick coat, I bought 20, which when killed were little better than cats. However, as no fresh stock is to be had for any money on the island, we were content; the inhabitants can hardly get a fresh meal in a week & if a sheep is killed it stinks in 4 hours, such is the heat of the climate.

Saturday 16th: It must be observed that with all the inconveniences of this settlement, that of getting a bed is most difficult, there being no houses of accommodation & as to our friends, they have scarcely room for their family, so that the Pilots, washerwomen & shopkeepers generally fix up a room or two & if you speak two or three days beforehand, it is then probable to succeed – my little Box stands in the midst of a garden & is both airy & pleasant, commanding a view of the town & harbour & at the back window of the Governor's Park, so called from a little barren land being enclosed, but there is the inconvenience of going half a mile uphill to it & no such thing as anything to eat or drink either for supper or breakfast; then all the folks being black & their little imps running or crawling about, has a curious appearance.

Sun: Remained on board the whole day, as did the Adml., who dined with us, nor does he find the shore at all congenial to his ideas, altho' the Governor, Sir James Cockburn's house and park is of course at a brother's disposal – he himself being unluckily in England now.

Sunday Jan.31st. 1813: Arrived several of the squadron with Prizes & among them the gallant Sir Thomas Hardy, Lord Nelson's Capt. (when he was killed). We hoped Sir Jn. Warren was coming, that we might commence operations – the weather getting quite cool.

Thurs. 4th Feb: Breakfasted with Mr. & Mrs. Holt. This gentleman belongs to the 9th Regt. & marryd. Miss Grant, a shopkeeper's daughter, but very pretty & will possess an immense fortune. He is a silly stupid fellow & a Methodist. Attended the sale of Prize goods & an opportunity of seeing how the things are literally given away, bought two casks of porter.

Watering tank, Bermuda

GREAT ENCOURAGEMENT.
AMERICAN WAR.

What a Brilliant Prospect does this Event hold out to every Lad of Spirit, who is inclined to try his Fortune in that highly renowned Corps,

The Royal Marines,
When every Thing that swims the Seas must be a
PRIZE!

Thousands are at this moment endeavouring to get on Board Privateers, where they serve without Pay or Reward of any kind whatsoever; so certain does their Chance appear of enriching themselves by PRIZE MONEY! What an enviable Station then must the *ROYAL MARINE* hold,---who with far superior Advantages to these, has the additional benefit of liberal Pay, and plenty of the best Provisions, with a good and well appointed Ship under him, the Pride and Glory of Old England; surely every Man of Spirit must blush to remain at Home in Inactivity and Indolence, when his Country and the best of Kings needs his Assistance.

Where then can he have such a fair opportunity of reaping Glory and Riches, as in the Royal Marines, a Corps daily acquiring new Honours, and here, when once embarked in BRITISH FLEET, he finds himself in the midst of Honour and Glory, surrounded by a set of fine Fellows, Strangers to Fear, and who strike Terror through the Hearts of their Enemies wherever they go!

He has likewise the inspiring Idea to know, that while he scour the Ocean to protect the Liberty of OLD ENGLAND, that the Hearts and good Wishes of the whole BRITISH NATION, attend him; pray for his Success, and participate in s Glory!! Lose no Time then, my Fine Fellows, in embracing the glorious Opportunity that awaits you; YOU WILL RECEIVE

Sixteen Guineas Bounty,

And on your Arrival at *Head Quarters*, be comfortably and genteely CLOTHED.---And spirited Young BOYS of a promising Appearance, who are Five Feet high, WILL RECEIVE TWELVE POUNDS ONE SHILLING AND SIXPENCE BOUNTY, and equal Advantages of *PROVISIONS* and *CLOATHING* with the Men. And those who wish only to enlist for a limited Service, shall receive a Bounty of ELEVEN GUINEAS, and Boys EIGHT. In Fact, the Advantages which the ROYAL MARINE possesses, are too numerous to mention here, but among the many, it may not be amiss to state,---*That if he has a WIFE, or aged PARENT, he can make them an Allotment of half his PAY; which will be regularly paid without any Trouble to them, or to whomsoever he may direct: that being well Clothed and Fed on Board Ship, the Remainder of his PAY and PRIZE MONEY will be clear in Reserve for the Relief of his Family or his own private Purposes. The Single Young Man on his Return to Port, finds himself enabled cut a Dash on Shore with his GIRL and his GLASS, that might be envied by a Nobleman.---Take Courage then, seize the Fortune that awaits you, repair to the ROYAL MARINE RENDEZVOUS, where in a FLOWING BOWL of PUNCH, in Three Times Three, you shall drink*

Long live the King, and Success to his Royal Marines

The Daily Allowance of a Marine when embarked, is---One Pound of BEEF or PORK.---One Pound of BREAD.---Flour, Raisins, Butter, Cheese, Oatmeal, Molasses, Tea, Sugar, &c. &c. And a Pint of the best WINE, or Half a Pint of the best RUM or BRANDY; together with a Pint of LEMONADE. They have likewise in warm Countries, a plentiful Allowance of the choicest FRUIT. And what can be more handsome than the Royal Marine's Proportion of PRIZE MONEY, when a Serjeant shares equal with the First Class of Petty Officers, such as Midshipmen, Assistant Surgeons, &c. which is Five Shares each; a Corporal with the Second Class, which is Three Shares each; and the Private with the Able Seamen, One Share and a Half each.

☞ For further Particulars, and a more full Account of the many Advantages of this invaluable Corps, apply to SERJEANT FULCHER, at the EIGHT BELLS, where the Bringer of a Recruit will receive THREE GUINEAS.

---

*T*he War of 1812 was, among other things, the only armed conflict between America and Canada. During the Anglo-French struggle in Europe, America's trade suffered greatly owing to the chief combatants' refusal to allow her to trade freely, for fear of supplying their enemies. Napoleon's Berlin Decrees of 1806 and Britain's Orders in Council of 1807 curtailed American trade with continental Europe and the West Indies. America responded with the Embargo Act of 1807, requiring all foreign ships to obtain official clearance before sailing from American ports. A great trading nation, America inevitably suffered from the long-drawn-out war between Britain and France, but because of Britain's naval supremacy, and past enmity, American feeling was more anti-British than anti-French. Sensing this mood, Napoleon cleverly revoked his Berlin Decrees, suggesting that rather than the war itself, Britain was America's greatest enemy.

There were close ties between American and British naval power. A large number of British seamen were to be found in the American merchant fleets – it has been estimated 2,500 British sailors were recruited annually. Americans also served in the Royal Navy, but roughly 1,000 Americans were impressed every year from American ships for service on British warships, further fuelling anti-British sentiments.

Rather than complex matters of maritime law, it is more likely that problems encountered in expanding America's western frontier, at the cost of Indians or loyalist Canadians, were the chief cause of the war. Ironically the British revoked the Orders in Council of 1807 some days before the Americans declared war in 1812, hoping for a peaceful settlement, but too late.

America was by no means the strong single nation popularly imagined. New England federalists owed their living to maritime trade; although aggrieved at British measures, they still felt a peculiar loyalty to the old country. When Congress decided that, rather than face the Royal Navy, an invasion of Canada by an army of 50,000 regulars and militia was the best action, they had little support from New England which was more or less on the front line. The New Englanders continued to trade with the British across a badly defined Canadian border throughout the war.

The Americans declared war on 18th June, 1812, and were forced onto the defensive almost immediately by British veteran Major-General Isaac Brock who captured Fort Dearborn, now Chicago. Shortly afterwards Detroit was handed over by the hopelessly inept American General William Hull. Moving to the offensive, the American Major-General Rensselaer established a bridgehead at Niagara for a full-scale invasion but was defeated by Brock, mortally wounded in the action at Queenston, Ontario. The war progressed with minor victories and calamities on both sides, the Americans sacking York (now Toronto) and the British pushing into American territory. American dreams of invading Canada were discounted for good upon arrival of British reinforcements from the Peninsular War. Similarly, stiff American resistance at Plattsburgh dashed British hopes of pushing into America; furthermore, the comprehensive defeat of Prévost's British naval squadron on Lake Erie rendered an invasion impossible.

The Royal Navy suffered intolerable defeats at sea against the American ships, in particular the USS "Constitution", a formidable battle ship that constantly surprised the British, who had grown used to defeating the French in almost every action. The ageing Admiral Sir John Warren was an ineffectual leader with little dash or imagination; but he was also hampered by limited resources and a lack of support from the Admiralty, more concerned with events in Europe. Admiral George

Cockburn was of a different mould. It was he who commanded the daring raids and attacks in the Chesapeake where Wybourn saw action against the 'Yankees', and succeeded where Warren had failed, by cutting at the soft underbelly of the Americas. His campaign led to the capture of a number of American warships, the occupation of Washington and the burning of the White House and the Capitol.

In the end the War of 1812 was fought for little gain, and to this day both American and Canadian children are taught that their side was victorious.

Thursday 18th Feb. 1813: Left this wretched miserable place, & preparing for broken heads amongst the Yankees. This morning we received our orders – the Commander-in-Chief, Sir John Warren, honoured Admiral Cockburn with a visit. This is a pompous & diabolical attempt at omnipotence. The whole ship's company, officers & strangers are warned of the approach of this Demigod, full dresses, humble looks on the one part, & terror mixed with forced adoration on the other; on his getting near the ship all the sailors man the yards aloft, as it is called, this is by running along & placing themselves at equal distances facing one way, while every man stands upright, extending his arms along a rope, fixed for the purpose, 500 men all thus stationed, then the soldiers under arms are placed around the ship facing outwards. This being now ascends to the Deck, under a discharge of great guns & is there received by the Admiral, Captain & all the Officers with the most abject humility, the timid shrinking behind the rest for fear of being annihilated. In this manner he struts to the front of the guard, mounted by a Captain & two subalterns who present arms or salute, the drums beating a march & the band playing "God Save the King". He is then ushered in to the Cabin & the Ceremony of secret conversation, & public gourmandising of a collation expressly prepared for the occasion being over, his ambition is gorged with a repetition of adulation on his return out of the ship.

On these occasions all the Commanders of other ships are obliged to attend, as so many satellites, & form a train in the rear of the almighty man, attend him on board, wait outside/in general/ & after escorting him on shore have some hours hard rowing against the wind & tide back to their ships, delighted with the scene of grandure [sic] at which they lick their lips, with vain senseless hopes of perhaps arriving one day to the same honor. O tempore! O Mores!

Feb.21st, Sunday: We are now a great distance from Bermuda.

Nothing material has happened, but abominably seasick, the weather is so boisterous. The Admiral dined with us.

22nd: Sent in a Prize to Bermuda – bad & rainy weather.

23rd: Experiments with a newly-invented elevated gun, made so as to fire nearly perpendicular. Had a long discourse with the Admiral upon gunnery, buck shot & American mode of warfare.

24th: Took two other Prizes & sent them in. A delightful but cold day. Did not visit the deck being unwell all day.

25th: Still contrary winds for the American coast.

26th: A most heavenly day – the Admiral suddenly gave orders to clear for action & all cabins were knock'd down & as great preparation made for fighting as if an enemy had actually been in view. A general exercise took place & several firing with shots, broadsides of ammunition being ridiculously thrown away. The Admiral says it puts everything in place for real service, but there is no possible prospect of having occasion to use the ship's guns against the Americans & all we have done is to render every officer uncomfortable at a cold, miserable season, for the Chesapeake is colder than England & nothing but canvas screens to keep out of frost & snow, while his own cabin is closed, well-carpeted & a large fire. This put us all out of humour, & dinner not ready till 5 o'clock, the cooks being fighting & the fire out.

Sun.: Past as the former ones, but the two American Captains (of our Prize ships) were astonished at hearing Lord Wellington & part of his army were coming out with 19 sail of the line; this we persuaded them of, as it was the intention to let them go on shore on our arrival.

Warren and Cockburn's squadron moved up the Rappahannock River, on their way to Chesapeake Bay. They encountered five American schooners, including the "Arab" (7 guns), "Lynx" (6), "Racer" (6) and "Dolphin" (12), which fled upriver and were chased by the smaller boats of the squadron. The Americans ran for 15 miles and drew up in line ahead, waiting. The British duly attacked. The "Arab" was boarded and taken by the "Marlborough's" two gunboats; "Lynx" hauled down her colours as Sir John Warren's "San Domingo" (74) came alongside and the "Racer" was captured, after a fierce resistance, by the lieutenant commanding the gunboats.

Chesapeake (America).
Lynhaven Bay

Wed 3rd March: Anchored in what the Yankees call their waters, & which they have so often forbade us to do. Cleared away for action again on approaching the shore, old Sir John Warren having told Admiral C. that the enemy had fortified the point we had to pass, which there was no appearance of, so much for wisdom; he had only just left the place, but at all events <u>why</u> was his information no better? This is a prelude to more – he is ignorant of everything we want to know.

4th March: Various emplts., of visiting the Admiral & receiving orders. A general dinner to all Captains – the officers of "Junon" came on board & singular to find my old ship (the "Ardent" in the Baltic) was by accident sent out to this station & he, Captain Honeyman, appointed to the "Marlboro", myself already here. Read, my subaltern of the "Ardent" in the "Junon" & one of the lieutenants in the "Rifleman," so that both ship & officers are removed from one quarter of the world to the other by detachments.

5th & 6th: Bitter cold, frost & snow – sent all the Prisoners on shore in flag of truce, our wardroom full of strangers, most of them slept on board. Guard-boats rowing about all night, men half starved with cold.

7th: Sleet & rain & shocking weathers, but taking Prizes every day. The boat service very wretched, yet vigilance necessary.

Tues. 9th: At daylight Boats in chase of an American, being nearly calm, a very pretty running fight for 5 hours, captured her with 500 barrels of flour, tobacco & other things.

Wed: Cleared for Battle & went with the squadron up the river to Hampton Roads near Norfolk with the intention of attacking the American frigate "Constellation". Passed within a few yards of their lighthouse point, which was not fortified.

Hampton Roads

Capt. Barrie of the "Dragon" and Capt Ross of the "Marlborough".

Thurs. 11th March: All Captains came on board to plan the attack, boats armed, Rockets prepared & all bustle & activity. Capts Barrie & Ross volunteer with about 300 men. They went away in high spirits at dark, a miserable cold night & 13 miles to go.

Fri. 12th: At 6 in the morning the expedition returned, not being able to effect their purpose – lost their way & currents & wind against them. At night a most formidable preparation made again, 600 men, all volunteers & a number of officers under the enterprising Captain Barrie, assembled round the "Marlboro", each having white bands round their arms & hats, to distinguish English from Americans; the enthusiasm was astonishing & everything was expected from such fine fellow & what added to it, a Packet arrived from England stating the Russians to have annihilated the French army & the Prussian General abandoned Boney & taken 20,000 men with him over to the

These Russian victories were doubtless skirmishes won by the highly mobile Russian Cavalry units, but there were no decisive defeats inflicted on the French, who were already in Moscow at this point.

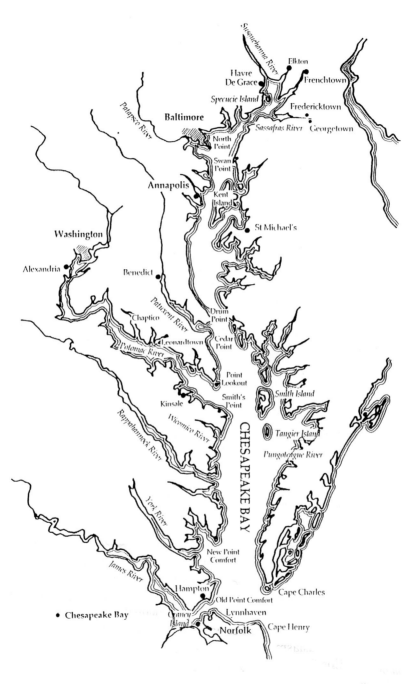

Map of Chesapeake Bay

SIR JOHN BORLASE WARREN BAR.^T KB.

Pub.^d by Bunney & Gold Shoe Lane. June 1 1800.

Russians – these things gave great spirits to us all & knowing Captain Barrie for what he is – a fire-eater (when fond of fighting) we made sure the American frigate would be in our possession. Accounts that Lord Wellington has entered France & Spain finally evacuated by the French. America is ashamed at our complete success everywhere & hearing there are 19 sail of the line, several frigates & 5 bombs coming out, with many troops.

Saturday 13th: A dreadful cold morning: at 6 all the boats arrived, everyone almost froze, having been 10 hours on the water & the night so bad nothing could be effected. This day we set two officers (prisoners) free on parole. The Admiral is in high good humour.

Sunday 21st: As usual. We all drank to the immortal memory of General Sir Ralph Abercromby killed in Egypt on this day, crowned with victory before Alexandria. The last 8 days employed as usual & practising every kind of discipline; almost every night the boats unsuccessful in their attack upon the enemy frigate. This day the secretary to the Russian Legation came on a visit to Admiral Cockburn, in a flag of truce, with the lieutenant of the American frigate, a consul & an officer of the army. As the admiral dined with us these people were all invited, & we were discussing politics pretty freely; it appears some idea of negotiation is attempted by the Russian Minister.

22nd: The Commander-in-Chief Sir John Warren arrived from Bermuda, our admiral went to Lynhaven Bay to meet him. I dined with Captain Ross, Talbot & Barrie, having caught some excellent fish, we had a princely dinner.

23rd: We turned out a Captain's Guard for the admiral, a great fuss as usual on this occasion – a most sultry hot day. Cleared for action, great doings expected.

24th: All boats armed again, chased three sloops, burnt two & brought one down; the enemy chased our boats, a flag of truce sent by us to Norfolk – an expedition by water planned.

Sunday 28th: Got under way, with all the fleet & gave up further attempts in these parts. The Admiral dined with us, a thoroughly wet day, 4 or 5 separate dinners. Arrived in the Lower Bay late. Long moral discussion.

29th: The "Junon" frigate & 7 of our most valuable Prizes sailed for Bermuda; sent my linen by my friend Read to get washed at that port – sent for stock, as we begin to live badly. The sun paid us a visit for a few hours & made us all cheerful. The Admirals visited each other; a signal made for an enemy in sight, supposed the "Essex"

A captured officer would be marched at gunpoint or held behind bars, like any enlisted man, unless he gave his word – his parole – that he would not attempt to escape. Paroled officers often fraternized with their enemies, and were grateful for the civilized company and understanding of their enemy brother officers; this was not treachery, but merely good manners.

Norfolk was visited under a flag of truce.

frigate – sent three frigates after her. Sent letter to England to Uncle & Dickinson.

31st: This morning an enemy Privateer came so close off the harbour, thinking nothing would go after her, that a frigate we sent out soon captured her with 12 guns & 87 men, out 4 months.

April 1st: Moved from Lynhaven Bay & proceeded up the Chesapeake River towards the Potomac River, which leads up to Washington. We left the "Victorious", 74, in the narrows towards Norfolk & the "Narcissus" frigate off Point Henry & put an American merchant ship in quarantine for her malpractices in giving information to a rich Bordeaux vessel who came in the night, that our fleet was up at Hampton, by which she escaped worth £60,000, but was stranded soon afterwards & we saved half her cargo. The severity of service now began, for no officer could get his dinner till 8 or 9 at night & then only salt beef, with a small proportion of corned pork – the Admiral in bad humour & generally 4 o'clock in the morning before we were in bed.

Friday 2nd: The weather suddenly changed to a sultry hot summer's day, a general indulgence of care on deck, the band playing almost the whole day, while the fleet glided along with a rapid tide, the shore on each side not being wider than the Thames & covered with verdure; passed several rivers branching from this channel.

Rappahannock River

Sat. 3rd April: At daylight this morning anchored at the mouth of this river & sent boats up it; in the afternoon we saw a very fierce engagement & the admirals were both much alarmed for the welfare of the boats; it being a perfect calm, no assistance could be afforded to them. At night we had the pleasing intelligence of the daring attack of our boats against an immensely superior force, being 4 vessels of war & a large India ship, one privateer of 16 guns & 103 men, two brigs of 8 guns each & 40 men & one of 6 guns & 35 men, the whole were boarded after much resistance & severe loss – our loss was only 13 killed & wounded, one lieutenant of the Navy wounded & one subaltern of Marines severely wounded, but the most unhappy thing was a fine enterprising officer who had lost his left arm on a former occasion, would volunteer on this, & almost the first great gun that the enemy fired took off his only remaining arm. He was brought on board of us & taken the utmost care of.

<u>Sunday</u>: A large force sent from each ship, foraging. No arrival yet from the little band of warriors up the river; being calm it is supposed to be difficult for them to bring the ships out. The Admiral, Captain & Secretary dined with us, being the last dinner we can give him, having reserved the little good things for this occasion, passed several very facetious hours. In the evening came one expedition of this morning with a lame account of their prowess, having being driven off by a handful of countrymen & would have been made prisoners, but for a strong detachment of my men & a subaltern, whom I fortunately ordered to follow in another boat. This evening the little signal officer (Mr. Roberts) came down to dinner late & in a most unhappy temper, so that I was compelled to destroy what little appetite he had, by a threat he had not the nerves for.

April 4, 1813
His Majesty's Ship "Marlborough"
In the Chesapeake River, America

Dear Brother [*in-law, Joseph Shipton*]

We arrived in "these waters" yesterday morning, and before night the boats were in action with four armed ships, which were only supposed to be small merchant vessels, and being calm no vessel of our force could be sent to their protection, their only alternative was to surrender or fight, and I am happy to say, two of the "Marlboro's" officers led, the result was honorable, as you will see by the papers. The subject is not of that nature to induce me to enter into detail to you, as it contains too many scenes of horror for the ear of a friend. It is sufficient to say it affords me the opportunity of sending you a letter which otherwise would not have occured, and I fear will be long before another happens. We are going on a most profitable expedition though blended with much cruelty.

Up this river a few days ago we made an unsuccessful attempt to destroy the American frigate "Constellation" and the town of Norfolk. Our force was not adequate so we swept James River, to use the Adml's expression, and sent 30 prizes to Bermuda. Our present object is to sweep all these noble and astonishing Rivers. The weather is now lovely and the shores look beautiful – it appears like a party of pleasure: 2 ships of 74 guns & Sir Jn. Warren's and our flags, two frigates and two smaller vessels compose our force, all the rest are sent to Boston, New York, Delaware, etc. Never was there a finer opportunity to make our fortunes, if we succeed to the extent we are informed.

We are now at the mouth of the Rappahanock (I will be particular in my description, as I know my dear girls will soon have their maps before them). We remained some days (too many) at Lynnhaven Bay, which they will see is between the two Capes Henry and Charles, we then went up Norfolk River, remained in Hampton Roads, and sent the Boats, armed, up James River, then returned to this wonderful Chesapeake. We sent boats up the York & Planhatank rivers, the first on our left hand, branching out of the grand channel; the Rappahanock we are now searching & have already captured the "Bordeaux Men", a large Privateer & flour ship. We next go up the Potomac, the finest of them all, and proceed to the Patuxent, Patapsco, Choptank, and to Baltimore, but the mine of wealth is at the pretty town of Annapolis about 90 miles from where we are. It is said there are 100 vessels protected by batteries; these they little think we disregard for in short we have been so familiar with cannon balls that I hardly know if one passed over our dining table whether it would be noticed or not.

If we take that nest, goodbye to the service say I, and I do not know whether I do not meet your ideas, that America might be a good place to do it.

Tell my dear Sisters that bright prospects are before me, and that Dame Fortune appears to be advancing on friendly terms after having been scared to so great a distance, that it was doubtful if her journey back could be accomplished.

Leonidas, King of Sparta, held the pass of Thermopylae against the invading army of Xerxes.

The gallant exploits of our little flotilla gives occasion to send dispatches, for it was certainly worthy of Leonidas. as a few open boats of ten and fourteen oars to attack vessels of force 40 guns and 438 men and carry them, says more than all their conquests with a vastly superior force. Their sweep against our frigates has caused such inveterate revenge, that I am sorry to say violence and brutallity [sic] are without control.

Report says every town, village and hamlet throughout these rivers are to be annihilated and plundered – We daily expect our two battalions from England with the 102nd Regt and artillery from Bermuda with five Bomb vessels. When we have done here it seems we are to return to Norfolk to carry death & destruction and take their frigates.

[*unfinished*]

Friday 9th April: These last few days passed in collecting all our scattered force, receiving and distributing prisoners. Early this morning we sailed up the River & the Commander-in-Chief got his ship the "St. Domingo" aground – it took the whole day for us to get him off. We however sent the small vessels up & several boats, also the 4 beautiful schooners, now our prizes, having put 50 men into each plus 3 officers; at night some of them returned having captured 17 of the enemy's vessels & had not the whole day been lost by the admiral's want of knowledge of the passage, or if he had let a frigate lead – we could, by following the boats up, have enabled them to capture above 30 other vessels.

10th April: The weather too foggy to move; a vessel came up from the bay with the news of two French frigates being taken who had come to assist the Yankees.

11th: Gales & wind & much danger for these large ships in such narrow waters.

City of Annapolis

Thursday 15th: Arrived off this beautiful town & every preparation making to storm the works, which attempt will be the destruction of the assailants, as we have neither Engineers or scaling ladders, but these sons of Neptune fancy it only necessary to conceive a plan & the execution is a mere chance work. I at all events sat down last night & made my will, also wrote letters to Caroline & Emily & Lawson in case of accidents. We made an excellent dinner having found calves, sheep & pigs in our Prizes as they were just ready for sea & had moved down to where our boats boarded them a few hours before we came in sight. After dark the boats & a brig went close in to reconnoitre & soon found the impracticability of a surprise, it being too shallow even for boats to get within musket shot & on the land side the redoubts were on the opposite side of small rivers – the object was therefore very prudently (for once) given up & preparations for proceeding upwards at daylight made.

16th: After a most violent gale of wind all last night, we this day moved up towards Baltimore & anchored near Poole's Island – the sail was truly sublime & elegant – conceive two large ships of the line, two frigates & about a dozen small vessels sailing in a narrow river nearly 200 miles inland from the anchorage in Lynhaven Bay, the water smooth as a mill pond & the shores covered with groves, gardens, gentlemen's seats etc., etc., every thing in full blossom & all the hills & valleys scattered with cattle, yet this country is said to be a wretched one & so it may [be] for the most part, but certainly for the last 50 miles & all around here, nothing can exceed the luxuriousness of the appearance, not even our Thames above Battersea.

Baltimore is just in sight about 14 miles off & too well-guarded by shoals & Batteries to get at it without 5,000 troops. Our boats proceeded up about noon & much firing has been seen, but no news this night can be expected as they are round a distant point. The Bay we lie in now commands four great rivers from which nothing can pass, one leading to Baltimore, the 2nd towards the shores near Washington City, the 3rd to the head of the Elk River, only 24 miles across from Philadelphia & the one we came up. Our chief object here it is said is merely to alarm & to get water.

Saturday April 17th: This morning Lieutenant Cairns who commanded the boats brought down four vessels & one of which a beautiful Packet full of passengers & a vast number of Ladies, who were terrified beyond measure; the firing we had seen & heard from a gun boat, the "Batteries", the Commodore was in it, but after a few shots he retired beyond his batteries & suffered the ladies to be taken. Although our boats were open ships' barges, we set all the ladies free & gave them a small Prize to reach home in – the Packet we kept, which was fitted up in a superior stile to our 'Margate Hoys'. They all appeared most grateful for they expected to find us savages & one old woman kept continually asking if they were not to be sunk or blown from the mouth of a Cannon. They at last petitioned for their husbands which was granted, the admiral very gallantly observing he was not warring against man & wife, nor would ever allow the peaceable part of the community to be molested. The vessels we broke up or burnt & one rich one being laden with goods we shared out; this kind of vessel, so-called by these people, is literally a large Country Shop, containing something of everything small villages stand in need of; they coast along the River & supply remote places from the great towns – & consequently such a Prize at <u>such</u> a <u>time</u> was most acceptable.

<u>Sunday April 18th</u>: A Brig arrived with newspapers to the 9th, from some of the American ports. I dined with the Admiral.

<u>Thursday 22nd</u>: Nothing particular determined upon yet, the last few days employed in chasing coasters & burning them & what was really too bad, the fools burnt the vessel laden with timber, oars & beams, worth an immense sum of money.

A Mr. McCoy went away with Cairns up to Baltimore in a flag of truce. This was a gentleman of genteel manners & good education & was supercargo in the "Arab", the finest schooner of all our Prizes: they were bound to France. Read this day 3 letters from my dear niece Mary, from Henry S. & from Richards.

<u>Friday 23rd</u>: A thorough wet day with heavy thunder & lightning. Papers from England to 13th Feb. containing great news: Spain for the most part evacuated by the French, Lord Wellington in full pursuit, the Russians crossed the Vistula after Boney, who is alarmed seriously & expects the Scheld fleet to fall. Revolution in Prussia & all the Continent in flames; so much for the vile, ambitious villain who would penetrate the depth of winter into the "frightful climate" as he termed Russia, while that noble people by sacrificing their ancient capital, the large & beautiful city of Moscow, defeated the usurper in all his plans & perhaps will cause his utter destruction before they rest.

<u>Sunday 25th</u>: After some quiet days a sudden order came for me & 80 men with a subaltern to proceed to the tenders & from there on board the "Fantome" sloop of war. As a vast number of men are ordered to join us from other ships, a formidable expedition appears to be planning. Accordingly we proceeded, armed & provided with everything necessary: canteens; camp kettles & a blanket each man.

<u>Tuesday 27th</u>: After sailing up two days, anchored off the entrance to Susquehanna River, which is the very utmost branch of the great Chesapeake River, or rather sea, for it is salt for the most part, whereas at Baltimore where the ships remain it is fresh, but off this river quite pure & fine tasted, the ships had only to fill from alongside.

After dark we were ordered into the boats: I had about 150 men under my command & there was one Rocket boat & three launches with 12lb. carronades & a proportion of seamen. A surprise was intended but we went up the wrong river, or at least of a branch of it

Rear-Admiral Cockburn embarked 150 marines, under the command of Captains Wybourn and Carter. Instead of entering the Elk River, the boats carrying the marines entered the Bohemia, delaying the attack. This enabled the inhabitants of Frenchtown to prepare defences including a six-gun battery which opened fire on the marines as they approached. Wybourn's marines ignored this and landed quickly.

Seeing this the American militia abandoned its guns and ran to safety in the nearby wood. The marines disabled the guns, destroyed some of the military stores and several vessels anchored close by. They then re-embarked and departed, suffering no losses, for Elk Town (now Elkton).

& at daylight our pilot saw his mistake & we returned 12 miles, when he discovered the right way. A Council was then held whether to go on, in execution of our orders, which was to attack some considerable magazines & destroy everything within our reach – or rejoin our ships.

French Town

Friday 30th: As we resolved to proceed (it having been very judiciously observed that we could row faster than news could fly across rivers) the men gave three cheers, although we had been 14 hours in the boats & the night very cold. About 11 o' clock therefore we saw the place, but did not expect to find a battery. When they opened fire upon us from 6 guns, our launches were a long way in the rear & we determined not to wait for them, but to land our men and attack by the town at the same time. This was effected under a smart fire which did no material mischief except disabling one boat & slightly wounding two or three men. In less than two hours we carried by the bayonet both battery & town, set fire to the magazines & burnt & blew up the vessels, after which we pursued the Yankees to a river which they crossed in boats & formed in good order at Elk Town, having a strong column with two field pieces at their head & a battery of three heavy guns, besides about 20 or 30 vessels.

It is evident that this was the place the Commander-in-Chief intended the attack upon, as it appeared a considerable place, the river washing it on two sides & a fine harbour for shipping, nor was it difficult with our force at this moment to have carried it. Captain Robinson & myself reconnoitred it & had nearly paid dear for it, not conceiving we were so near to them, when they opened a shower of musketry & field pieces, which only cleared our hats. We then consulted the officers & it was agreed to stay, but Lieutenant Westphal, whom the admiral entrusted the charge of the boats, opposed it & certainly called off two launches that were in the creek & almost within shot of Elk Town, only one got on a point, not waiting for a flowing tide, & was exposed to the enemy's fire, but would have got off & I am well assured, in half an hour the boats would have made their way up & at this point could have placed us across.

A general murmur followed this, but he was obstinate & we all reembarked & late at night reached our ships. I must, however admit that the admiral's information was incorrect, for he told us French Town, which we found, nor did we imagine there was any other place near, until I reconnoitred as I have before said & another thing against us was mistaking our road, by which we lost the whole forenoon, besides taking them by surprise &, as many cavalry were in sight, I will allow it would have been imprudent to remain all night, without having a position.

Island of Portsouci

<u>Sat. 1st of May</u>: It being no longer possible to remain without stock etc., the obstinacy of these people in refusing to supply us at their own price, compelled us to make a descent on this beautiful island covered with every kind of cattle, farms & grain. I was accordingly ordered to take possession of it, which we did without opposition, although it was only divided from the main by a narrow stream fordable across & the population of the island far more numerous than us. I immediately placed 200 men at this ford, which was 5 miles from the landing place. Parties were then detached across the island, assuring the people that if they made their slaves drive the bullocks, sheep, poultry, etc., down to our boats they should not only be paid by government bills, but their persons & property respected. This had the desired effect & we procured a prodigious quantity of everything. We then called in all parties & on the shore, covered by our boats & sloops of war, regaled with plently of good cheer & rest. After bathing & every man & officer glad to do this, in order to wash our shirts & dry them in the grass, not having had a change since we left the ships, or been undressed; in short, as it was supposed, 24 hours would have accomplished all our purposes up here.

Just as the sun set everybody embarked, when I discovered 4 of my best men had deserted. Only a few minutes before I had sent them as trustworthy men & against whom for 7 years no crime had been attached, to bring in some worthless stragglers, when, I imagine, an old Irish rascal who had been a labourer 14 years among the Yankees on this island, enticed them to leave us, for two were Irish. I, however, remained on shore with one subaltern (Lieutenant Barrie) a bold and enterprizing officer, two sergeants, a corporal & 4 privates, sent-off to the ships to be ready to support us if we fired our pieces & to leave a boat in hearing of the shore; we then took different directions for the other end of the island.

The Corporal & one man came up with them, just crossing. They had the start, however, & were 4 to 2; notwithstanding, these fine fellows got across, when the four villains tossed their hats up saying they were now Americans & tried to persuade the Corporal & man to join them but would not allow them to go up upon the rising ground they had reached. The Corporal had unfortunately left his musket behind, thinking they were only in the next farmhouse getting drunk, but on his discovering them just running off and guessing their design he called that one man after him. It appeared no use to endeavour to seize them as they would have shot them, they therefore, it appears, d ... d them for traitors & rascals & came back, as they feared to be surprised by the enemy's patrol only about a mile off. At 12 at night we got on board & I must confess, much mortified, but had boats been sent earlier in the afternoon (& we were a long while ready) all would have been well, as these very men were in the ranks waiting to embark, when I sent them for the stragglers.

<u>Sunday 2nd May</u>: Visited the island again to settle with the farmers, which the admiral did, to a fraction. I went to find the old Irishman, but he was not visible. Our 4 men, it seems, were met going to Havre de Grasse, a town of note about 7 miles from us & which this morning we intended to attack at daylight, agreeable to the information of the old Hibernian, who assured us they had only two brass guns & few troops there. Captain Robinson & myself reconnoitred it by his directions as well as our glass would afford & it appeared not difficult to access, so that we resolved to request the admiral to let us attempt it, which he immediately granted, but the weather did not admit.

At dinner this day we again mentioned it, but all agreed the deserters would alarm them as they knew our intention; however a larger force was appointed, not without some sneering, that the ambitious ones should prevail upon the admiral to attempt a forlorn hope, & when the admiral was absent, they croaked that we should all come back as wise as we went & that no attempt would be made to land; they did not know the men, or were themselves faint-hearted. At any rate it was ordered for Tuesday morning at daylight.

<u>Monday 3rd</u>: Preparations all day, making 350 men under my command, but my own Company left out as a punishment (such is

Once a breach in defences had been established, the first storming party to enter it was known as the 'forlorn hope'. Few survived this path to glory and promotion.

the zeal of men that they felt it so) for their 4 comrades deserting, excepting the Corporal & Private man, whom I promoted instantly, they joined our little expedition: three launches with 12 lbs. guns, one Rocket boat & about 200 sailors, the "High-flyer" Schooner, Lieutenant Lewis, son to our second Commandt. at Chatham – a brave & most gallant officer & Captain Robinson, a volunteer, with his 5 men.

Havre de Grasse [sic]

<u>Wed. 5th May</u>: In eight hours this fine town was destroyed, their troops dispersed, their forts dismantled, two stands of colours taken & fifty-one pieces of cannon, but only 12 mounted. Never was an attack carried with more courage or coolness, than every man displayed, with good order & humanity mingled with their operations, although the place was stormed by dawn of day. 2000 men drawn up in Battle array had not courage to await our attack though perhaps the circumstances of a Congreve rocket having been well directed at the onset put them into confusion. It passed through the Battery & struck a man in the back, when not a single vestige of him was to be found. This tremendous engine of death afterwards struck the ground & forced itself full a mile into the country, tearing up everything in its way.

The launches & Rocket boat attacked on the Town side & landed a mile & half from it, so as to cut off all retreat & the most laughable though distressing scene was the first enemy we met – about 400 women with their clothes or bundles under their arms, actually as they tumbled out of bed in the dark, for our cannon opened upon the town at 4 in the morning; the fright they exhibited on being met by us, was beyond anything – to go back was impossible for the rockets were then passing by them; they shrieked, ran & scrambled in all directions & it was some minutes before I could convince them Englishmen did not war with women. I halted my men & made an officer run towards them assuring them of our protection; they then requested to go up a hill to a fine noble house (a Mr. Pringle's) & I stationed an officer & 15 men to prevent any interruption to them by any of our parties. Daylight fast approaching, we assailed the town, secured all the

Cockburn's squadron headed for Specucie Island, but began taking fire from Havre de Grace, at the mouth of the Susquehanna River. The townsfolk had hoisted their colours and Cockburn reasoned that if they had thought it worth defending it was probably worth attacking. Once again, Cockburn's boats were assembled for another attack; Wybourn tells the story. Once Cockburn knew of the Principio Foundry, (Wybourn calls it the Cecil Foundry) the largest cannon factory in the States, he led a party which destroyed 51 guns and 130 small arms, five vessels in the Susquehanna and captured a sizeable depot of flour. A Lieutenant Scott recounts that once the Americans had run into the woods, they had failed to tell any of their countrymen that Havre was in British hands. About noon the stage coach arrived from Philadelphia on its way to Baltimore and stopped at the inn before the coachman and his affrighted cargo found they had fallen into the hands of the Britishers. Milliners with the latest fashions from Paris, merchants and tradesmen were alike pretty considerably confounded, wondering how we had reached the high road between their two most flourishing and principal towns. The passengers got off in safety without loss, except a luckless milliner, of whose finery some had been purloined by an individual who ought to have known better, but who was deservedly mortified by the Rear-Admiral [Cockburn] obliging him to return the spoils in propria persona to the forlorn damsel, with an impressive rebuke.' Compare Scott's words with Wybourn's. The American interpretation of the attack on Havre de Grace to this day paints Cockburn as some form of pirate or barbarian, rather than a commander in the midst of a war.

passes & the Prisoners & then 200 men lighted flambeaux & began to fire the houses.

The scene in the early morning must have been extremely ludicrous, for in one or two of the hotels we found all the beds had been occupied, but the clothes, shoes, hats, watches & in short everything remained in the room so that the inmates must have started off in the same <u>airy</u> dress as the unfortunate ladies. A most welcome Prize fell to my lot – a gentleman's portmanteau stood opened, in which clean white shirts were exhibited & a case of razors, neither of which I had seen since I left the ship, & when we embarked I instantly began my toilette in the boat. There were 5 shirts, those razors, a pair of nankeen pantaloons & waistcoats & neck handkerchiefs. I shared everything out, except two shirts & my razors: these were too great a luxury to part with. However, many others must have fared as well, for there were four stage coaches full of trunks which arrived from Baltimore & Philadelphia, only two hours before us; these were soon pillaged & the coaches shared the fate of the houses.

In the evening we sent all boats to destroy the vessels in all parts of the harbour; we all crossed the water & destroyed the Cecil Foundry & village & at 9 o'clock waded up to the middle to our boats & were pulling against wind & tide 7 hours, blowing & raining hard before we reached the tenders & there being no accommodation we were compelled to lie down, wet & miserable, to sleep. However, this day a beautiful hot sun & a whole day's rest revived us, hung everything up to dry & prepared for another midnight excursion up a different river.

George Town

<u>Friday 7th May</u>: At 12 o'clock on Wednesday night, the same force embarked, & at 9 yesterday morning we came in sight of George Town & Frederick Town, one on each side of the river, or rather creek, for it was only a pistol shot across. This was a most daring & difficult enterprise for our boats got aground every half hour from the narrow & muddy passage & just as we saw the towns, we discovered a battery on the summit of a hill perpendicular with the river, inaccessible on the outside & in front, and above 400 men posted, with a breastwork, also 150 men entrenched on the opposite side.

The admiral attended in person & shewed great personal courage, going ahead in a gig with only 6 men, under a shower of fire from the musketry. He came back & told me to pull as hard as possible past this position & instantly land on low sand & charge up the hill. On this occasion I never saw more good conduct & gallantry displayed in my life. We lost 44 men in passing, but was soon on shore & as all our men had been well trained and experienced, they formed in less than one minute.

The enemy were strongly posted & covered by thick wood & supported by a few cavalry on a plain on their right & by the battery on their left, yet in <u>ten</u> minutes we slew numbers & charged by the bayonet, routing their whole body, the Colonel & about 100 men taking refuge in a small wood, which after securing all the passes around it & having good information from the Negro slaves about us we explored but could not find the coward.

We now directed our course for Georgetown & destroyed every house in it. We had left the Rocket boat & launches engaging the breastwork on the other side of the river & in 9 hours we crossed over, routing all the vagabonds & pursued them 3 miles – afterwards returned &, with much regret, burnt the beautiful little well-built Frederick Town. On this day also we witnessed scenes of real distress, for pursuing the flying enemy with rapidity we came up with hundreds of poor women, old men, children & villagers crying & begging for mercy, some throwing themselves over hedges & into ditches, etc., etc. Among these a train of boarding school misses with governesses & teachers, about 40. These we shewed great humanity to & spared a village on their account. It was very singular but the admiral had information so correct that he knew of this school in Frederick Town – he is a droll character & witty in the midst of any danger, which I had often witnessed (particularly at the memorable Siege of Flushing when he was 3½ hours under the whole batteries of Flushing in an open boat, getting off a ship I was in, which had grounded). The gallant hero, when he rowed back to our boats, as I before said & pointing to various advantages, he added 'And, Captain Wybourn, at that town is a boarding school of young ladies.' I told them of this & that it caused so much mirth, tho' their foolish troops were then firing at us. I lament to say, however, that those poor girls' books, & even two pianofortes, found their way into the "Marlboro'", for the Jack tars, after pillaging & burning the houses reserved those things among others & conveyed them to the boats.

Before the sun set, we had travelled above 5 miles into the country & destroyed all the farms & every house, barn & rick. In the harbour were a few old vessels; these we burnt & all the storehouses, especially to our regret, a brewery filled with strong-beer, but as our small boats would not carry large casks, it was policy to destroy it, for the men would soon have got drunk had they been permitted to go into it.

Just before dark we all embarked & was compelled to row against tide 30 miles, so that if these <u>fine soldiers</u> had only laid in ambush in the thick woods on each side (as we apprehended they would) they could have picked off a man at every shot. This appears to be the last expedition in these parts, which is the upper part of all in the Chesapeake; at Frederick Town we understand it is only 30 miles from Philadelphia. No other town or harbour lies open to attack of boats. At night we felt all excessively fatigued having had nothing to eat for 20 hours & wet through wading to boats. Made an excellent supper & my friend Captain Lawrence made up a bed on the sofa, where I slept like an Emperor, perhaps much <u>sounder</u>.

Lawrence was Captain of the "Fantome"

<u>Saturday 8th May</u>: After a most hearty breakfast on board the "Fantome", paid my respects & congratulations to the admiral on board the "Maidstone" frigate, (Captain Burdett). We were all preparing to return to the fleet, but the admiral would have some more stock. I therefore accompanied him to the Main land with 200 men & no opposition to landing, & completely cleared two farms, which the admiral paid very liberally for & the farmers shewed much confidence by going on board the ships for payment, after which we made sail with a fine fair wind. I went on board "Maidstone" to dinner, but fared so badly, there being no wine, that I returned early to the "Fantome", had a cold fowl & ham & a bottle of old port wine.

Off Baltimore

<u>Sunday 9th</u>: Once more found myself comfortable in my own cabin, on board the "Marlboro'" after (at least) very harassing service & found the luxury of dressing from top to toe. Dined with the admiral & passed a most pleasant day, while our anecdotes amused those who had not shared our expedition. I never remember to have enjoyed my own bed with such satisfaction as on this night.

Monday 10th: Placed everything to rights, visited our friends on board other ships & watching the enemy's force in Baltimore river.

Sunday 16th: Nothing all this last week, but preparations for Sir John Warren's departure, collecting prizes together, etc. Admiral Cockburn & a Mr. Parkhurst, purser of the "Cleopatra", dined with us; we all moved down to the Bay.

Monday 17th May: Meeting of Congress at Washington, no doubt to abuse us all. Sir John sailed with all the prizes for Bermuda & Halifax. Wrote home public accounts of our proceedings to my Commanding Officer.

18th: Mr. Seventscoff, the Russian Secretary, came from Washington. I dined with him at the admiral's table; he tells us the master did not think our warfare did good, as we had many friends in America whom it irritated. He also brings glorious news that Russians are advanced to Poland, Holland in a state of insurrection, Spain evacuated & America humbled.

24th Monday: Yesterday a Prize valued at £30,000 came into our clutches & thought to escape. The "Fantome", returned from New York, brings intelligence that the "Sceptre" – 74 – was at Barbados the end of April, so that we may expect her daily. She's intended for our Admiral & we shall lose his noble society, with much regret. It is not usual for anyone but his Lieutenants, Captain & Midshipman to follow. My old friend Captain Honeyman (late of the "Ardent") I find commands the "Sceptre" so we shall once more sail together, for he must take the present Flag Captain's place. Mr. Westhall, first of "Junon" & Read, my old subaltern in the "Ardent" came on board to dine.

Tuesday 25th: In the evening arrived the "High-Flyer". She had been to cruize off the Roanoke river, to look for a schooner from France, when a heavy Privateer fell in her way, of 16 guns & 90 men. He had only 5 guns & 30 men, of which 15 & two midshipmen were killed & wounded. My poor friend Lewis, after all his gallant exploits, fell early in the action by a chance shot from a musket, but kept calling to the last to board the enemy. Strange to say, this vessel of force sheered off, hearing this & the little "High-Flyer" gallantly stood after him all night, but was so much crippled that she was obliged to come in here instead of proceeding to Bermuda. This is the Commander-in-Chief's hobby & never loses sight of her, but poor Lewis was so great a favourite he wanted to give him a prize. He was in chase of a Bordeaux vessel when by accident this privateer escaped past us in the night & crost his direction.

We now moved our position between the Horseshoe & middle ground so that nothing can pass in or out of the Chesapeake without our seeing them & the weather is getting so intolerably hot that this place lies in a current of air. News from Canada that General Harrison is shut up in Fort Meigs.

<u>Wed. 26th</u>: "High-Flyer" sailed for Bermuda with despatches. Sent letter to general Borblay.

<u>30th</u>: Sunday as usual, the admiral etc., etc., dined with us. Great news arrived thro' the medium of the Russian Legation at Washington: Austria has joined the Russians & beating the French who lost 35,000 men. Spain entirely evacuated by Soult, Holland in arms against the vile usurper & 50,000 Swedes under Bernadotte passed into Pomerania.

<u>June 14th</u>: Fired Royal salute in honour of our venerable & beloved King. Nothing material these few days.

<u>June 16th</u>: Except for a little expedition to Smith Island for stock, etc., which was conducted by my subaltern & 50 men, nothing material has occurred. A large party of Americans who had been civil to our boats on the Maryland shore were sometime since invited to come on board and we shewed them great attention, so much so that after a superb supper they began to find <u>we</u> were nearly all alike, for they had been told strange storys of us; we made them all completely drunk except one Methodist & he was getting on, but had resisted at first. They all "bundled together" as they call it hereabouts, and after breakfast they went on shore highly delighted.

We are all now getting impatient for the "Sceptre" & wish for some change. Several valuable ships came down to us, being forced out by their orders, or must otherwise submit to our embargo. We took possession of them & sent them to Halifax, worth £120,000.

Having caught a cold some time ago, have been very unwell for some days past, no sleep or appetite; the changes of climate vary here 3 & 4 times in one day. Thunder & lightening has been terrible. Dispatches from Adml. Sir John Warren arrived late.

<u>17th June</u>: In consequence of the dispatches moved the ships up higher to our old quarters off Hampton, close in with the enemy's advanced guard, all boats armed & the old harassing system again commenced.

At midnight a most tremendous hurricane with terrible lightning came on; let three anchors go, as we are surrounded with rocks & shoals – the weather is insufferably hot.

In May 1813 Napoleon defeated the Russians and Prussians at Lutzen and Bautzen, but French power was on the wane and Austria, now strong and hostile to France, induced Napoleon to sign an armistice. During this truce a congress was held at Prague and terms dictated to the weakened French. Napoleon hesitated too long before signing and the congress was closed, Austria declaring war on France.

Bernadotte was one of Napoleon's generals who had defected, and eventually became King of Sweden.

<u>18th</u>: Employed exercising, filling ammunition & various kinds of inventions for annoying the enemy, who have had ample time for completing their means of defence & had the force Sir John Warren is now bringing been with us at first we could have taken the City of Norfolk without much loss.

<u>June 19th</u>: The Commander-in-Chief arrived in the Bay below, having with him Sir Sydney Beckwith (the Quarter Master General in Canada) & a variety of troops, sailed from & collected at Bermuda. Sir Sydney is, or was, Col. of the 95th Regiment, a fine Rifle Corps & who have been so much distinguished in Spain with Lord Wellington; he is reported to be a brave & active officer. He has here the temporary rank of Brigadier General & has the 102nd regiment, two battalions of a thousand each of Royal Marines, a fine body of men – three companys of chasseurs (volunteers from the French prisons), two companys of artillery & a company of rocketeers. With this force & a Brigade of 1,000 of us from the ships we are to do wonders. It is supposed Adml. Cockburn will direct the whole.

<u>20th</u>: The advanced frigates were attacked in a calm by the enemy's gun boats & were beaten back with great loss. This evening all the force assembled at sunset round the two admirals' ships, the attack being intended for daylight tomorrow. I went with 90 picked men, my two subalterns, 3 corporals & two drummers, every ship sending their proportion – & we rendezvoused at the "Barrossa" frigate. It was 12 o'clock at night before we started from our ships – the sailors all manned the rigging as we rowed away and gave us three cheers, which we returned.

<u>21st</u>: The arrangements not being completed & quite calm, could not make towards the town & being 25 miles the men could not pull so far without great fatigue; we therefore remained on board the frigates, so crowded that no spot of the ship I was in was unoccupied; above 30 officers were crammed into a place intended for only 7. The officers & Captain Sheriffe of the "Barrossa" behaved with polite attention unusual upon such annoyance: they gave up their beds to such as were disposed to sleep & killed two sheep per day. In short, we remained till 10 o'clock on the 22nd, when we again started for some small vessels stationed just out of gun shot, off Craney Island, where final orders were given.

The 95th Rifles were one of a number of light rifle regiments identified principally by their dark green uniforms, and their highly accurate Baker rifles and known for their marching pace (nearly twice that of line regiments). The 'greenjacket', as it became known, was first used by the 60th Kings Royal Rifle Corps, originally the 'Royal Americans', who saw the success of the dark forester style clothing of the American minutemen in the American War of Independence.

When Sir John Warren arrived on the 19th, Cockburn had surveyed the approaches to Norfolk, which were guarded by batteries on Craney Island. Lieutenant Westphal had discovered shoals that would ground any attack boats some distance from the shore, easy prey for American guns. Cockburn knew it needed careful planning. He submitted his findings to Warren and offered to co-ordinate the attack, but was refused. Warren had completed the plans for the attack before he had arrived. Captain Pechell of the "San Domingo" was to be in overall command. Cockburn had little choice but to shift his flag from the "Marlborough" to the frigate "Barossa", where he would at least be close *enough to engage the batteries on Craney Island. The troops had had no rehearsal, but different units received conflicting commands. It was a complete disaster. It is not difficult to imagine Cockburn's frustration as he watched the debâcle unfold.*

Craney Island
June 22

The memorable Battle of this place, which is the key to Norfolk City & harbour, must be remembered for a few remarkable <u>facts</u>, which perhaps was never before witnessed on so insignificant a service, where it was scarcely possible to fail, even tho' the plan had been determined upon to fail, nor could operations [have] been better placed had the enemy been allowed to direct our movements. For the first time in my life I saw British sailors turn their backs, were again rallied, and finally ran away altogether.

But let me do justice to these brave people, I do not blame them, I blame the projectors, the superficial directors, & the want of <u>leaders</u> & of orders what to do &, in my firm and unalterable opinion, the want of co-operation in the two services, navy & army. The same men had rowed me, on six former occasions (where our force was never more than 300 men) against batteries containing more guns than we had now to oppose (that is, at the point we were to attack). We had on three occasions before taken about 15 or 16 boats – here we had above 100 & flat boats also which contained 60 men, had a thousand fighting men in them, and on shore, on our right, Sir Sydney & nearly <u>3,000 troops</u>, yet the expedition failed.

I had penetration enough to see the <u>discontent</u>, I was in the admiral's ship, knew his every look, but his language was convincing. I discovered on the evening I left the ship how things stood & that <u>he</u> was not to command, but to direct the floating service; an old army officer perhaps would not be under subjection to a naval one. Sir Jn Warren arranged that the one should be landed, the other, too indignant to be second fiddle where his rank gave him precedence, gave up the co-operation, but looked on, was sometimes afloat, sometimes a Volunteer on shore; we in the boats saw nothing of him.

Some captains of the navy had a sort of plan, understood by no-one that were to be the operators. These men were exalted on the gunwales of the ship we departed from, arranging the <u>divisions</u>, as they termed them, telling army officers they were to take the lar-board wing & others the starboard, a language unknown to them. Then all the men who had been in the boats of the ships they were passengers in & familiar with, were changed, & several applications were made to these exalted men to allow the men, particularly the Marines, to go in their own ships' boats, where a kind of emulation kept each other in good humour & one party would have been afraid to 'fight shy', for fear of the other. But no! not <u>one</u> boat was dispatched (to their position in the line of boats) with men known to each other.

At length a thousand men were set adrift & the right received orders to attack the gun boats (when no such intention was confessed by the admiral) – all this time edging on in gun shot of the batteries. One brave fellow was seen in a little 6-oared boat, under a shower of shot, sounding for depth of water & an engineer was in the boat, reconnoitring the landing place. These soon rowed towards us & kept continually waving so as to keep to the left, but we had no leaders, nor did <u>I know</u> who was the Senior Captain of Marines in all the fleet, who to apply to, what to do, or (had we landed, I must have had half my men cut to pieces before I could receive orders) what service I was to perform – on the other hand, several small vessels were to cover our landing, launches were to go ahead and two rocket boats to assist us – but to shew the want of Zeal, and that the cause tho' not left to one man was a general one & all parties should be unanimous, this was the fact with truth to assistance – the small vessels were 9 miles by my eye from us, the excuse was a shoal prevented them coming up, to this I say, boats could have shewed them, and there were 20 boats & upwards empty, owing to the want of calculation, & the others filled so full the men could not row easily; then the two rocket boats were anchored out of range from the forts; thirdly the launches, of which there were, or might have been, a dozen, only one had a cannonade in, & in <u>that</u>, one Commander of the Navy behaved well.

Then the mode of attack was infamous, all the launches, barges and heavy boats were in the front, cutters & large heavy ships' boats in the centre, <u>flat</u> boats (for going in the shallower water & of course best for landing in a hurry) were third, gigs (not bigger than wherrys) last – here was judgement!

Does not all the above mentioned facts clearly prove the fate of the evolution, somewhere, to fail? I as sincerely believe it, as I write this! – for let me remark, that on all occasions up the Chesapeake, tho' so unnecessary, as it turns out, we had a rocket boat & three launches with twelve and eighteen pounders, and the rocket boat under charge of the gunner (Mr. Hepburn) a brave man, was never further off than musket shot, and <u>he</u> proved that the rockets could be fired point blank, and we know that one of those horrid engines proves more destructive than 100 pound shot. It goes further, burns like a comet in appearance, & water will not quench it, and carrys such a tremendous appearance altogether & noise like near thunder that it terrifies & alarms far out of its vortex – what therefore ought to have been the proportion of assistance we had a right to expect? For a scene of magnitude that occupied the attention of 4,000 men? For tho' the <u>onset</u> might have succeeded and I pledge myself for it with our former little Band – yet here was a larger force to meet afterwards, 2,500 men supported by 17 gunboats, a large frigate, the town batteries, and two heavy batteries of 37 & 20 guns each, a crossfire – perhaps it is fortunate for us, the knowing one's fate so early, for with <u>such heads,</u> there would have been many wigs left in the field, had we come to serious action on shore. The event proved no quarter was to be given, a short detail I will commit to paper as an Eternal Momento of our Disgrace.

After all boats were filled, we moved forward and a few brave <u>somebodys</u> rowed about in great confusion (in the <u>rear</u> of us) giving some incoherent orders without authority, no doubt, for they differed from the confused directions some of our boats' officers had had given to them, and <u>in toto</u> from what was any how whatever possible to effect – at 12 o'clock noon day, under a burning sun, the action commenced, instead of our being placed in this position at midnight, to take the first dawn of morning for attack – and as the most ignorant man employed might easily foresee (by the warning from the engineer, in the small gig, to keep more left) we got aground in the <u>mud</u> just within grape shot distance.

In less than an hour a terrible scene of confusion ensued: those who were not aground stood towards the shore, the first boat was rowing 26 oars & had a body of the French Chasseurs in it. This was presently knocked to pieces & almost all the poor fellows drowned. Two other boats shared the same fate, the only man (naval) who shewed gallantry was in the launch that had the gun in it; she was sunk & the captain wounded. At length many other boats were struck & men killed & wounded, their shrieks & unmanly bellowings struck terror in the most part of others. All retreated in the utmost confusion, which was worse almost than going forward, for the enemy gained confidence by it, often halting out of reach of shot.

A general rally took place & getting in somewhat better order of line than before & seeing the light troops on shore engaging across the water that divided the island from the main, we all went boldly forward again, cheering all the way, but alas the fire was more tremendous than before, their guns were brought to the point, nearly 3,000 men appeared, the army did not <u>push</u> to engage their attention, our loss was immense & no hope of reaching the shore for the shallowness of the water, many men killed or wounded; & a second panic threw our expedition into confusion again, no leaders, no apparent object, or any one to look up to for encouragement. I was now in the headmost flat boat, nearly 70 men in it, 4 other boats near me & we thought certainly to reach the shore, when all our force put their boats round except us five, 75 or so boats, thus gave up the point.

We stood it for two hours pretty well & our five boats calling to the rest for support, calling them cowards for turning tail, hissed them & threatened to fire at them: nothing would do; we were now so close that their great guns & cannister shot went <u>over</u> us, nothing but musketry could affect us or interrupt our landing when from necessity we were compelled to follow, & gave all up.

The first boat was still floating, part of her at least. But the troops were in such numbers on the beach it was impossible to relieve the miserable poor fellows on her, whom the scoundrels were wantonly firing at. However one man swam for us & I resolved to pick him up, crowded as we were & hardly able to row, for which I nearly lost ourselves; a 24lb shot struck the side of our boat, carried off all the oars but 3, a second took off three men's right legs & a third shot the feather out of my drummer boy's hat, a boy only twelve years of age. We saved the man & hastened away.

Many of the rest waded on shore & were shot without mercy, three sailors excepted, whom the Americans called to & told them to get back "for they took no prisoners" they said. These men opened a new scene of regret to us & shewed the consummate folly of our directors – for finding they must drown or be shot & all the boats out of their reach – they waded up to their necks & made towards the main land, where our troops were & to our astonishment they got safe on shore without swimming, thus proving our want of information & how well the <u>secret service money</u> is laid out. We might all have attacked this way, at dawn in the morning without such heavy loss as we sustained & failed in the bargain, & why this was not afterwards done is surprizing. The fellows who drown the sailors & murder the soldiers, we suppose must be English, for those traitors to their country were supposed to be more than half the force opposed to us.

One anecdote of American barbarity I must relate, never having heard of civilised men acting so before – five chasseurs almost reached the shore & we concluded they were enticed to desert, but soon saw the villains on shore fire at them – three soon fell, one other reached the beach under a shower of fire & was soon sacrificed, the last man hesitated & stopt, there was no retreat & he saw death in his front, he therefore perhaps became desperate – we observed him take his musket from his back where he had slung it & primed – he then plunged on as fast as he could & two or three times stooped to the water's edge, his eye had no doubt caught the flash of one Yankee's musket who, more bold than the rest had advanced below the parapet or breast-work, & we had seen him a long time aiming deliberately at this unhappy fellow – at last he reached to about knee-deep, took a good aim & knocked the other fellow over like a crow. He still ran forward, as we imagine to use his bayonet as long as he could, but in a few seconds he had fifty balls through him & this brave fellow shewed them what they might have expected had all of us behaved as well.

We now gave over all thoughts of ever taking Norfolk & retreated to our old post – when it was intimated we were to join the main body on shore & once more try something – the joy expressed on this occasion, with the cheering, etc., made some amends for their conduct in the attack, as it proved sound bottom & courage in the men. All the boats pressed for the shore, each exacting a vow from the other to give no quarter for their conduct to our troops. However, the incapable directors, ashamed of themselves, had no longer any nerves & we were kept till near sunset in a state of suspense, broiling at anchor in the burning hot sun & no water or provisions for the men. I had, as an old campaigner, foreseen this & had charged the coxwain of our boat with a basket of provisions & some wine & grog, with which & a few friends near us, we regaled, amusing ourselves with the anecdotes of the day, smoking cigars & abusing the wise heads of our leaders, against a country of <u>Infants in War</u>.

Here the Journal ends

An original letter, torn, to: Miss Wybourn, c/o Edw. Morley Esq., Herne Hill, near Dulwich, England – forwarded to: at Mr. Wybourn, Craig Court, Chareing Cross [sic], London.

Since Emily is not at her own address, she may have been working as a governess.

Nov. 5, 1813
"H.M.S. Marlboro' "
St. Thomas

In the Virgin Islands

My dear Emily,

Just after I had written you on 29th Sept., your letter arrived, as also my uncle's & one from Nelthorpe. I need not say how acceptable [this was] for we were going out of harbour to this boiling place & of course I could not expect to hear how you were, or any accounts of those I most dearly value; it was some months since [I had heard] from England <u>then</u> & I had begun to fancy everyone dead – yours & Uncle's were dated June.

We have just left Antigua & as Mr. Cootes' residence was at English Harbour 12 miles from us, I did not venture in a <u>vertical sun</u> to visit there. We only staid two days at the island & have since enjoyed a most delightful sail thro' these astonishing islands & have at length reached St. Thomas's. The convoy are to rendezvous here & we expect to be on our way for England in <u>less</u> than 3 weeks. We have faint hopes of even eating our Xmas dinner in England, but I fear it will be far into Jany before we see dear Albion cliffs again; I do not know whether I shall let anyone know of my arrival till I recruit a little, and my dear Caroline must nurse me a month or I shall not be right. I am now broke out in what is called the prickly-heat (a very certain token I am safe from the <u>Yellow Fever</u>) a most distressing disease, making you appear like a child with the small pox & some people can neither bear to lie or sit – mine is not yet so <u>bad</u>!

I must remind you that these foreign letters are to be charged to <u>me</u>. I do not know that I shd. have written, being so near return, but these vile Yankees are taking all our Packets, & reports say our last letters are all at the bottom of the sea & I am fearful you will see by the papers that the "Marlboro'" is at the West Indies & not know that we are only to stay a short time – and the kind anxiety you are always so good to shew might create unnecessary apprehensions. I certainly

Cockburn was determined to do the job properly and returned on 25 June. The boats landed in good order to the west of Hampton before daylight. Cockburn then repeated his successful formula witnessed by Wybourn on several occasions: the launches and rocket boats engaged the American batteries while the landing troops marched on the enemy and captured the town. After keeping it for ten days and resupplying the squadron from the captured stores, Cockburn destroyed the batteries and ordnance, and re-embarked. However, the Canadian Chasseurs, the French prisoners enlisted as the 102nd Regiment, had pillaged the town and killed a number of captives, to the disgrace of British Arms. A subsequent court of enquiry investigated their conduct and they were returned to Bermuda, never to be employed again.

shall wish to see old England again & try my influence for the Brevet rank, for I was Senior Officer in Chesapeake the whole time and was in all the actions. I see the papers mention my name, but with much less justice than I merited for I actually <u>commanded</u> at all the attacks; the Navy seldom speak of <u>us</u> except where they cannot help it. Will the people of England believe that we lost 200 men, after the gentle & trifling manner the dispatches were written in, and as to the affair of <u>Craney</u> Island and <u>Hampton</u>, never was anything so disgraceful to the projectors, or the sacrifice greater to the assailants, but for a special providence over us – and now I am upon the subject it may at least afford satisfaction to your male readers of this, to hear that we were put in boats at 11 at night, 1,000 men without any assignment being understood – & 2,000 men landed on our right, contrary to our information. At 12 o'clock, at noon next day we in the boats were ordered to attack the Batteries and remained under showers of shot for some hours, all the boats aground, some sunk, others cut to pieces & it finished in a disgraceful retreat, thus did 3,000 fine resolute fellows lose all their Credit before a handful of Yankees. Had we landed on the other side Norfolk would have fallen [yet] we were told over & over again that it was the only mode we could pursue with success.

At Hampton we were more successful, having taken the enemy's Camp & Town, but we had all their troops in our power, <u>yet let them escape</u>. In neither of these affairs was I <u>named</u> even though senior officer in the boats that we landed, would have commanded 1,000 men, & at Hampton full companies were under my command & we were in the advance under Col. Napier of the 102nd Regiment, who was the only officer above me. I mean to make a great fuss on my return, you may be sure, & I sincerely hope the House of Commons may take the whole Chesapeake business in hand. I will be in voluntary evidence against the whole, for I have seen too many desperate engagements and have always been fortunate before, not to boil with indignation at the disgrace our arms have met with. This I should like you to shew our friend Mr. Bull. I shd not have said so much upon war to you, only I wish you to shew it my friends – & indeed as you know I must fill my paper; I really have nothing else to write of unless I wished to frighten you with a description of this vile tropical climate. I very much lament being within a few hours sail of Trinidad & not having it in my power to go there.

I suppose Portsmouth will be our first Port & I hope the ship will

George Cockburn as a Colonel, RM, by John James Halls

T. Marmaduke Wybourn in middle age

be paid off at Chatham & I shall hope to find a letter from you, telling me all the news of everyone, that I may make my arrangements for leave. I shall certainly pay you a visit (upon private leave) as soon as the ship arrives, but it may not be necessary to let anyone in London know it as I will not go there till I have been to Birmingham, for only consider in 12 months I have undergone eight changes of climate from the worse extremes. Adieu my dearest sister – may all hopes … and serenity attend you.

Your ever affec. Bro. TMW

Love to dear Susy – there are no more relatives left but Uncle! How strange.

Wybourne retired on half-pay on 12th April 1826 with the rank of Brevet Major. He settled down with Emily, but lived only another six years. Perhaps, if he had to take 'Jesuit's bark', he suffered from malaria. He died in 1832, aged fifty-four.

A Private of the Royal Marines, courtesy of the Parker Gallery

The Marines/Royal Marines of Wybourn's Day

The Royal Marines had been first known as The Admiral's Men, or the Duke of York and Albany's Maritime Regiment of Foot. Their anniversary of foundation is considered to be 28th October 1664 – during the early part of the Second Dutch War. However, the Corps was always disbanded after each conflict and re-formed in the event of subsequent wars. It was not until 1755, on the eve of the Seven Years' War, that the Marines were in constant service; an Admiralty Office order of 26th April authorised the raising of 20 companies at Portsmouth, 18 at Plymouth, and 12 at Chatham: 5000 men in all. Thus began the Corps' continuous existence until today, for some of their number was always retained, often as dockyard guards, thus providing a seasoned nucleus for rapid mobilisation. In 1794 the Corps was expanded to 12,000 and in 1805 the demands of the Napoleonic wars prompted a further expansion to 30,000 men.

Marines served in small detachments aboard ship, originally acting as part of the crew. Because every warship of over 10 guns had its detachment of marines, they figured in nearly every naval engagement of the Seven Years' War and the American War of Independence. Deployment in action, though it varied according to a ship's size, was typically: poop: Captain of Marines and two/three lieutenants plus 12 marines; the rest distributed in ones, twos and occasionally threes among all the gun crews, usually acting as powder men.

In the eighteenth century, several famous army regiments acted as marines, e.g. the 69th Regiment had a detachment on board HMS "Captain" with Nelson at the Battle of Cape St Vincent (1794). Marines were often the spearhead of amphibious operations and were occasionally involved in protracted military campaigns on land, such as the capture of Belleisle, the attack on Bunker Hill, and the first landing in Australia's Botany Bay in 1770.

The chief role of the marines was to fight as seaborne infantry. As early as the Spanish Armada, soldiers had made up roughly a third of a ship's company. By the 1650s, however, the standard marine arms of musket and sword were regarded as secondary weapons and, by the 1790s, only a tenth of a 74-gun ship's complement of 120 marines was used as small-arms men. The aggressive tactics employed by Nelson increased the importance of boarding enemy ships, and here the nimble sailors, with cutlass and pistol, complemented the marines' musket and bayonet.

The marines who worked the great guns alongside the seamen had no special training in this role during the eighteenth, and early nineteenth centuries. Indeed in 1740, when they were re-formed for service in the War of Jenkins' Ear, they were seen as a training group primarily for future sailors, who would learn the necessary skills of seamanship from within their ranks. Even in the nineteenth century there was still some vestige of this attitude; marines were often encouraged to go aloft for training purposes, but were never 'to be obliged to go aloft or be beat or punished for not showing an inclination to do so'. By 1806, however, Naval Regulations provided that no serving marine could be discharged and entered as a seaman without a specific order from the Admiralty.

In 1759 King George formed a new establishment of Marine officers of superior rank, to be chosen from officers of the Royal Navy. Thus Captain Horatio Nelson was appointed Colonel of Marines in 1795, and Admiral Sir George Cockburn was made Major-General of Marines in 1821.

At the close of the eighteenth century, in the Napoleonic Wars, the marines' role was dramatically expanded; as well as enforcement and guard duties aboard ship, their most important task was the suppression of mutiny. Apart from during sea duties and working with the guns, it had been normal practice to segregate marines and seamen, with their own messes and berths. Under Admiral Lord St Vincent in 1797 – the year of the great mutinies – the segregation was strongly reinforced, supposedly providing a ship's officers with a contingent of loyal, fully armed soldiers at their command. Marines were to stand guard whenever punishment was to be carried out, and were kept at drill and parade when the ship was in harbour – the likeliest venue for mutiny. As a result of these efforts, there were no major mutinies on any ship under the Admiral's command.

St Vincent's regard for the Marines was such that he recommended to King George III that they be awarded the title 'Royal'; this was granted on 29th April 1802. Shortly before his death he said: 'In obtaining for them the distinction of Royal, I but inefficiently did my duty. I never knew an appeal to them for honour, courage or loyalty that did not more than realise my highest expectations. If ever the hour of real danger should come to England, they will be found the country's sheet anchor.'

It must be said that in the mutinies at Spithead and the Nore, some rebellious marines played a full part alongside the seamen. Most were extolled for their loyalty, whilst those who supported the mutineers were hanged or flogged. Admiral Philip Patton believed trust in them to be misplaced, saying that 'they feel a very great inferiority to the seamen when at sea.' However, in subsequent mutinies, the Marines behaved with conspicuous discipline and loyalty.

Amphibious operations threw up many problems for the army and the navy. Soldiers at sea would still be under military discipline, not naval, and the blurring of the lines of command often produced tactical impotence and incompetence. Marines, however, were clearly under naval discipline, used to life aboard ship, and were more effective specialists in landing operations. The role of amphibious warfare was expanding continuously, and proved very effective under that enterprising commander, Popham, during the Peninsular War. In 1804, companies of Royal Marine Artillery were first formed, based at Chatham, and in 1805 at Woolwich and these would probably have been active in the bomb vessels and in landing the guns during some of Wybourn's service.

There was always the danger of seamen deserting when landing for resupply in friendly ports or foraging for victuals in outlying regions. The well-drilled and uniformed marines, in contrast to the sailors' more relaxed appearance, were used to impress enemies and allies alike when landing, and to remind sailors of their true allegiance. In these instances they were sometimes used as reinforcements to press-gangs and guards to prevent seamen from escaping. This was a fate no marine had ever undergone – because they were landsmen, marines could not be impressed; they were volunteers.

The recruiting system of the marines was similar to that of the army. Recruits were raised in market towns all over the country, tempting healthy young men with the promise of action and adventure and financial reward. This proved insufficient. In wartime, a bounty was raised; in 1794 this was eight guineas per recruit. This was raised again to 15 guineas. By 1801 this had risen to £26 per man and in 1808 £30 was offered. Poorer areas could provide a steady flow of recruits, doubtless more interested in these comparatively vast sums and the promise of regular meals than tempted by action and adventure. In 1809 the marines of the "San Domingo" included 50 former agricultural labourers among 121 NCOs and men; there were also 20 weavers – tradesmen whose livelihood had been swept away by industrialisation. But in wartime there were never enough recruits. In 1795 the navy expanded greatly, but the marines could not keep up. Soldiers were used instead, to take up the shortfall, acting as marines. Some were allowed wives to accompany them aboard ship and many of these women were present during naval engagements. The use of soldiers caused difficulties in discipline, and naval officers insisted on having marines aboard to keep order. To get round this, many of these soldiers were offered a bounty of five guineas to leave their regiments and join the marines permanently.

The Royal Marines, desperate for recruits, also saw foreigners as a potential source, and went round the prison ships and hulks seeking men who had been taken unwillingly unto the French flag, such as the Dutch, Swiss and Polish. In 1803, when the "Hercules" attacked Fort Piscadero, 30 of her 67-strong marine company were Poles, who had been captured and imprisoned in the West Indies. When a recruiting station was opened in the Caribbean, free negroes were also taken to the colours.

When a new ship was commissioned, the captain would apply to the nearest marine barracks for a detachment. These would be selected by the local commandant and sent to the ship. If the captain wished, he could return any marines he considered below standard as unfit, giving his reasons in writing.

The size of a shipboard detachment varied according to the size of the ship, and the period; in 1801, roughly one sixth of a ship's company would be marines. By 1808 this was increased to one fifth, perhaps for fear of mutiny. On board, the ship's captain was obliged to post a 24-hour sentry at the hatch of the ship's magazine; he would also post a man at his own cabin door, and others to guard the store rooms and the 'spirit room'. On a 74-gunner, some 30 marines would be kept in full uniform as a rota of sentries. The orders on the "Centaur" in 1803 states that sentries were to 'walk brisk on their posts, backwards and forwards, never to sit down, read or sing, whistle, smoke, eat or drink, but be continually alert and attentive to the execution of their orders, not ever to quit their arms on any pretence whatsoever'.

The relationship between seamen and marines was not always one of guard and prisoner, however. They were, in the end, two parts of an effective war-machine. According to one captain during the Napoleonic Wars, the differences between the two were never in doubt.

No two races of men, I had well nigh said two animals, differ more from one another more completely than the "Jollies" and the "Johnnies". The marines as I have said before enlisted for life, or for long periods as in the regular army, and, when not employed afloat, are kept in barracks in such constant training, under the direction of their officers, that they are never released for one moment of their lives from the influence of strict discipline and habitual obedience. The sailors, on the contrary, when their ship is paid off, are turned adrift, and so completely scattered abroad that they generally lose ... all they have learned of good order during the previous three or four years. Even when both parties are placed on board ship, and the general discipline maintained in its fullest operation, the influence of regular order and exact subordination is at least twice as great over the marines as it can ever be over the sailors.

One Captain Glascock had this to say as well:

The sailor of our wars with France had so much *esprit de corps* for his own branch of the national service that he genuinely and heartily – not to say unreasonably – despised all that pertained to soldiering and pipeclay. But in most of the affairs we are able to relate, marines and seamen were able to work more perfectly together, the former, efficient soldiers as they were, holding the enemy's troops and covering the no less efficient cutting-out and demolition work of the seamen.

Marines played a vital liaison role between the two branches of the armed forces. The navy's power lay in its ability to destroy coastal installations and encampments, and control seaborne trading, and limit an enemy's ability to return the compliment, by sinking his ships. However, this in itself would not win a war. The only way to consolidate naval success was to land men to seize and hold enemy territory. The marines, a peculiar naval/military hybrid, were the only men for such a task: able to undertake long sea-journeys and willing to participate in ships' duties, especially under fire, under rigid, ingrained discipline, they fought alongside soldiers and seamen alike, spearheading vast invasion forces, holding enemy positions until reinforced by land or sea, and besieging the enemy within his fortresses. In 1827, King George IV had difficulty in selecting battle honours from so many glorious deeds and directed that the Corps should have 'The Great Globe itself' as its emblem, surrounded by the laurel wreath.

Respected by the sailors amongst whom they lived, often like guards and prison warders rather than comrades, the Marines instilled in friend and foe a sense of awe at their self-discipline, courage and pride. As these diaries and letters testify, a young ambitious officer in the service of his country could take part in great sea-battles and seek glory amidst shot and shell in far-off lands, dine with exotic allies and beard enemy lions in their dens. Wybourn's story is, indeed, the very stuff of empire.

J. Downs

BIBLIOGRAPHY

Britain's Sea Soldiers, a History of the Royal Marines and Their Predecessors, by Colonel Cyril Field, R.M.L.I., The Lyceum Press, Liverpool 1924

British Battles and Medals, by Major L.L. Gordon, Spink & Son Ltd., London 1979

Encyclopaedia Britannica

The Great Mutiny, by James Dugan, Andrew Deutsch, London 1966

The Illustrated Companion to Nelson's Navy, by Nicholas Blake and Richard Lawrence, Chatham Publishing, London 1999

Life in Nelson's Navy, by Dudley Pope, Chatham Publishing, London 1981

The Line of Battle, the Sailing Warship 1650–1840, ed. Robert Gardiner, Conway Maritime Press, London 1992

The Man who Burned the White House – Admiral Sir George Cockburn 1772–1853, by James Pack, Kenneth Mason, Emsworth 1987

The Napoleonic Sourcebook, by Philip J. Haythornthwaithe, Arms and Armour, London 1990

The Naval Chronicle, 1797–1813

The Naval War of 1812, ed. Robert Gardiner, Chatham Publishing, London 1998

Nelson's Navy, by Brian Lavery, Conway Maritime Press, 1989

The Oxford Illustrated History of the Royal Navy ed. J.R. Hill, O.U.P. 1995, 'The Struggle with France 1689–1815' by J.B. Hattendorf

Royal Naval Biography, by John Marshall, London 1823

Shipboard Life and Organisation, 1731–1815, ed. Brian Lavery, Navy Records Society, London 1998

'*Steel's List', Original and Correct List of the Royal Navy, 1793–1815*, by D. Steel, 1793–1815

Wellington's Military Machine, by Philip J. Haythornthwaite, Spellmount, Tunbridge Wells 1989

INDEX TO THE MAIN TEXT
Numbers in bold refer to illustrations